GABRIEL POWELL'S

SURVEY OF GOWER

1764

GABRIEL POWELL'S

SURVEY OF THE LORDSHIP OF GOWER 1764

Edited and introduced by
Bernard Morris

A Gower Society Publication

Lunnon village, near Parkmill.

Peter Douglas-Jones

A

SURVEY

OF THE

Seigniories of Gower and Kilvey
with the several Members of which the most Noble
Henry Duke of Beaufort is Lord
Made in the Year 1764

By
Gabriel Powell the present Steward, Coroner,
Bayliff of the Liberties, and Recorder of the Courts of
the said Seigniories; from several antient and
authentick Papers, and the observations and Experience
of Gabriel Powell his late Father deceased and Himself
for above Sixty three Years

At the Desire of the most Noble Elizabeth
Dutchess Dowager of Beaufort (Mother and
Guardian of the said Duke) to whom this Survey
is most humbly presented by

Her Grace's
most faithful and Obedient
Servant
Gab: Powell

First publication – October 2000

ISBN 0 902767 27 5

© Bernard Morris 2000

Published by
The Gower Society

British Library Cataloguing in Publication Data.
A catalogue record for this book is available
from the British Library.

*Printed in Wales by
Dinefwr Press
Rawlings Road, Llandybïe
Carmarthenshire, SA18 3YD*

The Gower Society is a Registered Charity

Typeset in 12/15 point Garamond

FOREWORD

How deceptive a title can be! *A Survey of the Lordship of Gower* could be a rather dull, historical accountancy of some indeterminate time in the past. What we have here, however, is a lively, exciting account of a particular place and a particular time in history.

The Steward of the most noble Henry Duke of Beaufort "ought to be a person of fortune and consequence in the country, to support the dignity and respect due to his office". Gabriel Powell was just such a man, though the politics of profit frequently made him unpopular, particularly with the burgeoning industrialists of the late eighteenth century. His Survey was an attempt to compile an accurate and definitive list of holdings and rentals within the Seignories of Gower and Kilvey.

Here we learn of the boundaries (and boundary disputes), of ditches, hedges, brooks and rivers, many still visible on the ground. Of the early industrial activity, coal, limekilns, mills, quarries, copper and shipping. Of the fees due for grazing on commons, for building boats, for fishing and crabbing. Of taxes due to the lord with such improbable names as Ferry Corn, Toll Pixie, Mises, Prisage, and Butlerage of Wines. We learn of individual inhabitants, their duties of 'suit of court' and 'suit of mill' (with a 3s 4d fine for non-attendance) and "doing service with oxen and horses when required". Of rents, which range from a bow and halbert, a pair of gilt spurs or six swallow-tailed arrows to two fat pullets or two capons. By 1764 most of these had been commuted to financial equivalents, from 6d to 20s, but fortunately no equivalence is found for Maysod Dawkins' due of "a rose at midsummer".

Henry Duke of Beaufort was fortunate to have a steward of such vast local knowledge and with such a meticulous attitude towards recording the facts. The Gower Society is fortunate in having a man equal in local knowledge, and equally meticulous in editing and introducing this Survey. As a long-standing editor of, and major contributor to, *Gower*, the Gower Society's journal, and a prolific writer and lecturer on local history, Bernard Morris is uniquely qualified to undertake this edition.

Despite its importance, the Survey has, until now, only been available in two original manuscript copies and a late-nineteenth century manuscript transcript. With this publication, it is made available to a wider audience – researchers, historians, local inhabitants, and descendants of the tenants recorded in its pages. From a wider viewpoint, this 'Domesday Book' of Gower is a microcosm of many parts of Britain on the eve of the industrial revolution.

Bernard Morris's masterly introduction illuminates the context of the Survey in both historical and personal terms. The Gower Society is proud to have had a part in the publication of this important work, but the praise belongs, alone, to the editor.

Malcolm Ridge
Chairman,
The Gower Society

ACKNOWLEDGEMENTS

In editing and preparing for publication Gabriel Powell's comprehensive 'Survey of Gower' I have received ready encouragement and help in a variety of ways, directly and indirectly, from many people and organisations, not least from the following: Mr Jeff Childs; Dr F.G. Cowley; Mr Peter Douglas-Jones; Mr Thomas Lloyd; Dr Prys Morgan; Mrs Olga Rogers; Mr W.C. Rogers; Mrs Sandra Thomas; Miss Susan Beckley, West Glamorgan Archivist and her staff; Mrs Elisabeth Bennett, Archivist, University of Wales Swansea and her predecessor, Mr David Bevan; Mrs Margaret Richards, Badminton Archivist; the staff at Swansea Museum (City and County of Swansea); the National Library of Wales; and Mrs Marilyn Jones, Local Studies Librarian, City and County of Swansea Central Library. Acknowledgements for the provision of illustrations appear on page xvii. I am particularly grateful to my wife, Pam, for valuable comments as the text and the commentary took shape. I am also indebted to the Gower Society for agreeing to publish the Survey. If this encourages interest in the history of the lordship of Gower and leads to further research into this fascinating area, the venture will have achieved its purpose. Finally – love him or hate him – thanks are due to Mr Gabriel Powell, gentleman, without whom there would have been no 1764 Survey of the Lordship of Gower.

Bernard Morris
Swansea
October 2000

CONTENTS

Introduction

THE LORDSHIP AND THE SURVEY

THE STEWARD AND HIS STEWARDSHIP

EDITORIAL MATTERS

The Text of the Survey

THE SEIGNIORY OF GOWER

MESNE MANORS, HELD FROM THE LORD

THE OFFICERS OF THE SEIGNIORY

GOWER ANGLICANA

* Bold entries indicate that the items include lengthy lists.

THE BOROUGH AND MANOR OF SWANSEA

THE BOROUGH AND MANOR OF LOUGHOR

THE MANOR OF PENNARD WITH THE FEES OF KITTLE, LUNNON AND TREWYDDFA

Pennard

Kittle

Lunnon

Trewyddfa

THE MANOR OF OYSTERMOUTH

BISHOPSTON MANOR

THE SEIGNIORY OR LORDSHIP ROYAL OF KILVEY

APPENDICES

List of illustrations, and acknowledgements

Items indicated as 'Swansea Museum' are reproduced by permission of the City and County of Swansea, Museums Service. The aerial photographs were all taken by Mr Peter Douglas-Jones. We are grateful to the owners of the various original illustrations for their permission to use them in this book. All unattributed illustrations are by the editor.

Sources mentioned in footnotes, and other relevant works

Works mentioned in footnotes

Jeff Childs. 'The Parish of Llangyfelach, 1750-1850: . . . with particular reference to changes in landownership' (unpublished MA thesis, University College Cardiff, 1988).

Jeff Childs. 'Landownership Changes in a Glamorgan Parish, 1750-1850: The Case of Llangyfelach' in *Morgannwg* XXXVIII (1994).

A Dictionary of the Welsh Language (University of Wales, 1957 onwards).

Lewis Weston Dillwyn. Diaries. 'Calendar of the Diary of Lewis Weston Dillwyn'. Typescript volumes prepared by National Library of Wales.

G.H. Eaton. 'A Survey of the Manor in Seventeenth Century Gower' (Unpublished University College of Swansea MA thesis, 1936).

George Grant Francis. *Charters Granted to Swansea* (Swansea, 1867).

George Grant Francis. *The Smelting of Copper in the Swansea District* (London 1881).

William Hickey. *Memoirs 1791-92*. Quoted in J.E. Ross ed. *Letters from Swansea* (Swansea, 1969).

House of Commons Journal, 1787.

W.H. Jones. *The History of Swansea and the Lordship of Gower*, I (Carmarthen 1920), and II (Swansea 1992).

W.H. Jones, *History of the Port of Swansea* (Carmarthen, 1922).

Joanna Martin. 'Private Enterprise versus Manorial Rights . . . in Glamorgan' in *Welsh History Review* 9 (1978-79).

Prys Morgan. 'The Glais Boundary Dispute, 1756' in *Glamorgan Historian* IX (Barry 1973).

Robert Morris. 'The History of the Copper Concern', 1774. Unpublished mss. volume in University of Wales Swansea (Local Archives).

T.B. Pugh. 'The Ending of the Middle Ages' in Glanmor Williams (ed.) *Glamorgan County History* III. (Cardiff 1971).

David Rees. 'Neuadd Wen: Changing Patterns of Tenure' in H. James (ed.) *Sir Gâr: Studies in Carmarthenshire History* (Carmarthen 1991). Also his 'The Gower Estates of Sir Rhys ap Thomas' in *Gower* XLIII (1992).

David Rees. 'Gower Divided', in *Gower* L (1999).

W. Rees. 'The Union of England and Wales' in *Transactions of the Honourable Society of Cymmrodorion* 1937, reprinted separately under that title (Cardiff, 1948).

W.R.B. Robinson. 'The Litigation of Edward Earl of Worcester, concerning Gower, 1590-1596' in *Bulletin of the Board of Celtic Studies* XXII, pt. 4 (5.1968) and XXIII pt 1 (11.1968).

W.C. Rogers. 'Swansea and Glamorgan Calendar' (Unpublished typescript volumes. Copies are held at: National Library of Wales, Swansea Public Reference Library; and University of Wales Swansea (for Swansea Museum).

J.E. Ross (ed.). *Radical Adventurer – The Diaries of Robert Morris 1772-1774* (Bath, 1971).

C.A. Seyler. 'The Early Charters of Swansea and Gower' in *Arch.Camb.* LXXIX (1924) and LXXX (1925).

J. Beverley Smith and T.B. Pugh. 'The Lordship of Gower and Kilvey ' in Glanmor Williams (ed.) *Glamorgan County History* III (Cardiff 1971).

South Wales Record Society Publication No. 1 (1949).'Lordship of Kilvey, Account of the Receiver of Mines & Coals, 1399-1400'.

Peter Thomas. 'Glamorgan Politics 1688-1790', in Glanmor Williams (ed.) *Glamorgan County History* IV (Cardiff, 1974).

M. Fay Williams. 'The Society of Friends in Glamorgan 1654-1900'. (Unpublished MA thesis, University College of Wales, Aberystwyth, 1950).

A selection of other relevant works

Charles Baker and George Grant Francis. *The Lordship of Gower in the Marches of Wales.* Supplementary volumes to *Archaeologia Cambrensis*, comprising many Gower surveys (1861and 1864, ed. Francis; 1870, ed. Baker).

John Cowell. *Law Dictionary* (1727).

David W. Howell. *Patriarchs and Parasites: The Gentry in South-West Wales in the Eighteenth Century* (Cardiff, 1986).

Philip Jenkins. *The Making of a Ruling Class: The Glamorgan Gentry, 1640-1790* (Cambridge, 1983).

David Jouneau. 'Les Seigneuries de Gower et de Kilvey: Deux seigneuries du Pays de Galles à travers une étude manuscrite de 1764'. Unpublished thesis, Universite de Poitiers, 1995

Llewelyn B. John. 'The Parliamentary Representation of Glamorgan 1536-1832' (unpublished University of Wales thesis, 1934).

David Leighton. 'A Fresh Look at Parc le Breos' in *Gower* L (1999).

Joanna Martin. 'The Landed Estate in Glamorgan: c.1660-1760' (unpublished PhD thesis, University of Cambridge, 1978).

Tom Ridd. 'Gabriel Powell: the Uncrowned King of Swansea' in *Glamorgan Historian* V (1968).

New and forthcoming publications

Stephen Hughes. *Copperopolis: Landscapes of the Early Industrial Period in Swansea.* Royal Commission on the Ancient and Historical Monuments of Wales (Sept. 2000).

The Court Book of the Manor of Pennard, 1673 to 1700 (ed. Joanna Martin). South Wales Record Society (forthcoming, 2000).

Abbreviations used in footnotes and references etc.

Arch. Camb.:   *Archaeologia Cambrensis.* The Journal of the Cambrian Archaeological Association.

BBCS.:   *The Bulletin of the Board of Celtic Studies* (University of Wales).

Bn: The Badminton manuscript of the Survey of 1764, now in NLW.

Cambrian, The: Swansea weekly newspaper, published from 1804.

'Copper Concern':   'History of the Copper Concern . . .'. Mss. volume compiled by Robert Morris junior in 1774 from the family's business letter-books. In UWS. Library (Local Archives Collection).

Gower: The Journal of the Gower Society.

GCH.:   *Glamorgan County History.* Ed. Glanmor Williams. Vol.III, and Vol.IV (Cardiff, 1971,1974).

GRO.:   Glamorgan Record Office, Cardiff.

NLW.:   The National Library of Wales, Aberystwyth.

NLW.II: Badminton (Beaufort) manuscripts, Group II, at NLW. The ref. nos. and dates of correspondence etc. are quoted.

Sa: The Swansea manuscript of the Survey of 1764, now in UWS (held for Swansea Museum).

UWS.:   University of Wales Swansea.

WGRO.:   West Glamorgan Record Office, Swansea.

WHJ. *History.*:   W.H.Jones. *The History of Swansea and the Lordship of Gower,* Vols I and II (Carmarthen 1920 and Swansea 1992).

Introduction

i. The Lordship of Gower

In modern usage the word 'Gower' generally refers to the peninsula lying west of Swansea, but as a medieval lordship it also included the area lying between the Tawe and the Llwchwr and extending more than thirteen miles to the north of Swansea, reaching to the rivers Amman and Twrch[1]. Gower was not just a lordship but was a *marcher* lordship, a lordship of the march in Wales. This meant that its lord had royal rights and privileges within its boundaries, and that those rights and privileges were almost independent of the king.

The early conquests of Welsh lands had proceeded under what amounted to 'private enterprise' ventures by powerful Norman lords. Having quickly secured England following his victory near Hastings in 1066, William needed to secure his western borders and also had to offer further rewards to his followers. He granted his close associates the right to seize what land they could from the adjoining disunited land of Wales, and allowed them to create new lordships from their conquests. Within these lordships were set up feudal systems echoing that newly established in England, with the significant difference that within his own boundaries the new lord and his successors stood in the place of the king. His were the only courts which could deal with criminal offences or civil disputes in his lordship, and at the outset the whole lordship was his. Needless to say, the marcher lords, although autonomous within their own lordships were not completely independent of central authority[2]. Every one of them owed personal allegiance to the king, and could lose all that he possessed if he failed in this, or was considered to have failed. Even then the marcher lordship remained as a legal entity and the new owner for the time being received it with all its previous rights and privileges intact, but subject to his personal fealty and allegiance to the king. Sometimes the lordship came into the hands of the king himself, but it still retained its distinctive rights and privileges, which passed on to the next lord.

Until shortly after the year 1100 the boundaries of what became the lordship of Gower were those of a Welsh commote known as Gŵyr[3]. This was part of a larger territorial division, or cantref, which included also Cydweli and Carnwyllion, the two commotes which lay between the Llwchwr and the Tywi rivers. The ancient links of Gŵyr alias Gower were thus with south-west Wales and the new lordship and its western neighbours had once been part of the dominions of the rulers of Deheubarth, the pre-Norman Welsh kingdom centred on Ystrad Tywi. It could be

---

1. At some time after 1203, and probably during that century, the parish of Bettws was removed, and the north-west corner of Gower was pushed back to Cwm Cathan. See C.A. Seyler. 'The Early Charters of Swansea and Gower' in *Arch.Camb*. LXXIX (1924), p.304 and W.H.J. *History* I, p.193.
2. Although English common law did not apply in the marcher lordships, the specifically enacted statute law did. See *GCH*. III, pp.572, 573.
3. For details of this and much of what follows, see J. Beverley Smith and T.B. Pugh. 'The Lordship of Gower and Kilvey' in *GCH*. III, pp.205-283.

1

expected that Welsh counter-attacks would be repeated and violent and they were, continuing intermittently for two centuries after the seizure of Gower. The first Norman lord of Gower was Henry de Beaumont, first Earl of Warwick and confidant of King Henry I. The last Welsh lord had been Hywel ap Goronwy, though he had gained it through services to the English king. He was killed near Carmarthen in 1106, and the next appearance of Gower in history is in 1116 by which time Henry de Beaumont had already become its lord. He had established his principal castle at Swansea, perhaps as early as 1107, and it was the unsuccessful siege of this by a son of the late ruler of Deheubarth which led to its first mention in the contemporary chronicles. Sometimes Welsh attacks were successful and caused devastation within the lordship, but Gower still continued in the hands of the invaders.

Whatever the military situation, the ownership of the Lordship of Gower changed hands quite frequently. The Warwick tenure ended when the last earl died, and it then passed through various hands, including three kings (Henry II, Richard I and John) and a native Welsh prince (Rhys Gryg) until the long tenure of the de Breos lords began in 1220. It was in their time, in 1306, that Gower's status as a marcher lordship was first challenged in a royal court of law. The matter was not pressed to a conclusion then but was to be raised again half a century later. When the male line of the de Breoses ended the lordship passed by marriage to the de Mowbrays, Dukes of Norfolk. They held it until 1468 when, by an exchange of properties, it passed to Lord Herbert of Raglan. His grand-daughter brought Gower by marriage to Charles Somerset, who was created the first Earl of Worcester in 1514. In the Civil War the Earl of Worcester steadfastly defended Raglan Castle for the king and forfeited his estates for his loyalty. Oliver Cromwell became lord of Gower in his place, but at the Restoration the then Earl of Worcester received his lands again. It was his grandson, Henry, who was created the first Duke of Beaufort by Charles II in 1682, and the Beaufort line continues today as lords of the seigniory.

The all-important claim that Gower was a marcher lordship, bringing to its lord royal rights within its boundaries, was challenged in 1306 during the great lawsuit when his principal tenants complained of William de Breos' oppressions. No conclusion was reached then, because the case was settled when de Breos agreed to grant favourable charters to Swansea and to Gower. The issue arose again in 1369, when the Earl of Warwick (not of the original Warwick family) had briefly reclaimed Gower from the de Mowbrays, only to have his claim to marcher lord status immediately disputed by the Prince of Wales' advisors. This case, which turned on legal points which the Warwicks were less able to counter than the de Mowbrays and the de Breoses, went against Warwick, but the prince then regranted marcher status by way of a royal charter, which subsequent lords could point to as their title. The specific and remarkable royal powers of the marcher lords in Wales were abolished by Henry VIII's Acts of Union of 1536 and 1542/3[4]. These applied the law of England uniformly to all the various manors, lordships and other jurisdictions in Wales and, apart from the manorial courts, abolished their independent legal systems. Other powers and perquisites of the marcher lords, however, were not removed. The Acts[5] also created or extended the county system to cover the whole of Wales. As part of these reforms the lordship of Gower

---

4 . T.B. Pugh. 'The Ending of the Middle Ages' in *GCH*. III, pp.555-581.
5.   The Act of 1536 contained the principal provisions. For its text see W. Rees. 'The Union of England and Wales', *THSC*. 1937, reprinted separately under that title (Cardiff, 1948).

was joined, not to its western neighbours, but to the marcher lordship to the east, known as Morgannwg and Glamorgan,[6] to create the new county of Glamorganshire. It was thus that Gower and other marcher lordships finally lost their independent legal systems and their unique status.

Until 1986 the lordship's boundaries, modified by the early withdrawal to the Cathan at the north-west corner, remained in being as those of the Gower parliamentary constituency (allowing for the deduction of the Swansea East and West constituencies). Otherwise, the extent of the ancient lordship had long ceased to have real significance but this has been changed by the most recent reorganisation of local authorities. The peninsular part of Gower had already been included as one authority with Swansea in the local government changes in 1974. Then in 1996 a large part of the Lliw Valley District Council's area was added to create the City and County of Swansea, the current unitary local authority. Part of the Lliw Valley area, being the parish of Llangiwg plus a part of the Rhyndwyclydach division of Llangyfelach parish, was not included in this, but was joined to the adjacent new Neath Port Talbot authority. Apart from this latter omission the City and County of Swansea's area now covers virtually the same ground as the ancient Lordship of Gower, which is perhaps of some help in understanding the extent and complexity of the lordship and its administration.[7]

ii. The Lordship and the Survey of 1764

Surviving original documents from the medieval period provide a certain amount of information concerning the extent, ownership and organisation of the Lordship of Gower, but there are many gaps and uncertainties in the evidence. Fortunately, records become increasingly available and more detailed as the centuries pass, and without these more recent documents the medieval picture would be obscure indeed. Gabriel Powell's 'Survey of Gower', completed in 1764, provides a clear and detailed description of the Duke of Beaufort's rights and ownerships as lord of Gower as they stood at that time. It is a contemporary working document and is concerned with facts. However, it was prepared as a statement to be used on behalf of the Duke in the likely event of a continuation of recent acrimonious disputes and challenges to his rights, and cannot therefore be impartial. It was not compiled, as manorial surveys usually were, by a 'jury' made up of tenants of a manor to provide an (in theory) impartial record, but was a statement based on rent rolls, court records and leases, drawn up by one individual who knew the lordship intimately. In terms of such records it was more properly described as a 'particular', an owner or agent's record of rights and property, rather than a 'survey'. Having said that, it is clear from its content that Powell's Survey is essentially a record of facts rather than of convenient opinions.

Although necessarily containing many lawyers' terms and concepts the narrative text within the Survey is clear and easy both to follow and to understand. It is largely self-explanatory and terms

---

6.   A major factor must have been that both Gower and the eastern lordship were then in the hands of one lord, the Earl of Worcester. *GCH*. III, p.571.
7.   David Rees. 'Gower Divided', *Gower* 50 (1999), pp.15-19.

which appear daunting to modern eyes, and no doubt to those of eighteenth-century laymen also, are quickly followed by explanations. The spelling of place-names is sometimes unusual and often erratic, but the most obscure often can be recognised if read phonetically. In the rural areas the majority of the farm names can be found still on the modern 1:25000 Ordnance Survey maps. More obscure locations and boundaries can often be identified with the aid of the tithe apportionment maps and schedules, many made less than eighty years after the Survey. They can also be sought on the Penrice and Beaufort estate maps, prepared around 1780 and from 1800 to 1826 respectively[8].

Within the lordship the greatest detail is given for those manors which the Duke held in his own hands, his *demesne* manors, where there were no intermediate 'lords of the manor' between him and his tenants, or their rents. The Survey has very full accounts of Oystermouth, Pennard, Lunnon, Kittle, Trewyddfa, and Bishopston (the latter, which formerly belonged to the Bishops of Llandaff, having been purchased by the Duke c.1702). The Duke also held in his own hands the two manors known as Welsh Gower above the wood, and Welsh Gower below the wood (Gower Wallicana Supraboscus and Subboscus[9]), the former covering most of the hill country north of Swansea, the latter a much smaller area in the north-east corner of the peninsula. He also held the manor of English Gower (Gower Anglicana). Covering rather more than the peninsula, in its strict sense this included the intermediate (*mesne*) manors of west Gower (Penrice, Reynoldston etc.). In practical terms it was principally composed of many individual properties and farms etc. which paid rents directly to the Duke, lying in a swathe from Swansea and Blackpill across to Loughor and even to the Cathan brook in the north-west. All of these demesne holdings together with the names of their tenants are listed in the rent rolls in the Survey. The mesne manors held by the various lords of the manor are not described in such detail, but they are listed in full, even including some which were very small, effectively defunct, or both.

The Survey describes in detail the boundaries of nearly all of the manors, demesne or mesne, sometimes using descriptions contained in earlier surveys made many years before. In these cases care was taken to update the references to owners and tenants mentioned in the older surveys. Manorial boundaries sometimes followed parish boundaries for part of their length, but often they went their own way, and only rarely in Gower did parish and manor coincide to any great extent. A serious study of the origins of these boundaries would be a welcome addition to local historical literature. However, not all manors had defined boundaries, nor were their land-holdings always grouped together, and some manors had holdings in faraway places (e.g. Kennextone in Llangennith was held of Oystermouth manor, as was part of Scurlage Castle farm). The specific reasons may have been long forgotten, but 'administrative convenience' may explain some. Several manors had detached portions, including Reynoldston and Weobley. In the latter case, half of Weobley manor was in Bishopston parish, lying between Barland Common and Upper Killay. Manselfield, near Murton and Bishopston, was a detached part of Nicholaston manor, four miles distant. Part of Oxwich manor was near Cheriton, also four miles distant from the main body of the manor.

8.   Held in WGRO. Ref. D/D P 808-821 and D/D Beau. E/1 & 2.
9.   Seyler argued from the Welsh forms, Uwchcoed and Iscoed, that the meaning was 'upper wood' and 'lower wood'. See Seyler op. cit. note 1 above, 1924, p.312.

The Lordship of Kilvey is described in detail in the Survey and was always associated with and held with the Lordship of Gower. It comprised a large area of land east of the Tawe, and although it would be extensive as a manor, it is surprising to find it designated not only as a lordship, but as a 'lordship royal'. This was an alternative title for a marcher lordship, similar to its much larger neighbour Gower. It had many small farms, often very small indeed, but by 1764 it had become the location of coal mines, waggon-roads and several copperworks and other industrial undertakings. It had much in common with the Welshry areas of Gower, both in its soils and also in the almost exclusively freehold tenure within it, each tenant paying a fixed quit rent to the Duke. By 1764 most of these small freeholds had come into the hands of one major owner, with two lesser ones holding most of the rest.

Pennard was a demesne manor, and is likely to have been held directly from the lord of Gower from the time of its conquest. It was large and fertile, and had three lesser manors, referred to as fees, belonging to it. Two of these, Kittle and Lunnon, were contiguous to Pennard. The third, Trewyddfa, was an oddity, for it lies seven miles from Pennard, away in the Swansea Valley. It has been plausibly suggested that before the conquest of Gower, Trewyddfa had been a demesne of its Welsh lords, subsequently acquired as a unit by their successors and added to their major holding at Pennard. 'Administrative convenience' may explain this and other manorial links between widely-scattered holdings, but in this case, as no doubt in others, the convenience was the lord's. The tenants of Trewyddfa had to attend the twice-yearly manor courts and these were held in Pennard, nine miles journey from their homes, on foot or horseback. Compared with Pennard, Trewyddfa's soil was indifferent, and there were extensive 'wastes' or commons within it. There were, however, large reserves of coal below it and the navigable Tawe gave convenient access. In the eighteenth century Trewyddfa became one of the most valuable of manorial properties, with many coal mines and several copperworks within it, and it was here that the bitter disputes over mineral rights developed, disputes which were to lead to the creation of the 1764 Survey. That the Survey was compiled by the Duke's officers rather than by a jury of the lordship's tenants is not surprising in view of the opinion expressed by Powell in June 1756 that:

> *In the temper of the Seigniory as at present, I think it will not be proper to attempt making any Surveys or doing other public acts of that kind . . . but . . . I will take care not to let it slip*[10].

In September 1760 formal written instructions were issued to Gabriel Powell and his colleague Mr Gardiner to prepare a survey of the lordship[11]. The instructions, issued by Mr Duthy, the duke's principal agent at Badminton, are lengthy and detailed, and the contents and form of the completed survey follows them closely. It is likely that Gabriel Powell had as large an input into their preparation as he had in creating during the next four years his unique Survey of Gower and Kilvey.

10. NLW. II, 2396 (–. 6. 1756).
11. NLW. II, 1494 (9.1760).

iii. The Lordship, its Manors and its Tenants

Until 1536 and the first of the Acts of Union, the Lordship of Gower was, like other marcher lordships, almost an independent realm. It was bound to the English crown only by its lord's fealty to the monarch and by the statute law. However, within such lordships the manorial systems were broadly similar to those of other more ordinary lordships in England, though those in turn varied greatly. The details are complicated, but the marcher lord 'owned' the lordship and in his lordship everyone who had land held it as the lord's tenant. If the lordship had not been a marcher lordship all its land-holders would have been tenants of the king, including its lord, and he would have the king's 'tenant in chief'. In the first three centuries or so after its conquest Gower, as a marcher lordship, had its own hierarchy of landholders headed by the marcher lord, with below him his own tenants in chief, who held their manors from him by knight's service. These were the local 'lords of the manor'. Some manors had been granted to the Church and these were held 'in free alms' or similar concessionary tenures. Next came a large number of free tenants who paid fixed rents and had to attend the lord's courts, grind their corn at his mills etc. Below them were the many 'bondmen' who held their lands from the lord in return for their labour services on his demesne (the land kept for his own use), in addition to rent and other services. Unlike the freeholders these tenants were 'unfree' and could not move away from their manor or lordship without the lord's express permission. Below them in status, in a society where land and tenure were the basis of social standing, came the landless labourers, usually having just a cottage and garden held at the will of the lord.

There had been major changes in the manorial system within the lordship by the time of Gabriel Powell's Survey, six and a half centuries after the conquest[12], but the main landholding categories can still be recognised and another had been increased substantially. Following a statute of Charles II, the lords of the manors no longer held by knight's service, but in common soccage. They were freeholders, and had to attend the lordship courts and make certain specified payments to the lord. The general body of freeholders had seen little change, though the rents they paid, fixed at the medieval levels, were gradually becoming nominal. However, great changes had occurred in the position of the former unfree tenants. Their compulsory labour on behalf of the lord had gradually been replaced by payments of fixed rents, which in turn had, like the freehold rents, gradually become nominal through inflation. The onerous requirements which tied them to a lord and his lordship or manor had withered away, and even the former stigma of holding such lands had long gone by the eighteenth century. They had become known as 'Copyholds' or 'Customary tenancies' and there are many references to them under both names in the Survey. Nominally they still held their lands 'at the will of the lord', but the lord's freedom of action had become circumscribed by the acceptance in law of the over-riding requirements of 'the custom of the manor'. Manorial customs varied greatly, but were generally clear within individual manors. Although copyholders had to seek the consent of the manorial court to any transfer of their tenancy (otherwise it could be forfeited to the lord), transfers to heirs and even sales to third parties were usually approved. The position of these once unfree tenancies had improved to the extent that by the eighteenth century they were almost as desirable as freeholds. In the nineteenth

---

12. The period from the conquest to the Survey was almost three times as long as from the Survey to the present day.

century this was recognised by Acts of Parliament from 1841 which enabled copyholders to purchase the freehold interest in their holdings. Copyhold tenure was finally abolished in January 1926 by the Law of Property Act of 1922.

Tenancies which were truly at the will of the lord continued to be granted, and there are many of these in the Survey. They usually applied, as in earlier centuries, to small cottages or pieces of land encroached from the lord's commons, and also to cases where a lease had expired and had not been renewed or surrendered, the former lessee being permitted to remain in the meantime 'at the will of the lord'.

Leases were a form of tenancy found in medieval times, but which had come into greater use from the sixteenth century onwards, and many are described in detail in the Survey. They operated much as modern leases do, and granted a named lessee or lessees the right to occupy land for a defined period at a stated rent. They were granted in respect of lands which were in the lord's hands either as his original demesne, or as land forfeited to him by misdeeds of the former tenants or by extinction of a tenant family. Leases could be for so many years, or for the terms of the lives of several specifed persons, usually three and usually the lessee and his family. They could also be for both, e.g. for ninety-nine years or the longest surviving life of three, whichever was the shorter. There was normally provision for the lease to be assigned (sold). Subject to the economic situation, leases usually gave landlords the chance to get an up-to-date initial rent, often with a lump sum as a starting premium or 'fine'. Additional payments and conditions were also included, many of which required standard manorial services or a cash equivalent. Leases granted in the early 1700s and recorded in the Survey contained requirements for the lessee to do service for the lord "with oxen and horses when required", resurrecting the old impositions once placed on unfree tenants. The opportunity was also taken to require the lessee to grind his corn at the lord's mill, and to attend the manorial courts. A common requirement was the free supply of two fat capons on St Thomas' Day yearly (or a cash sum in lieu). St Thomas' Day is 21st December, so the festive season would be well provided for. Leases were written documents which set out their terms in detail, and the Survey is at its most informative when it refers to them, the entries often being paraphrased directly from the original document.

In the more anglicised manors copyholds were common, existing alongside freehold tenancies. Powell specifically pointed out that Pennard was a "meer Copyhold" manor, except from a few freeholds in Kittle. He needed to stress this because distant Trewyddfa was part of the manor of Pennard, and here the disputes over rights to coal and other minerals were intense. Freeholders could properly claim the minerals under their land, but copyholders could not, hence Powell's emphasis of the point.

In the extensive Wallicana manors, the parts of the lordship where anglicised settlement and interference was least, copyholds were entirely absent. Apart from minor tenancies at will and the leases of demesne land, all the tenants were freeholders, individually holding the many scattered farms which are still characteristic of much of these parts of the lordship. In the Welshry, the Wallicana areas, compact 'English' style villages were absent before the new settlements of the industrial age, and even where ancient churches provided a focus few, if any, houses stood close by them. Following the conquest these areas were clearly treated differently from the peninsula, but their old ways were still subjected to major changes. The ancient Welsh land-holding system consisted of groups of related persons which each held a specific and quite large area of land on a communal basis, in return for rents and services due to their lord[13]. How quickly this was changed by the new lord we cannot say, but it may have been at an early date that the Welsh system was replaced by the numerous individual freeholds listed in the Survey[14]. By Powell's time many of the freeholds were owned by landlords who had let them to the occupiers. The location and extent of most of them can be found on the tithe maps of the 1840s, and many of the names are still on the 1:25000 Ordnance Survey maps.

One interesting anomaly deserves particular mention. At the far north-east corner of Gower was the manor of Caegurwen, a mesne manor held of the lord of Gower on the same basis as the manors in the peninsula. It lay at the furthest edge of the Welshry and it appears that this manor was at first part of Gower Supraboscus, until the aftermath of the failed rising of Rhys ap Maredudd of Dryslwyn in 1287. The Welsh freeholders in this northern part of Gower had supported Rhys and subsequently forfeited or surrendered their lands, which were then combined to form the new manor of Caegurwen. Initially it was held by the lord himself, but later became a mesne manor similar to those in the peninsula[15].

Although Gabriel Powell's Survey is so valuable as a record of the manorial system within the ancient lordship, it must be remembered that, as mentioned, the period which had elapsed between the conquest of Gower and the writing of the Survey was nearly three times greater than that between the Survey and the present. There had been great changes which its author was well aware of, for example commenting in introducing his description of Gower Supraboscus:

> . . . *it must be observed by the rent roll of the Chief Rents that the Englishery and the Welshery were in ancient times greatly intermixed.*

He well knew of valuable rights of the lord which had been lost or fallen into disuse, such as rights of Admiralty which gave jurisdiction over offences committed at sea near the lordship and entitlement to Prisage and Butlerage of Wines – a duty of ten per cent on imported wines, increased to twenty per cent if the vessel concerned was foreign. The greatest changes, however, had been brought about by the abolition of the lordship's independent legal jurisdiction by the Act(s) of Union. The manor courts had not been abolished by the Union and they continued to function actively through the eighteenth century. Weakened in the nineteenth century by the gradual enfranchisement of copyhold tenure, their basic purpose ceased with the abolition of that form of land-holding on 1st January 1926[16].

As well as his rights relating to land tenure and the holding of courts, the marcher lord had many other feudal rights and entitlements to customary payments and although they gradually

---

13. G.H. Eaton. 'A Survey of the Manor in Seventeenth Century Gower' (Unpublished UCS. MA thesis, 1936), p.239, quotes the *Black Book of St David's,* re the continuance of this ancient 'gwelyau' system in Llangyfelach as late as 1326. See also *GCH.* III, 214, 215.

14. But for an indication that the freehold tenancies in Wallicana manors may once have been customary tenancies, or, more probably, had been subject to onerous customary payments etc., and that in the mid 1500s these had been converted to freeholds in return for a payment, see W.R.B. Robinson, 'The Litigation of Edward Earl of Worcester, concerning Gower, 1590-1596'. *BBCS.* XXII, pt. 4 (5.1968), p.362 and XXIII pt 1 (11.1968), pp.67-68.

15. David Rees. 'Neuadd Wen: Changing Patterns of Tenure' in H. James (ed.) *Sir Gar: Studies in Carmarthenshire History* (Carmarthen 1991). Also his 'The Gower Estates of Sir Rhys ap Thomas' in *Gower* XLIII (1992), pp.31-41.

16. Under the provisions of the Law of Property Act 1922.

came to appear anachronistic, the surviving ones are carefully recorded by Powell. Of these the most onerous was that known as 'Mises', set at the very large sum of two hundred pounds due from the lordship as a whole, and to which every manorial tenant had to contribute[17]. This payment became due whenever a new lord succeeded on the death of his predecessor and its timing was always uncertain, and could be frequent. Although Gabriel Powell had written to the new duke in March 1745 pointing out his right to collect mises following the death of his predecessor[18] nothing seems to have been done about it, and the last recorded collection was in 1714[19].

Another apparently anachronistic annual payment due to the lord was that recorded as 'Toll Pixie', a fey title for a levy on practical persons, for it was charged on all craftsmen and buyers and sellers within most, but not all, of the parishes of the southern part of the peninsula. It has the appearance of an ancient measure to ensure that those who made a living in the lordship other than from the land should still contribute to the lord's income. The boroughs did not pay it because they had been created for purposes of trade and manufacture, but the exclusion of Reynoldston, Llanmadoc and Rhossili is interesting, as also is the use of parishes rather than manors in selecting the payment areas.

More appropriate in modern eyes are the provisions for payment of 'Ferry Corn', entitling the inhabitants of the lordship to use the ferry at Swansea[20] in return for an a single annual payment, assessed at a specified number of sheaves for those growing corn, and two-pence to four-pence for other householders. The Swansea ferry was the only way of crossing the lower five miles of the Tawe, and in return for these payments the lord had to provide and maintain a ferry boat. The payment areas were based on parishes, and Llangyfelach, Llangiwg, and Llandeilo Talybont are not included in the listing. The first two comprise most of the Supraboscus Welshry, but the latter was largely Englishry. The distinction is probably that the northern part of the lordship was nearer to bridges over the upper parts of the Tawe and had less need for regular use of the ferry at Swansea.

The Survey also records that the lord was entitled to various other rights and payments, the most valuable being those arising out of court actions and decisions. These even included receipts from penalties imposed by courts which were no longer within his jurisdiction as a result of the Act(s) of Union. It seems clear these various rights were but a shadow of the lord's former privileges, and that it was wise for his Steward to direct his energies towards the preservation of his master's landed interests, and particularly to the protection of his new-found mineral wealth.

iv. Gabriel Powell and his Times

The Powells were an established family of Breconshire gentry, long active in the affairs of the County and of the Borough of Brecon, who in the eighteenth century became prominent in the

17. W.R.B. Robinson. 'The Litigation of Edward, Earl of Worcester concerning Gower, 1590 to 1596'. *BBCS.* XXIII, p.74. The sum due had been set at £200 in 1596, but the entitlement was ancient.
18. NLW. II, 2327 (16.3.1744/5).
19. W.R.B. Robinson. op. cit. note 14, p.75.
20. The ferry was on the site of the present Sainsbury's car park, Quay Parade, Swansea.

affairs of Swansea and Gower[21]. Among the generations of Powells the names William, Thomas, Daniel, Hugh and John occur frequently, but Gabriel was much used, and it was some of these Gabriel Powells who became prominent in the Swansea area in the 1700s.

John ap Howell, Rector of Cantreff, who died in 1626 had taken the anglicised form 'Powell' for his surname, and his third son was a Gabriel, the first in this family to bear the name Gabriel Powell. He died in 1685, and although none of his children then surviving were Gabriels, there were three of them amongst his grandchildren. One of these, the eldest son of William (second son of the Gabriel who died in 1685), was the first of the family to become active in the Swansea area. Styled Gabriel Powell of Pennant in the Borough of Brecon and also of the Borough of Swansea, he had been born in 1676. As a lawyer he is recorded as acting for the Swansea Corporation in 1693, and in 1701 was admitted as a burgess of Swansea, qualified for this privilege by reason of his marriage in 1696 to the daughter of a burgess. He moved rapidly through the local hierarchy, becoming portreeve (approximately equivalent to mayor) in 1705 and again in 1713 and 1726.

His family background, his profession as a lawyer, and his Breconshire origins must have helped him advance still further, when, in 1708, John Watkins of Pen yr Wrlodd[22], another Beconshire man and the steward of the Duke of Beaufort's Lordship of Gower, died and Gabriel Powell soon replaced him in this prestigious office. He continued acting on behalf of many important local families, as well as representing the duke, and he was also actively involved in some the major industrial ventures which were beginning to transform Swansea into a major copper smelting and coal mining centre. Amongst his business partners and clients were James Griffiths and Silvanus Bevan, who in 1720 set up the first (and last) copperworks within the Borough boundaries, and also Robert Morris, whose similar works in the Swansea Valley proved much more successful, and whose son John later founded the town of Morriston.

He died on 5th November 1735 and was buried in the Priory of Brecon (now Brecon Cathedral), but his place was soon filled by one of his sons, yet another Gabriel Powell, the active, able and long-lived compiler of 'The Survey of Gower'. Gabriel Powell the father was survived by three sons. The eldest son, John, was born in 1704 and was admitted as a Swansea burgess in 1728, as an alderman in 1731, and served as portreeve three times between 1733 and 1747. He was a lawyer and sometimes acted for the Duke of Beaufort in manorial matters. He died in February 1769.

It was the second son, Gabriel, who became steward of the Gower Estate of the Duke of Beaufort and who is therefore of particular interest. He was born on 8th May 1710 and became a solicitor, being admitted at Lincoln's Inn in November 1730. His first wife died at Swansea in December 1733 and he married his second wife, Mary, in July 1740. Following his father's death in 1735 he had succeeded him as steward of the Beaufort Estates in Gower. Already, in September 1732, he had been admitted as a burgess and as an alderman of the Borough of Swansea, thus acquiring influence and seniority at the age of just twenty-two. To attain both of these positions

---

21. This chapter outlining the family history is based on the researches of W.C. Rogers, who in turn had the benefit of information passed to him by living representatives. In 1946 he produced the careful, complex and lengthy account of the family's history which can be found in the unpublished typescript pages of his 'Swansea and Glamorgan Calendar', which quotes his sources. Copies are held at: NLW.; Swansea Public Reference Library; and UWS (for Swansea Museum). His account of the Powell family is in Part I, Vol. I, as Appendix 5, pp.310-375.

22. Near Hay on Wye. Gellihir, Ilston, was his Gower home for a time. There is an eroded memorial to him in Ilston churchyard, near the tower.

together on the one day was an event most remarkable in itself. Such was the standing of the family in Swansea's ruling circles that in September of the following year, at twenty-three years of age, he was nominated as one of two candidates for portreeve. The other candidate was his brother, John, and it was John who was then selected for this, the most senior office of the Corporation. Having again, in 1735, been nominated but not selected, Gabriel eventually became portreeve in September 1740. The following twelve months period was the only time during which he served as portreeve, but his influential and responsible position as the duke's steward, combined with his standing in civic affairs as burgess and alderman, one of the small and exclusive body which governed the borough, ensured that he became a dominant figure in the affairs of Swansea and its neighbourhood from the 1730s until his death in December 1788. In reporting that event the *Hereford Journal* of 5th January commented that:

He was commonly called "King of Swansea", a nominal dignity arising from an old custom.

The connection with "old custom" seems unlikely, but this Gabriel Powell's position and actions during a long and influential career would appear to have been sufficient to have earned him that regal title, though, perhaps, not entirely as a compliment. His professional and business activities are discussed in more detail below.

His elder son was another Gabriel, who was knighted in 1800, thus making it easier to distinguish him from the many other similarly-named Powells. He was born at Swansea in 1753 and admitted into Lincoln's Inn in 1770, thus following his family's involvement in the law. He was admitted a burgess of Swansea in 1771, but being then still under twenty-one years of age he had to wait until 1774 before he could be formally sworn. Elevation to alderman soon followed and in September 1776 he became portreeve, serving again in this office in 1795. In 1778 he married Mary, one of the two daughters of Joseph Price of Ilston, co-heiresses of his Gellihir estate. Their home, the ancient mansion of Gellihir, burnt down on the night of 13th January 1788, and Mary died in 1793. Her husband had moved first to Fairwood Lodge, Killay, and became prominent in moves to defend the Swansea area during the Napoleonic wars, raising and commanding the Fairwood Troop of Yeomanry Cavalry[23]. He became Sir Gabriel after attending with many other dignitaries on King George III, to congratulate him on escaping an attempted assassination. He was knighted at St James' Palace on 2nd July 1800. It is a familiar story, but one well worth repeating, that, on hearing of Sir Gabriel's knighthood, the general comment in Swansea was "Now we *know* the King is mad!". His last residence was Heathfield Lodge, Mount Pleasant, where he died on 11th November 1813.

His younger brother was the Rev. Thomas Powell, born at Swansea in 1755. He was admitted a burgess of Swansea in 1771, on the same day as his brother, but was not sworn until 1776 when he came of age. His main interests lay in Breconshire, although he maintained some Swansea connections. He became portreeve in 1778, and acted as deputy portreeve for his brother on occasions during 1795-96. It is he who has been identified as the fighting clergyman in the 1787 cartoon of the Swansea Corporation "discussing harbour improvements" (see below, p. 29). He

---

23. Raised in 1798 as the Fairwood Troop of Gentlemen and Yeomanry.

lived at Peterstone Court, and was the rector of Cantreff, Brecon, a living which had been in the hands of the Powells for generations.

The Powell family produced many children in each generation, and appear to have been a robust lot with a high survival rate, so there will be many who can claim descent from them today. This present account is only intended to mention the near relatives and descendants of the Gabriel Powell who compiled the 'Survey of Gower' but will, in conclusion, mention just one more Gabriel, one of his grandchildren, elder son of the Rev. Thomas Powell. He had been born in 1788 and was admitted and sworn as a Swansea burgess in 1810, being described as "of Cantreff". He was active in Swansea Harbour Trust affairs and in January 1816 had been appointed Comptroller of Customs at Swansea. Lewis Weston Dillwyn records in his diary entry for Tuesday 7th November 1820:

> *Went with Mary in the carriage to dine at Mr Gabriel Powell's in Rutland Place where we met the Morrises, Vivians etc., who together formed a pleasant party, and had the best dinner we had either of us seen in Swansea*[24].

With both the company and the food, this Gabriel evidently was still making his family's mark on Swansea society. He was elected portreeve on 29th September 1826, and to mark the occasion gave what was then described as a "sumptuous dinner" at the Assembly Rooms for the Corporation and gentry of Swansea and the officers of a Royal Navy vessel then surveying the harbour[25]. This may be, perhaps, a suitably high point on which to end this overview of the Powell family and their involvement with Swansea.

The Steward and his Stewardship

Stewardship, but no Sinecure

It will be seen from the account of the Powell family given above that they were newcomers to Swansea in the eighteenth century. Gabriel Powell the elder became the Duke of Beaufort's Steward of his Lordships of Gower and Kilvey in about 1708 and held this responsible and powerful position until his death in 1735, serving two successive dukes in this time. The offices of the lordship lapsed automatically at the death of each duke, and the making of new appointments rested with the new duke. The officers held their positions at the will of the lord, so that existing holders could never feel entirely secure even during the life of the duke who had appointed them. The office of steward of the lordships seems often to have passed quite quickly between various local notables, and during some periods the duty of holding the lordship courts seems to have been shared between several gentry[26]. It was the elder Gabriel who established the singular hold on the office of steward which, after his death, was held for most of the remainder of the eighteenth century by Gabriel Powell, his second son. Despite the (no doubt ironic) local reference

24. NLW. 'Calendar of the Diary of Lewis Weston Dillwyn'. Typescript volumes.
25. *The Cambrian* 7.10. 1826, p.3 col.1. The vessel was H.M.S. Shamroc, Capt. Martin White R.N., which had been surveying Swansea harbour for the chart published in 1830. A copy is in WGRO. ref. D/D WCR/P1/26. The vessel is named as "Shamrock" in *The Cambrian*, but as 'Shamroc' on the chart.
26. See the 'List of Stewards' in Appendix I below. Also the summaries of names of persons holding the Seigniory Courts, given in NLW. Badminton Group II Schedules – vols. I-III.

to this latter Gabriel as 'the King of Swansea', the succession of the son to the father's position was in no way automatic, nor could his subsequent life-long tenure have been relied upon. Influential economic and political rivals of the Dukes of Beaufort, as well as other senior members within the lords' own legal and financial organisation, could object to or question the actions of the steward, for good or bad reasons, and if he lost the reigning duke's trust professionally or personally, his successor would quickly be sought[27]. To be Steward of the Lordships of Gower and Kilvey was neither a job for life, nor, as we shall see, a sinecure.

In May 1736, just six months after his father's death, the new steward was having to defend himself and indirectly his late father, against allegations of inefficiency. These came not from those who were the opponents of the ducal interests, but from Mr Robert Morris[28] and Mr Gardiner, the latter being the receiver (effectively, the chief accountant) for the Beaufort estates and the former the local industrialist who worked within the fee (i.e. sub-manor) of Trewyddfa. Powell defended his conduct robustly and showed that already he had a firm grasp of the history of disputes in the manor[29].

It appears from the surviving correspondence that it had been alleged that Gabriel Powell, and his father before him, had not taken adequate steps to safeguard the Duke's commons in Trewyddfa against encroachments. Powell confirmed[30] that the customary tenants had always pastured their livestock on the commons there, and that the lord's agents had claimed rent from them for this, "but I can't find that that rent has been particularly (i.e. identifiably) paid ever since the Civil Wars". He then makes the point that since "the time your Grace's Estates were sequestered by Oliver Cromwell" the customary rents had nearly doubled, and he thinks the rent for use of the commons is included as part of the higher rent. He further refers to the sale of some of these commons to the Herbert family (this was in 1556[31]) and to later attempts by their lessee to enclose them – "but at the Revolution the tenants broke down the new inclosures". In 1714 the late Duke had begun court action to recover these lands, but both parties to the action died before any judgement had been obtained. However, Gabriel Powell senior had prevailed on the occupiers of the many cottages which had been erected on the commons to acknowledge the lord's ownership and to pay rent for their small but numerous encroachments. The cottage people kept horses on the commons, and some kept cattle and sheep there, to the prejudice of the rights of the copyhold tenants. Powell would be taking action on this complaint. The essence of Powell's answer to the allegations of apparent inaction was that there was a complicated legal background, and that he and his father had done remarkably well on behalf of the duke in all the circumstances. In an earlier response[32] he had indignantly declared:

> *My father knew and I believe preserved your Grace's rights as well as any man that ever lived in Gower; and he took some pains to make me thoroughly acquainted with them. And I can*

---

27. Sir Edward Mansel, Steward and Receiver of Gower, was dismissed by the Earl of Worcester, (his brother in law) in 1578. See W.R.B. Robinson. 'The Litigation of Edward, Earl of Worcester concerning Gower, 1590-1596, in *BBCS.* XXII, pt.IV (May 1968) p.367.
28. Founder of the Morris family fortunes in Swansea and usually allied with the Duke's representatives. Not to be confused with Robert, his son, their fierce opponent. See below p. 28).
29. NLW. II, 2321 (15.5.1736) & 2323 (1.7.1737).
30. NLW. II, 2323 (1.7.1737).
31. WHJ. *History* II, p.80.
32. NLW. II, 2321 (15.5.1736).

venture to defy Mr Gardiner or Mr Morris to show one single right that was lost during his whole service under your Grace.

Pressure came on the steward from many quarters, as will become evident, but it is clear that sometimes he had to answer to those within his own circle also. Some aspects of a busy professional life have, perhaps, changed little.

Valuable Wastes

The prevention or control of encroachments on the commons and 'waste' lands of the Lordships of Gower and Kilvey was an important concern of the steward. From early medieval times these unenclosed lands had formed a valuable resource for the Lord's tenants, providing pasture for livestock additional to that on the enclosed holdings, as well as economic benefits, such as the right to cut furze (gorse) for feed, and fern for bedding, and to dig turf, quarry stones, and to a limited extent, in some cases, to dig for coal for their own use. As the 'Survey' makes clear, these benefits were rarely free, but the rents payable to the lord by the commoners were not large. Encroachments were not necessarily unwelcome to the lord, provided that he received a suitable financial return and adequate legal acknowledgement, and the erection of cottages with small gardens on the commons was usually accepted, as long as rent was paid. Many of these latter encroachments occurred in Trewyddfa, providing impromptu self-build housing for the growing workforce in the coal and copper industries.

The manorial copyholders and freeholders took a different view of the enclosure of commons, unless they had a direct interest in a particular case. Enclosure, even by the erection of small cottages, reduced the area over which their common rights could be exercised, and – as shown above – the workers in the cottages soon began putting their livestock on the common in competition with the rights of the long-standing manorial tenants. When, occasionally, the lord attempted to permit new large-scale encroachment on the commons, spontaneous pulling-down of the new hedges and fences by the existing manorial tenants was likely to result.

Lost Lands Remembered

In the Lordships of Gower and Kilvey in the eighteenth century there were two other major considerations affecting the Beaufort Estate's attitudes to its common lands, one historical, the other very contemporary. The first of these was the need to prevent surreptitious enclosure, amounting to theft of the Estate's lands, which had apparently happened on a very large scale two centuries earlier. During the time of William Somerset, Earl of Worcester (Lord of Gower from 1549 to 1589), the administration of his Gower Estate had become very lax. Many of his tenants took advantage of the situation to enlarge their holdings by large-scale encroachment on the lord's commons and wastes and it appears that some local office-holders, whose duty it was to safeguard the earl's interests, had been amongst those who had benefited. Corruption had been added to negligence. Remedies at law were not sought until near the end of Earl William's life, and were continued more actively by his son and successor, Earl Edward (lord from 1589 to 1628). Too much time had passed, and the alleged encroachers on the ground had the advantage over their absentee lord when it came to providing evidence of former boundaries so many years before.

The defence in most cases was that the land alleged to have been encroached had always been part of the legitimate tenancy. Litigation, of which a detailed record survives, continued until 1594, when the lord's case against the tenants who were alleged to have encroached on his lands was dismissed by the Court of Wards and Liveries[33]. In 1755 Powell could still refer to Queen Elizabeth's reign as a time when there were "great disputes between the Lord and the Tenants". The Worcesters, and the Beauforts after them, had had a hard lesson in the dangers of neglecting their more distant estates, one which was unlikely to be soon forgotten.

Coal and Copper

The second, more contemporary, consideration was the continuous increase during the eighteenth century in the exploitation of mineral resources, particularly coal. Mining for coal in Gower and Kilvey was not new, and is documented both in general and in some detail in the fourteenth century[34]. Most of the lordship's extensive commons and wastes were in the duke's own hands. They were subject to common rights, but these did not include rights to mine and sell the coal beneath them. The duke also claimed coal lying beneath the extensive copyhold lands in his various demesne manors. After all, when the copyhold tenancies were originally created, the digging and selling of coal was unlikely to have been seen as something of particular value to have been passed from the lord to the tenant. In the Lordship of Kilvey, the duke claimed a right to have four pence for every weigh[35] of coal dug and "sold to sea", irrespective of the nature of the tenure of the land in which it was found, and this comprehensive levy probably originates in the relatively early exploitation of coal seams on that side of the River Tawe.

Most of the known and potential coal resources lay under what had been the agriculturally less productive parts of the Lordships of Gower and Kilvey, the greater part being in the Welshry areas, and here the commons were more extensive than in other parts of the lordships. By Gabriel Powell's time no one had any illusions about the considerable value of these commons and the minerals below them. In 1759 he warned the duchess (as legal guardian of the young duke) that the commons and wastes must be safeguarded, as otherwise it:

> . . . *may be a very great loss to my Lord Duke, for the coal under the wastes is worth several thousand – I am sure I may with safety say several hundred thousand – pounds, and if once the tenants get beyond their inclosures, they will know no bounds*[36].

These were large, indeed immense, sums. While tensions between new industrialists and the older aristocratic order would have played some part in the acrimony which developed between the duke's officers and some of his major tenants in eighteenth-century Gower, the basic argument was about money, and about who was entitled to have it. The successive dukes had no objection to industry or to industrialists as such, and happily encouraged incoming entrepreneurs, such as the Morrises and Chauncey Townsend to mine coal, construct waggon roads and watercourses, and to erect copperworks within the lordship, provided appropriate financial benefit came to

33. W.R.B. Robinson, op. cit., note 14 above, describes the litigation in detail.
34. G. Grant Francis *Charters Granted to Swansea* (Swansea, 1867), p.7 (Charter of 1306); and South Wales Record Soc. Publication No. 1 (1949), pp.180-187, 'Lordship of Kilvey, Account of the Receiver of Mines & Coals, 1399-1400'.
35. The 'weigh' or 'wey' could be variable, but averaged around 5 tons in the Swansea area. See 'Copper Concern' 1774.
36. NLW. II, 2404 (29.11.1759).

them. It was with some of the long-established local gentry families, themselves anxious to exploit the valuable coal seams beneath their ancestral lands, that the often fiercely- acrimonious disputes arose. The principal antagonists of the duke's interest – and certainly of his steward – were the related families of the Prices of Penllergaer and the Popkins of Fforest, both long-established in the area. They held much of their estates as copyhold tenancies from the lord, who claimed ownership of all minerals (which included coal) therein. This was initially accepted, with reluctance, by the tenants and a number of leases had been granted to them giving the specific right to mine the coal beneath their copyholds, in return for a rent payable to the lord based on the amount of coal actually mined.

On the manorial commons the copyholders had rights of pasture, but the lord claimed the minerals beneath these also, and looked for a proper share of the value arising from any mining there. In addition, the lord claimed ownership of all highways, and even where tenants had leased the rights to work coal under their copyhold lands, they could not (without permission – and payment) continue their workings under the highway to link with other mines on the other side of the road. Matters became more contentious where the local gentry concerned were also themselves lords of one of the Gower manors, and claimed all rights in, and under, the commons there. With the duke also claiming the same rights, and with potentially large sums involved, conflict was almost certain.

Personal Rivalries

Other factors aggravated the commercial disputes between the Dukes of Beaufort and the Prices of Penllergaer, and more particularly, between Gryffydd Price and Gabriel Powell. Thomas Price, Gryffydd's father (or perhaps it was his similarly-named grandfather) himself had been steward of Gower in 1706[37] and perhaps in other years, as one of the local gentry who had shared the office for short periods before the incoming Powells had established their virtual monopoly of it, one which was to last for most of the eighteenth century. It was certainly the father of Gryffydd Price who was steward of the Bishop of St David's Manor of Clase when its boundary was disputed in 1749[38]. Powell was a solicitor and well-versed in the law and in the courts and their procedures. Gryffydd Price was a barrister, who became a King's Counsel, and also achieved other substantial distinctions in a professional career which was mainly pursued away from Swansea. It is not surprising to find rivalry between these two able professionals fuelling the disputes between the duke's interest and the claims of his tenants. Another factor is that the Prices clearly regarded themselves, and seem to have been regarded, as champions and protectors of their neighbours and tenants in the 'upper parts' of Gower, otherwise the Welshry of the lordship[39], and as such were acting out a traditional role of great antiquity.

Litigation and Violence

However great the effect of these various factors may have been, disputes in the Price/Popkin parts of the lordship became increasingly bitter in the middle years of the century, sometimes

37. See the list of Stewards, Appendix I.
38. NLW. II, 2395 (–.6.1756, referring to earlier events).
39. NLW. II 2359a (11.4.1751); 2360 (13.4.1751) & 2361 a/b (27.4.1751).

leading to violence and even death. In 1724, when Robert Morris was becoming active in the Swansea area, he was involved in the affairs of the Llangyfelach copperworks. It stood just inside the boundary of the parish of Llangyfelach, hence its name, and it had been built at Landore in 1717, the pioneer copperworks in the Swansea Valley. Acting first as receiver for the former owner's creditors, Morris and his partners took over the works in 1727. Under the terms of the lease their coal supplies had to come from Thomas Popkin, who had coal works on his own freehold lands. He also later obtained from the duke a lease enabling him to mine the coal under his copyhold lands (see p. 163, folio 91). The poor quality of the coal supplied by Popkin had caused problems and disputes, and so the copperworks owners had obtained their own rights to mine coal under the duke's Trewyddfa Common. There, between modern Morriston and Plasmarl, Robert Morris senior, owner with Richard and John Lockwood of the Fforest copperworks, had opened his own coal mine under a lease from the duke.

In November 1753 Gabriel Powell was able to report to the duke, with evident personal satisfaction:

> *Mr Morris has at last been so fortunate as to discover the Great Penvilia Coal Vein in its full perfection at the bottom of Trewyddfa Common, just above the copperworks, which will in all probability yield great profit to your Grace, as well as the Company, and be a means to discover other veins of coal there and under Lower Forrest farm, which have hitherto been attempted in vain*[40].

Morris was working his coal by vertical shafts or pits, as well as by levels driven into the hillside, and in December 1754 Powell wrote:

> *Mr Morris has at last got his new pit down and again works at his level, so he is out of Popkin's and Price's power*[41].

He also mentioned that Morris was erecting a new 'fire engine' (a steam-powered pumping engine) on the coal vein he had lately discovered on Trewyddfa Common.

Mr Thomas Price had taken direct action to disrupt Morris' operations, but:

> *Mr Price took so much pains in stopping the air from Mr Morris's (coal) works and did it so effectually, that he has for the present entirely destroyed his own*[42].

and, far worse:

> *. . . the workmen (Mr Morris's) that were imprisoned were employed to keep open the air hole, which Mr Price did so effectually shut up, that the poor fellows lost their lives . . .*

---

40. NLW. II, 2374 (15.11.1753).
41. NLW. II, 2376 (19.12.1754).
42. NLW. II, 2377 (2.1.1755).

Gabriel Powell proceeded to indict Mr Price's workmen for their actions. Two months later he succeeded at Hereford Assizes, in a trial lasting nearly seven hours, in winning two cases for the duke against Mr Popkin, having the previous day succeeded on behalf of "Mr Lockwood & Co." against "[John] John and Terry[43] for smoking their works". His opponent in the courtroom had been Gryffydd Price, barrister and son and heir of Thomas Price of Penllergaer. This younger representative of the Price family was a professional and personal rival of Powell, and the focus of most of the opposition to the duke's interests in the lordship. Powell's satisfaction, and relief, at the outcome of the trial are clear from the ending of this letter informing the duke of the outcome:

> *I hope it will cure him [Popkin] of his rashness, and convince Mr Price that he may possibly be mistaken in his law, and that it will produce Peace and Quiet in the Seigniory of Gower[44].*

None of these hopes was to be realised.

Politics and the Lordship

Some of those involved in the growth of industry and the exploitation of natural resources endeavoured to increase profit for themselves by attempting to deny the duke's rights as a landowner. Their efforts were sufficient in themselves to cause stresses within the lordship. When the opposed sides were led respectively by Gabriel Powell and by Gryffydd Price, strong characters, men of substance and standing, experienced in the law and in litigation, the prospect for "Peace and Quiet in the Seigniory of Gower" became remote indeed. The Beauforts, as the inheritors of the position and what remained of the powers of the medieval lords marcher, had a hold on most of the local organisations which performed the functions of government. The manorial courts in the extensive and valuable manors which lay in the duke's hands were presided over by his steward, who kept the all-important court rolls, and who selected the annual officers of the manors from pairs of candidates put forward by the manorial tenants. The same system of selective election was used in the Boroughs of Swansea and Loughor, though in the boroughs the burgesses who constituted the electorate were far less representative of their community than were the juries of tenants in the other manors. Rural Pennard was one of the duke's own manors and attached to it as a fee, or sub-manor, was valuable and rapidly-industrialising Trewyddfa, where many of the Price v Powell disputes originated. Yet although his manorial powers strengthened the duke's position, it was not easy for him (or his steward) to use them arbitrarily against his opponents.

The dukes took an interest in national politics, and, in a time-honoured way, looked to those of their tenants who formed part of the local electorate, to vote for their favoured candidates. Although the Beauforts had substantial influence in the choice and election of members to represent Cardiff (and its 'Contributory Boroughs', of which Swansea was one) in the national

---

43. Robert Terry, yeoman, Gryffydd Price's 'Coal Steward', was bequeathed £10 p.a. for life in Price's will, dated 6.6.1783 (copy in GRO. ref. D/D 1/184), "for his long service to my father & myself". I am grateful to Mr Jeff Childs for this particular reference.
44. NLW. II, 2380 (26.3.1755).

parliament, they were but one of several aristocratic families which involved themselves in Glamorgan elections. County politics were complex, and groupings of allies, whether aristocrats or gentry, could and did vary from election to election. Personalities outweighed policies in these alliances and although stresses between resident gentry and an absentee lord could be expected, it was squabbles over profit, not politics, which in Gower underlay the unhappy relationships between the duke and some of his substantial tenants. Even so, sanctions could be used against political dissidents and waverers, and there is a sinister note in Gabriel Powell's letter to his master in March 1745, following a parliamentary election in January which was lost by the duke's favoured candidate[45], when he assures him that he will follow the direction he received:

> . . . *in regard to the persons that voted in the late election and don't doubt but to convince most of them of their error*[46].

The duke's most effective power came from his ownership of large areas of land[47], and particularly common land, and the opportunity it gave of 'obliging' friends, and, more importantly, of 'disobliging' opponents. It was considered wise not to offend the duke openly even if working against him, for as Powell wrote to the duke in June 1750, referring to Mr Mathew Price and his family and old Mr Popkin:

> . . . *[they] are at the bottom of all the trouble your Grace has had in this County, particularly the affair with Mr Roger Powell, but they avoid as much as possible to appear openly, lest they should lose the benefit of your Grace's favour*[48].

That the duke's position as landowner made his favour worth keeping is made starkly clear by his steward in a letter of October 1753. He explained that Mynydd Bach y Cocks was in the Parish of Llanrhidian, and that the coal under it had been granted to Mr Lockwood and Co. Mr Price (it appears this is Gryffydd, not Thomas his father) had asked Mr Morris (Robert Morris senior, Lockwood's partner) for leave to make a level under this common, and Mr Morris has consulted Gabriel Powell, who wrote:

> *It was considered as a very fair opportunity for your Grace to let the gentleman see it was in your Grace's power to serve them, and that they must deserve favours, before they received them . . . This gentleman is one of the most vehement in the opposition to your Grace, and carries it so far as to show it in what he is in no way interested.*

Powell therefore advised the duke to refuse Price's request, otherwise:

45. Of the 641 votes polled by the unsuccessful candidate, 216 came via Lord Mansel (Briton Ferry and Margam), 300 via Lord Windsor (Cardiff) and others, and just 125 via the Duke of Beaufort. See: Peter Thomas. 'Glamorgan Politics 1688-1790', in *GCH.*, IV, pp.413-4.
46. NLW. II, 2327 (16.3.1744/5).
47. He was by no means the largest landowner in the area, but he had about 1200 acres in Glamorgan in 1870, despite over 4,000 acres in the Lordship having been offered for sale by auction in 1837. Sale particulars are in WGRO., ref. D/D P889. See also Joanna Martin 'Private Enterprise versus Manorial Rights . . . in Glamorgan', *Welsh History Review* 9 (1978-79), p.156.
48. NLW. II, 2348 (23.6.1750).

> *It will appear to the people in the County that no distinction is made between your Grace's friends and others*[49].

Other ways in which a distinction could be made between friends and others were more direct. Writing to the dowager duchess in March 1761, the steward reported:

> *A few weeks ago a Sturgeon weighing 123 li. was brought me as being a Royal Fish, which, as it could not be conveyed to your Grace or my Lord Duke, I had distributed amongst his Grace's friends in the neighbourhood*[50].

Gabriel Powell in the Field

Gabriel Powell's profession of the law meant that, in addition to his duties at the manorial courts, he was fully occupied with negotiations and discussions, preparation of leases and agreements, correspondence, and preparatory work for various cases before the higher courts, the latter usually at Hereford. He spent a few months in London in most years, generally in the late autumn, and usually called in at the duke's mansion at Badminton in passing[51]. He could thus maintain the necessary personal contact with his important client. Although the office of steward was one for a lawyer, the holder had to (or chose to) carry out many of the functions which would soon come to be regarded as the particular work of a land agent. It is clear from his correspondence that Gabriel Powell was in no way bound to his desk, and that he knew the ground within the lordships and manors for which he was responsible as well as he knew their deeds and records.

The Fee of Trewyddfa, where many of the more serious disputes were centred, was about two miles from Powell's home at Swansea, an easy journey on horseback, and he knew the ground there well. In January 1750 he was called upon to point out where he thought the duke's boundaries were there, in relation to the lands of an adjoining owner, Mr Roger Powell, who had just made a new road for carrying his coal, and who intended to form a waggon way on it[52]. The steward thought that it would cross some of the duke's lands, but the matter was settled later when Roger Powell agreed to take them on lease. On other occasions more serious matters required attention. In September 1763 Gabriel Powell wrote to the duchess, guardian of the young duke:

> *. . . I was informed that some labourers by the direction of one Dorset had diverted the Brook which was the boundary of the Fee of Treweyddva.*

> *I went immediately to view it and found that they had not only diverted the water but had also filled up and levelled . . . the channel in such a manner that there will not in a year or two be the least traces of the ancient Boundary.*

> *. . . they have also taken in a piece of the waste within the Fee and thereby shut up the old way, which went to my Lord Duke's tenement of lower Forrest.*

49. NLW. II, 2373 (15.11.1753).
50. NLW. II, 2407 (12.3.1761).
51. e.g. NLW. II, 2365 (26.9.1751) etc.
52. NLW. II, 2345 (18.1.1749/50).

There are a few small incroachments on the wastes within the Seigniory, which I will lay before your Grace, when I come to Badminton[53].

Activities west of Swansea also came into Powell's view, and in March 1750 he had written to the then duke:

As I rode out this morning I observed a deep trench carried up for twelve or fifteen yards along the side of the highway at a place called Dyvnant [modern Dunvant] *within your grace's manor of Gower Subboscus. Upon enquiring how it came to be done, the workmen informed me that they were employed to do it by Mr Robert Popkin, who was about carrying up a coal level from thence under the adjoining tenement*[54].

In 1753 a court action between the duke and his Penllergaer antagonists was likely to stand or fall on the issue of whether trees had been cut down within the boundaries of an alleged highway which ran near their mansion and the ancient estate of Nidfwch. Powell had been out on site. He had been shown:

. . . the spots, which Mr Price's witnesses marked as the places where Mr Price's witnesses had cut or remembered the cutting of trees on. I carefully sought them in the presence of two others. I pulled up the turfs, I poked the ground afterwards with a knife and could not find the least footstep [?] *of an old stump, not even a root of any size . . .*[55]

For a detailed description of a site inspection and dispute along a manorial boundary the account at the beginning of the description of the Lordship of Kilvey cannot be bettered (see the 'Survey', folios 125 to 127, pp. 205-207). There is another reference in the correspondence to boundary disputes affecting the Manor of Trewyddfa and involving the Prices, which occurred in about 1749. Then Gabriel Powell had walked the boundary between the latter manor and the Bishop of St David's Manor of Clase, in the company of a jury composed of the tenants of both manors, and also Mr [Thomas] Price, then steward to the bishop. In Powell's words:

When we came to the Common [Mynydd Carn Llwyd], *Mr Price was taking in a large part of the Common* [i.e. claiming it for Clase] *upon which the people called to him and told him he was mistaken. I thereupon offered him a pickaxe, and told him that if he thought himself right, he might break the ground and I would sue him. Upon his declining to do that, I ordered several holes to be cut along the boundary and told him that if he thought me wrong, he might sue me. Whereupon he acquiesced, and sometime after I put up mear stones, which are still in the same place*[56].

One more example shall suffice to show the readiness of the duke's steward to visit in person the various parts of the extensive lordship. On the 12th March 1761 he wrote to the Duke's mother:

53. NLW. II, 2413 (26.9.1763).
54. NLW. II, 2346 (12.3.1749/50).
55. NLW. II, 2371 & 2 (30.7.1753 & 16.8.53).
56. NLW. II, 2395 (–.6.1756), referring to events "about 7 years ago".

I was last night informed that on Friday last a young whale came on shore near Whiteford Point in the Lordship of Lanmadock, a mesne manor held by Mr Aubrey in the Seigniory of Gower. It measures 65 feet in length, 17 feet in heighth as it lay on the sands, and 7 feet from eye to eye, and seems to have had a bruise on the head. It is a male fish of the Sperma Ceti kind. The country perceived it sometime before it reached the shore and took it for the wreck of a vessel, so that they were prepared to receive it. As soon as the tide left it they attacked it with hatchets, and in about five hours killed it. As it is a Royal Fish it belongs to my Lord Duke as Lord of the Seigniory. . . . I could not go down myself as it is twelve computed miles from hence[57] . . . and am busily engaged in settling the evidence for Mr Lockwood's trial . . .[58]

However, the lure of the whale could not be resisted, and as soon as the court case had been dealt with he was writing again, on the 26th March:

I returned home on Monday, and yesterday went down to see what I could make of the whale, but found about two-thirds of it had been plundered by the country, and the other third lies buried in the sands, and is now so nauseous that no one will work on it[59].

He admitted ruefully that whales were new to his experience. He had enquired at Bristol as to the value of whale oil, but no one offered to buy it. He had told the local people that if they would bring to Swansea the oil they had taken, he would make reasonable allowance for their trouble in getting it:

. . . but what effect this may have on the country I do not yet know. I shall do all in my power, but I am afraid that for want of knowledge and conveniences I shall make but a bad hand of it.

Gabriel Powell and the Past

In June 1750 Powell told the duke that he had seen a copy of a grant by John de Mowbray, dated the 13th year of Edward III (1340-41), to Neath Abbey, of a weir in the River Tawe. The document belonged to Mr Morgan of Gwernllwynchwith (who was not well-disposed towards the duke or his steward). It was shown to Powell secretly by a third party, and he was unable to take a copy. This tantalising situation was somehow resolved by the following January and the duke was then sent a copy of the old grant. The steward certainly, and the duke probably, would have had no difficulty translating such a document, but the letter contained some notes on the editing of the text, which must have some appeal to modern editors:

. . . I have wrote most of the words at length, though in the original most of them are abbreviated and written in an old Court Hand[60].

57. The riding distance from Swansea is about sixteen miles (26 km).
58. NLW. II, 2407 (12.3.1761).
59. NLW. II, 2409 (26.3.1761).
60. NLW. II, 2347 (11.6.1750); 2354 (21.1.1750/51).

In February 1755, writing from George's Coffee House, near Temple Bar, London, Gabriel Powell quoted to the duke a Latin passage from the "Bishop's Black Book" [of St David's] detailing some of the customs of the Manor of Clase, which could be useful in their on-going litigation with the Prices of Penllergaer:

Gouheria. Langevelach
Jenkin ap Griffith et alii Super Sacrementum dis—— quod Dominus et Tenentes sui habent
Communiam in Bosco Domine Goherie de Supraboscus pro housebote et Heybote et pro Pastura
Animalium per Cartam Domine in Supraboscus[61].

A further example of the use of early charters in eighteenth-century estate work is provided by the account in the 'Survey' of the aftermath of the Glais boundary dispute ('Survey', folio 127. p. 207), when Powell and Mr Thomas Edwards of Cardiff, the steward of Cadoxton Manor, argued fine points in the translation and interpretation of the Latin text of an early document.

Interest in antiquities of less practical use is evidenced in a letter to the duke dated September 1749, where in the middle of discussing matters relating to the Gower Estate, his steward comments:

I have also enclosed a copy of the inscription on Sir Hugh Johnns tomb, which stands in the
middle of the Chancel of Swansea Church, with a short description of it[62].

The enclosure is no longer with the letter, but one senses that although the original enquiry about the tomb may have come from the duke, Gabriel Powell had enjoyed answering it.

Powell was very aware of the value to his professional work of ancient documents, which might provide him with information on ancient rights and boundaries, useful in case of litigation or arguments with other landowners. He seems also to have enjoyed them for their own intrinsic interest as historical documents, and allowing also for his penchant for seeking buried features with a knife and his dexterity with a pickaxe (see p. 21 above) one may perhaps wonder whether, if he had lived a century later, he might possibly have joined George Grant Francis and Llewelyn Morgan as one of Swansea's distinguished pioneer antiquarians.

Home and Office

Gabriel Powell's home was in the town of Swansea, on the eastern side of High Street 'below the gate'. At that time the town was still small and rich and poor lived close to one another, though with very different homes and lifestyles. High Street was a 'good' address and its eastern side overlooked the river and the green fields of St Thomas. Industry had already become established further up the river and there the smoke from the copperworks had begun to blight the countryside downwind, but its effects were less noticeable in the town. Gabriel Powell senior had actively supported the building of a copperworks not far from his house (later the home of his

61. NLW. II, 2378 (1.2. 1755).
62. NLW. II, 2339 (23.9.1749).

son), on the site later occupied by the Cambrian Pottery. In answering complaints that the copper-smoke would be harmful to the town and its people, he had robustly responded:

> *It was insinuated unto me (who has been at £150 about my garden) . . . that it would spoil my garden – but that I look upon as the least of their pretences*[63].

His confidence was ill-founded, and when, in 1764, the Corporation granted a new lease of the copperworks site for the pottery, the lease expressly excluded use of the site for copper-smelting. The garden at the rear of the Powells' large house is well-shown in the Buck print of 'The East View of Swansea', published in 1748. Neatly divided by hedges and/or paths, it slopes steeply to the Strand, the road along the riverside, which is busy with the loading of coal and the building of ships. The house is shown as having a double-saddle roof running parallel with High Street, and it has two floors plus a dormered attic. The window layout is symmetrical each side of a large staircase window, and taken with the location of the chimneys on the end walls, suggests that the house had four rooms on each of its two floors, arranged around what was probably an imposing central staircase, plus an attic for servants and perhaps basement rooms. It was offered to let, furnished, in 1804, when it was described as a spacious house in High Street. The accommodation was listed as three parlours and a kitchen on the ground floor, four bedrooms on the first floor and five attic bedrooms. There was a large walled garden, stables and coach house and the advertisement stated that the house had formerly been in the occupation of Gabriel Powell, deceased, and lately of Mr Thomas Lynch[64]. The frontage of the house to High Street is well-shown in a later view of Swansea from the north-west, drawn by Paul Padley in about 1795, and this complements and confirms the information in the Buck view. It was not the largest house in town, but it would have been one of the best and when, in 1749, the duke was preparing to visit his Welsh estates, Powell was able to express the hope "that your Grace will do me the honour of making use of my house"[65].

It is likely that, in accordance with common practice at the time, Gabriel Powell's home and his office were one and the same. We know that he employed a clerk, Mr Jones, who rode with his master to the boundary confrontation at Glais, and there may have been others to carry out the many tasks of a busy solicitor's office, not least the preparation of the handwritten leases, conveyances and other legal documents, and the extensive correspondence. While his senior clerk may have done some of this work, it is certain that Powell did not, for his handwriting is distinctly crabbed and awkward, both in his signature and also in the notes he has added to his copy of the 'Survey'. As well as his own office staff, Gabriel Powell could also use appropriate officers within the various manors which were in the Duke's hands. These men were not professionals, but were elected each year from the tenants of the manor, to whom appointment to the 'enforcement' offices could be unwelcome. In October 1748 Powell sent his servant (probably one of his

63. George Grant Francis. *The Smelting of Copper in the Swansea District* (London 1881) p.98.
64. *The Cambrian*, 14.4.1804, p.2, col. 5. The house was offered for sale by the family in 1817, when it was occupied by a Mrs Patton – *The Cambrian*, 18.1.1817, p.1, col.5. By an interesting coincidence, by 1826 it, or a new building on its site, had become the premises of John Francis, coachbuilder, father of George Grant Francis the Swansea antiquarian, as evidenced by Land Tax records in WGRO, and the Swansea town tithe map and schedule, ibid.
65. NLW. II, 2335 (31.5.1759).

clerks) and the bailiff of the manor, to Llanguick, ten miles north-east of Swansea, to break down the fences of an enclosure on a common there. He had also arranged for them to be accompanied by one of the sergeants at mace from Swansea (one of the town burgesses). By December he had to report to the Duke that all had suffered abuse for their involvement and that the bailiff had since been waylaid on the highway.

Although much of Gabriel Powell's work was concerned with his wide-ranging duties as the duke's principal officer in Gower, he also acted for other landowners and for the Corporation. In and before 1736 he had been agent to Mr Herbert[66], and he acted for the burgesses in successfully guiding the Townhill and Burroughs Enclosure Act of 1762 through the Parliamentary processes. In 1753 he had the whole charge of a case on behalf of Lady Mansel, mentioning to the duke that the whole Estate of Sir Thomas Stradling depended on it[67].

Getting About

Even in the eighteenth century, people of Gabriel Powell's standing could be surprisingly mobile. He visited London regularly, usually in late autumn and stayed for several months[68]. While there he continued his correspondence with the Duke, his letters being addressed from "George's Coffee House, near Temple Bar", in the capital's legal quarter. The journeys to or from London also provided opportunities for the steward to call at his master's mansion house at Badminton for face-to-face discussions of the lordship's affairs. On 26th September 1751 Powell wrote that he would be setting out from Swansea on the 15th or 16th October and "would be pleased to wait upon your Grace". Hereford was also visited when necessary for attendance at the Assizes[69]. Brecon, the Powell family's earlier home was also visited on the occasion of the king's audit[70]. The journeys to London may have been by stage-coach, but those to Hereford, Brecon and Monmouth were probably made on horseback, as were all local site visits. There is an illuminating description of the eighteenth-century equivalent of present-day 'car allowance' in the Survey. Writing of his position as Coroner of the Lordship, Gabriel Powell comments:

> *This Office was a burden and expense to the Coroner, till the late Act of Parliament for allowing Coroners twenty shillings for every Inquisition, and nine pence a mile for every mile they were obliged to travel to view the body and take the Inquisition[71].*

More, unreimbursed, travelling was involved because the coroner had to attend both sittings of the Courts of Great Sessions and the four Quarter Sessions and it seems that he could recover only the costs directly incurred by his attendance at inquests.

The Swansea Scene

As mentioned in the foregoing account of the Powell family and Swansea, Gabriel Powell became a member of the exclusive ruling body of the town of Swansea when still only twenty-two years of

66. NLW. II, 2312 (15.5.1736). The Herbert lands in the Swansea area subsequently passed to the Calvert Richard Jones family.
67. NLW. II, 2373 (25.10.1753).
68. e.g. NLW. II, 2353 (24.11.1750) & NLW. II, 2378 (1.2.1755).
69. NLW. II, 2358 (30.3. 1751/2); 2380 (26.3.1755).
70. NLW. II, 2390 (26.10.1755).
71. 'Survey', Sa. fo. 28.

age, being admitted as a burgess at Michaelmas 1732. Remarkably, he was at the same time admitted as an alderman of the borough, one of the twelve-strong inner ruling body, from whose number the office of portreeve, the chief magistrate and chairman of the Corporation's meetings, was filled. By 1740, at the age of thirty, he had been elected to that leading position, having been nominated, unsuccessfully, as early as 1733 (when his brother, John, was elected) and again in 1735. He was entitled to be admitted a burgess because he was the son of a burgess, but his instant promotion to alderman must have been due to his father's status and abilities, and, perhaps, the belief that the younger Gabriel might well soon succeed him as the duke's representative in the lordship and the town. The burgesses of Swansea, and of most if not all boroughs at that time, were an exclusive group who saw their first duty as being the preservation of the ancient rights and privileges of their Corporation, and of the benefits in kind which they received from it. Some of their duties benefited the town and its people in general, such as the regulation of the market, maintenance of order and the management of the harbour, but the income which was received from some of these activities and from the town's substantial landed estate was regarded by the burgesses as their own.

In his capacity as a leading member of the Corporation, Gabriel Powell sought to maintain the position of the Duke of Beaufort, but he was ready enough to seek the duke's help on behalf of the burgesses if, as was usually the case, there was no conflict of interest between them. Both sides appear to have been anxious to maintain harmony, and the issue of who owned the seaweed on Swansea's foreshore tends to confirm this. Early in 1749 the Swansea Corporation granted to one of their aldermen the right to gather seaweed (valuable as a fertiliser and in some industrial processes) along the beach within the borough boundaries. Mr Gardiner, the duke's receiver (accountant) then claimed that the seaweed belonged to the duke, not to the burgesses. Mr Hugh Powell, the alderman involved, then said he would relinquish the right as he did not want to cause dissension, but the burgesses requested the duke to agree that the weed was theirs. Gabriel Powell researched the issue, but could find little information on it:

> . . . *As there never was any difference during the whole time of my father's service, he never drew up anything in writing in regard to it. So that I am entirely ignorant of the right any further than what little appeared to me from the Corporation's books and papers, and what I have heard talked of in the place . . .*[72]

The detached approach to this issue contrasts with the acrimony with which some other disputes with certain families were conducted. A much larger matter was amicably arranged between the burgesses and the duke when the Townhill and Burroughs at Swansea, owned by the duke but subject to the common rights of the burgesses, were inclosed by Act of Parliament and parcelled out between them. Mr Gardiner had been opposed to the scheme, but Gabriel Powell had supported the Corporation and had pointed out to the duke that although he would get only about a tenth of the total area after inclosure, it would be difficult to get more as many parties were involved – and the duke got nothing from the land at present[73]. Powell also pointed out that

---

72. NLW. II, 2333 & 2337 (18.3.1748/49 & 30.6.1749).
73. NLW. II, 2399 (11.8.1757).

there were about eighty burgesses, including the aldermen. Only four might achieve immediate profit, but the rest would expect something in their turn[74]. In the event the duke got rather more of the total area and the mineral rights, including coal, were specifically reserved to him, which was to be expected after all the arguments at Trewyddfa. On behalf of the burgesses the steward was able to get the duke's agreement to the Burroughs, the extensive area of grass-covered dunes along the bay as far as Brynmill, included in the scheme[75]. Having achieved agreement between the duke and the Corporation, Powell then oversaw the passage of the necessary Act through Parliament until it became law early in 1762. The inclosure of Townhill shows how the duke and the burgesses could work together, but it also emphasises how few townsfolk were represented on or by the Corporation. As the eighteenth century moved on and Swansea's trade, industry and population grew, it became ever more apparent that the powers, resources and interests of the old Corporation were increasingly inadequate and inappropriate. Gabriel Powell had been born in 1710, and he found himself more and more having to defend the old order, on behalf both of the duke and the Corporation, as he himself moved into old age.

One of the ancient functions and duties of the Corporation was the control of the town's harbour, always an important part of the town's economy. They had in the past dealt with this seriously, ensuring that ships' crews did not throw their ballast into the navigable channels (or fining the captains of those that did), and initiating major improvements, such as the first stone quay and the first 'dry dock'. With the increase of trade during the eighteenth century, particularly in vessels proceeding further up river to load coal and copper and unload copper ore, the Corporation's control became far less effective. The gentlemen who owned the up-river works and collieries began to demand action to keep the river channels clear of silt and gravel, but few of them were burgesses. In 1768 there was a public meeting in Swansea of those concerned, which was chaired by Gryffydd Price of Penllergaer. Gabriel Powell was present, in his usual double (or multiple) capacity, with other members of the Corporation. The presence of both Price and Powell ensured dissension. The meeting agreed that action to reduce the obstructions in the river was necessary, but Gabriel Powell stated that the Corporation was opposed to such a move. Another leading burgess then said that was not so, most of them were in favour, but that they had not yet considered the matter as a body. Soon afterwards it was found that the income from the number of ships using the harbour and the river was insufficient to fund the proposed improvements (which Powell probably knew from the first). In fact, it was not until the number of vessels had nearly tripled, from 690 in 1768 to 1803 in 1791, that it was finally agreed by the burgesses, the duke, the industrialists, and others to seek the first Harbour Act, which was passed in 1792[76].

Gruffydd Price died in July 1787, aged sixty-nine, and his bitterness towards the Powells is expressed in unequivocal terms in his will which describes how his landed property had suffered "through the treachery of the Lord's present Steward and that of his father"[77].

Gabriel Powell, reached the greater age of seventy-eight years. His last years were as active and contentious as his earlier ones, and a new, younger, equally formidable and more vociferous

74. NLW. II, 2400 (8.9.1757).
75. NLW. II, 2408 (21.3.1761).
76. W.H. Jones, *History of the Port of Swansea* (Carmarthen, 1922), passim.
77. Copy in GRO. ref. D/D 1/184.

adversary had replaced the departed Price. In the first part of the eighteenth century Robert Morris and his firm of Lockwood, Morris & Co., had been allied with the Duke of Beaufort and his steward in the disputes and litigation with Prices and Popkins over the Trewyddfa coalworks. Robert Morris had two sons. John (later Sir John) was the younger, but took on the management of their industrial undertakings when his father died in 1768. The elder, another Robert, became a barrister and actively involved himself in radical politics, as well as in an unwise elopement[78]. Feudal rights and powers angered him, and the authority of the aristocratic lords of Gower, and in particular of their autocratic and elderly steward, soon came under his direct attack. In 1787 Robert Morris and some of his local supporters came to several of the Manorial Courts being held in Swansea by Gabriel Powell, and directly challenged his right to conduct them alone, without a jury of manorial tenants. Powell was indignant, and wrote to the duke:

> . . . *my duty will not permit me to be silent when your Grace's rights and privileges as Lord of the Seigniory of Gower are openly attacked by Mr Robert Morris in such a manner as I never knew before or ever heard of*[79].

On "Monday last" Mr Robert Morris had come into the court being held by Gabriel Powell for the Borough of Swansea and Manor *(sic)* of Kilvey and, without interrupting the proceedings, had made a show of reading from a large folio volume which he had brought. Two others had also arrived immediately after Morris, evidently as supporters:

> *Mr Moses Harris, one of this Town, and a Clerk of Mr Cockayne, each of them with a large folio book under his arm . . .*

The stage had been set for a legal challenge and that soon followed. "Yesterday", Gabriel Powell had opened the court, when Robert Morris got on the Bench with a large book open before him, and questioned the legality of the proceedings. Powell accused him of delaying the business of the court, to which Morris responded with some heat that he was a freeholder of the manor concerned, and was therefore entitled to act as a judge in its court. He declared that he intended to disrupt every court accordingly, and challenged the steward to distrain on him. Faced with this attack on the authority which he had long exercised, Gabriel Powell wrote to the duke, confessing himself perplexed, and seeking instructions[80]. Counsel's opinion was sought on the Duke's behalf, but gave little comfort, advising that as the courts affected by Mr Morris appeared to be Courts Baron then the Suitors or Freehold tenants[81] were the judges, so a steward could not hold a Court Baron alone. Powell had been taking courts as steward alone for at least twenty years, for whatever reason, and it seems that Morris' attack was well-founded.

It is not surprising to find Morris involved in another confrontation with Powell shortly afterwards, in an incident which has been commemorated in one of a small group of political cartoons which then originated in Swansea. The issue of improvements to Swansea Harbour, mentioned above, had been discussed at a meeting of the Corporation on 2nd November 1787, not long

---

78. J.E. Ross (ed.). *Radical Adventurer – The Diaries of Robert Morris 1772-1774* (Bath, 1971).
79. NLW. II, 2415 (1787 – no day or month quoted).
80. Ibid. note 54.
81. i.e. in their capacity as the manorial jury.

'A Welsh Corporation Meeting'.
A cartoon by Moses Harris depicting a fracas at a meeting of the burgesses of Swansea on November 2nd, 1787.
The Rev. Thomas Powell kicks out at Charles Collins. Gabriel Powell, Thomas' father, has snatched
Collins' wig. Robert Morris restrains Powell senior. See page 30.

A rough sketch by W.H. Jones of a small cartoon used in an political pamphlet in 1789,
probably drawn by Moses Harris. Captain Windsor R.N., prospective candidate for Glamorgan in
a forthcoming parliamentary election, was being drawn through the streets of Swansea in a wheeled
boat, preceded by a drummer. The contraption fell apart, tipping Windsor onto the road so that his
fine clothes were bedaubed with mud. The tall person in boots is the Rev. Thomas Powell, defying
the mob in characteristic fighting stance. Behind him stands Thomas Morgan of Penderry,
successor to Gabriel Powell as the Duke of Beaufort's steward. See note 83, page 30.

after the disruption of the manor court by Robert Morris. At its meeting the Corporation resolved to oppose new moves to obtain a Harbour Improvement Act. According to the text on a cartoon, drawn by 'Mos(es) Har(ris)' and published in London as a print, the meeting at one point descended into violence, involving overturned benches, kicking and wig-snatching. The text blames the Powell faction, and Robert Morris is depicted as the peacemaker, bursting in to separate the parties. The cartoon is, however, the only source of information on this incident, and "Mr Moses Harris, one of this town" was a leading supporter of Robert Morris when he disrupted the Court Baron a few months earlier[82].

Another of Moses Harris' three[83] Swansea cartoons is familiar to local historians. Entitled "The Steward", it shows Gabriel Powell standing in Wind Street in front of a building clearly displaying its name as "Swansea Theatre". The text quotes Gabriel Powell's evidence before Committees of Parliament which had been considering representations seeking a Paving Act for the town. Contending that Swansea was too small a town to require such a measure, he countered opposing evidence that it was sophisticated enough to have its own theatre, by claiming he knew of no theatre there, but then (probably under cross-examination) grudgingly admitting that he may have heard of one – but he never was at it![84] The Corporation and, no doubt, the duke, objected to such measures as a Paving Act and the proposed Harbour Act because they would introduce new administrative bodies into the town, "to the manifest destruction of many of our most valuable rights and privileges". Moses Harris' association with Robert Morris[85], an active supporter of the proposed Paving Act, must make him a biased witness, but we are indebted to him for what appear, despite their function as political cartoons, to be genuine portraits of Gabriel Powell. They are the only representations of him which are known, but his dignified if autocratic demeanour, his upright stance and his smart but rather old-fashioned clothing are not at variance with what might be expected. One small piece of additional evidence may come from a photograph of a descendant of his who visited Swansea in 1972, and whose distinctively dignified features have much in common with those depicted by Moses Harris nearly two centuries before[86].

By the last decades of the eighteenth century pressures on surviving ancient privileges were increasing, leading in the nineteenth century to many reforms and changes. Gabriel Powell's earlier struggles with the Prices and their relatives the Popkins placed economics first, with ancient rights and privileges a distant second. By the end of the century the two issues ran side by side – but the

82. I have been unable to locate Moses Harris as having been baptised, married or buried in St Mary's, Swansea. However, a Moses Harris had a son Aaron baptised there 1.2.1765, and a daughter Anne ditto on 7.7.1779. The Glamorgan Family History Society's excellent index to the parish registers. has been of great assitance in this search. W.C. Rogers' typescript 'Swansea and Glamorgan Calendar', pt.I, vol. I, (lease no. 171, 6.9.1779) records "Moses Harris of Swansea, Mercer" witnessing a lease from the Corporation to Moses Harry, of Swansea, Collier, on 6th September 1779. Also ibid. Appendix 7, p.420, has Moses Harris of Swansea listed as a Trustee under the Glamorgan Turnpike Roads Act of 1785.

83. Two are mentioned here. The third, much smaller, is known only from W.H. Jones' sketch and commentary on p.15 of his notebook, UWS. Library, Archives. ref. 24 (held pp. City & County of Swansea Museum Services). Although it might not be Harris' work, its date (1789), its subject (Swansea electioneering), and the inclusion of the Rev. Thomas Powell suggest that it probably is his. Reproduced here on p.29.

84. The *House of Commons Journal* for 1787, p.645, confirms that witnesses for and against the Bill were examined on 19th April, and Gabriel Powell's name appears re a further petition considered on 4th May, p.719. Sadly, the evidence itself is not quoted.

85. Robert Morris, following his various personal problems, left Britain to practice as a barrister in India, arriving in Calcutta in December 1791. His reputation caused the Judges of the Supreme Court to refuse to allow him to plead cases before them. After this severe rebuff he left Calcutta for the interior "making himself conspicuous by his violent conduct wherever he remained twelve hours. Happily for society this dangerous and troublesome man was carried off by an attack of liver about eight months after he left Calcutta". William Hickey. *Memoirs 1791-92.* Quoted in J.E. Ross, ed. *Letters from Swansea* (Swansea, 1969) p.57, 58.

86. *South Wales Evening Post*, 14. 9. 1972. Photograph of Mrs Gladys Gabrielle Athy, then an elderly lady living near Kingsbridge, Devon, visiting Swansea's Mayor, Councillor Chris Thomas. Mr W.C. Rogers, then Borough Estate Agent, was present and confirmed that she was a direct descendant of the Gabriel Powell who compiled the 'Survey'. The facial resemblance is remarkable. See p.31.

'The Steward'.
Moses Harris' cartoon of Gabriel Powell, published in 1787.

Gabriel Powell's house in High Street, Swansea, seen
from across the river, as shown in the Buck brothers'
'East View of Swansea', published in 1748.

Mrs Gabrielle Athy, direct descendant of
Gabriel Powell, visiting Swansea's Mayor,
Councillor Chris Thomas, in September 1972.
She is accompanied by Mr and Mrs
W.C. Rogers and their younger son, Philip.

steward had stood loyally by the old ways throughout a long professional career. It seems that he could do no other.

Gabriel Powell appears to have held a court for the last time early in 1788 but his signature endorsed the accounts of the overseers of the poor on the 4th August in that year.[87] He died at Swansea on 29th December 1788 and was buried on 2nd January in a vault in, or adjacent to, St Mary's Church.

Editorial Matters

The Manuscripts of the Survey

Two original copies of the Survey are known to exist, and there is possibly a third, whose existence is unproven. There is also a large and impressively-bound volume containing a fine transcript made in 1890 and certified by the then agent to the duke's Gower Estate. The two originals and the certified copy have all had adventurous lives, as will be seen.

Of the two known originals, one is now owned by the City and County of Swansea (Museums Service), as trustee of the collections transferred from the Royal Institution of South Wales in 1991[88]. This is at present (October 2000) held for safekeeping in the Local Archives Collection of the Library of University of Wales Swansea. In 1876 this copy had been given by Joseph Joseph of Brecon to his friend George Grant Francis, a prominent Swansea citizen and notable antiquarian[89]. Joseph had acquired it in that year on the death of Gabriel William Powell, a Brecon solicitor, whose great-grandfather had been Gabriel Powell of Swansea, compiler of the Survey. It is this copy which bears numerous contemporary notes in the steward's own rather awkward handwriting, and Grant Francis is probably correct in assuming that this copy was his own original which had passed by descent to his great-grandson. When it returned to Swansea it was in poor condition, without its back and with many of the leaves worn through at the folds, but Grant Francis arranged for it to be thoroughly repaired and conserved, adding some illustrations and an index. After his death this original of the Survey came by gift of his son in 1895, to the Royal Institution of South Wales together with many other important historical collections left by his father.

During the 1939-45 War the Swansea Museum, home of the Royal Institution of South Wales and its collections, was severely damaged by bombing. Fortunately, most of the contents, including the Powell Survey, had been moved elsewhere for safety, much of it to Kilvrough mansion in Gower. There were other dangers than bombs for, writing in 1959, the former Honorary Librarian of the Royal Institution recalled how he and two other members had recovered the Institution's

---

87. WGRO. P 123/22.
88. The legal transfer was effected on 21st August 1991.
89. See Grant Francis' own account in Appendix V.

original of the Survey from Kilvrough where it was in danger of being damaged by damp. It was then taken to the National Library of Wales for restoration[90]. It was returned to Swansea Museum but, with the other manuscript collections, it was later moved to the care of the archivist at the University College (now University of Wales Swansea). The then archivist, Mr David Bevan, arranged for it to be further conserved and rebound, the Grant Francis additions and some miscellaneous early papers being bound as a separate volume.

The second known original, now at the National Library of Wales, has had an even more fraught existence. According to W.C. Rogers, only two originals existed "one of which, almost miraculously survived the Swansea blitz of 21st February 1941, when the building housing it perished in flames"[91]. The building concerned was No. 7 Picton Place, the office for the Duke of Beaufort's Welsh Estates[92], which was indeed destroyed at that time. The pages of the National Library's original are sound, but the volume lacks the front and back covers, and also almost all the leather of the spine is missing, but what small fragments remain have been scorched and partially melted. Between the last page and the old cardboard wrapping around the book is a single sheet of paper bearing in pencil the statement that:

> *"This volume was in the German air raid on Swansea where the Beaufort Estate Office was 'blitzed' and burnt to the ground. It was salved from the strong room there in this condition. Date of the air raid was Feb. 1942".*
>
> *[1942 is an error for 1941. There was no raid on Swansea in Feb. 1942]*

The note bears the initials WCR in monogram form, which would indicate W.C. Rogers, but I doubt that either the monogram or the writing are his[93].

Having survived this ordeal, the volume seems then to have been returned to the muniment room at Badminton, for it was from there that it was transferred to the National Library in 1988. This, or yet another original, is listed in a muniment room index compiled in 1913, so it appears to have moved to the Swansea Estate Office between then and the war. There is another intriguing possibility that the volume listed in 1913 was the third original which Grant Francis believed existed. In his introduction to the volume given to him by Joseph Joseph, written in 1876, he mentioned that before he became aware of that volume he had expected that there would have been a total of three originals: one compiled by Gabriel Powell, one made for the duke's own use at Badminton, and one for the Estate Office at Swansea. Referring then to the latter two, he stated that he had *seen both* (prior to 1861), but without power of inspection or extract. If the scorched volume had always been the Swansea Estate Office copy and had gone to Badminton only after the air raid, one must wonder if the 1913 inventory volume is the third original – yet it appears to be unknown at Badminton today[94].

---

90. *South Wales Evening Post*, 30.1.1959. Note by the then Hon. Librarian of the R.I.S.W.
91. W.C. Rogers, 'Swansea and Glamorgan Calendar' (typescript volumes, 1946). For location of copies of this work, see note 1 above. The account of the air raid is in Part I, Vol. I, Appendix 5, p.21.
92. *South Wales District Telephone Directory*, 9.1939.
93. The note is probably a copy of an original WCR note, and his involvement seems clear.
94. Mrs Margaret Richards, Badminton Archivist, has kindly supplied the information relating to the collections there.

The fine 1890 handwritten transcript of Powell's 'Survey', magnificently bound and with a brass clasp, was prepared by Walter W. Goddard, a well-known local artist[95]. It is now in the West Glamorgan Record Office[96]. It contains a clear contemporary statement of its origins on folio 239:

> *Copied from the original Survey*
> *in the possession of*
> *His Grace the Duke of Beaufort*
> *by me the 10th October 1890.*
> *W. Goddard.*
> *[signature]*
>
> *Examined with the Original Survey*
> *and certified to be a correct copy.*
> *F.H. Glyn Price*
> *[signature]*
> *Agent to His Grace the Duke of Beaufort*
> *for the Seigniory of Gower.*
> *June 1891.*

If, in 1890, the duke's agent found it necessary to have a high-quality copy made from the Badminton original, one must wonder what had become of the local Estate Office original which Grant Francis, a reliable witness, claims to have seen before 1861? Theft, more innocent loss, or destruction by fire are possibilities – but we can only speculate. Certainly, the 1890 transcript is an almost exact copy (some very minor transcription errors were noted in pencil by Price), of the National Library (ex Badminton) original.

In common with the two known originals, the 1890 transcript has had some adventures. The transcript had been deposited in the Glamorgan Record Office, Cardiff, in 1955 by the Plymouth City Archivist. Its provenance was unclear, but in correspondence at that time he was able to say that it and a related document had "formed part of a collection which was found submerged in a basement"[97]. Fortunately the submergence seems to have been metaphorical as far as the transcript was concerned, because it now shows no evidence of having suffered such a potentially terminal fate. In 1992 it came to the West Glamorgan Record Office, Swansea, when the former Glamorgan Archives Service was divided to serve two areas, one centred on Cardiff and the other on Swansea.

Of the two known originals, one at Swansea and the other at the National Library of Wales, the former is clearly the earlier. Its provenance and the numerous added notes in Gabriel Powell's handwriting confirm this, but there is also ample internal evidence, such as persons named as landowners or tenants in the Swansea version having been replaced by their sons or other heirs, or by their widows, in the National Library (Badminton) one.

95. His line drawings illustrate several of the volumes of J.D. Davies' *History of West Gower* (Swansea 1877-1894).
96. WGRO. ref. D/D MG 13.
97. Information from Glamorgan Record Office, March 2000.

In preparing the text for the present publication, the 1890 certified copy, the clearest version was first transcribed[98] and then word-processed. The text was then compared word for word with the two originals. As expected, the 1890 version followed the Badminton original, but as indicated above, there were some minor differences between that and the Swansea version. As the latter was the initial version it has been used as the basis of the text as now published, but the differences in content between it and the Badminton version have been indicated where they occur.

Editorial Practice

Punctuation is erratic by modern standards in both originals. Colons and semi-colons frequently appear where stops and commas would be used today. Short oblique strokes are also used, which can represent either stops or commas. Longer oblique strokes are used for brackets. Often there is no punctuation where it would now be expected, and this is not only in the extracts from leases and similar documents, where punctuation was (and is) usually avoided as a matter of practice.

In the present edition, punctuation has been brought substantially into line with current usage. Very occasionally it is omitted altogether where the original has none and it is not clear what its wording may require. (e.g. 'Cottage garden and croft' may mean 'Cottage, garden and croft', or it may not.)

In the original, capitals are used frequently to start words where they would not now be used, often as a form of highlighting. In this edition their frequency has been much reduced, though they have been retained for many words used in a legal or quasi-legal sense. Abbreviations have usually been expanded, but less so in lists of tenancies, fields, etc. where space is a consideration. Italics are used for specialised Latin or French terms, but not for commonly-used examples, such as 'Anno'.

Headings which are in the original are set in roman text, those which for clarity have been added to the present edition are in italics.

Place names and personal names have been kept as in the original, even where they are, or appear to have been, mis-spelt, and even where variant versions appear in the original, sometimes on the same folio. Styles and titles, whether abbreviated or in full, are given in modern form.

Words or letters which have been omitted from the original, but which are clearly required, have been added in square brackets in roman. Modern editorial additions or emendations are shown in square brackets, in italics. Brackets which are in the original manuscript are given here as round brackets[99]. 'Sa' indicates the original now in University of Wales Swansea, and 'Bn' indicates the Badminton version, now in the National Library of Wales.

The folio numbers which appear in the transcript which follows are those of the Swansea version. Badminton folio numbers differ but are the same as those of the 1890 transcript.

Spelling has been modernised (except, as previously indicated, in personal names and place names). Few old forms, such as 'antient', 'ye', 'thence', etc. appear in the Swansea version and fewer in the. Badminton one. They have been modernised here, but where the 1764 originals are quoting earlier documents describing, e.g. manorial boundaries, the older forms have been

---

98. In pencil in accord with Record Office practice. The volumes were too large and too vulnerable for photocopying.
99. Brackets in the original are usually represented by oblique strokes.

retained. In the 1890 copy, hyphens have been used in place names such as Tyr-y-Bont, with a circumflex over 'y'. Neither of the 1764 originals uses hyphens in such cases, but circumflexes are used. Neither are used in this transcript.

The majority of the farm names mentioned can be found on the modern 1:25000 Ordnance Survey maps, and more can be found in the tithe apportionments of the 1840s. There is a good Beaufort Estate map-book of 1801-03 in the West Glamorgan Record Office, which is supplemented by detailed particulars prepared for the intended auction of the Gower Estate in 1837[100]. There is an excellent tracing by W.C. Rogers of Lewis Thomas' map of Trewyddfa, prepared in 1761[101], contemporary with the 'Survey', but the original is now lost. Although place-names are sometimes oddly spelt, they can usually be 'translated' if read aloud, phonetically (e.g. 'Keven Mothvay' becomes 'Cefn Myddfai'). Overall the rendering of place-names, English or Welsh, shows a clear knowledge of both language and locality on the part of the compiler of the Survey and his assistants.

Ampersands are rendered as 'and' in the general text, but usually left unaltered in columns or lists where space is limited. 'Al's' or 'als' is given as 'alias' throughout.

The names of tenants and holdings have been set in bold text in many of the descriptions of holdings, as a finding aid. In most cases this has been used only for the lead tenant and the name of the overall holding.

---

100. Map-book: D/D Beau E1. Sales particulars: D/D P 889.
101. A copy is in WGRO.

A Brief Glossary

i. LEGAL TERMS

Affeerors:	Members of a manorial court deputed to assess the reasonableness of financial penalties imposed by a steward.
Amerciament:	A fine imposed at a manorial court.
Constat:	Certification of a court record.
Court Baron:	The manorial court which dealt with transfer of customary tenancies and the internal customs and activities of the manor.
Court Leet:	The manorial court which dealt with matters affecting the wider public and with minor criminal matters.
Curtesy:	Where a wife died owning land, and in legal possession of it, provided she had had a child her husband could keep that land for his lifetime 'by the Curtesy'.
Deodand:	Weapon or implement used in crime and forfeit to the king, or, in Gower, to the lord.
Destringas (distringas):	A writ requiring distraint on a person indebted to the king or, in Gower, to the lord.
Disseisin:	Unlawful dispossession.
Dissessin en le post:	Further unlawful dispossession despite reinstatement.
Distrain/Distraint:	Seizure of property, which was then held until a court's requirements had been met.
Estrays:	Any stray beasts (not wild), not owned or claimed within a year and a day after being 'cried' in a nearby market. Ownership then passed to the king (in Gower, the lord).
Femme Covert:	A married woman.
Flotsam:	Wreckage or goods found floating at sea.
Free Bench:	Where a customary tenant died his widow was entitled to retain all his copyhold lands as her 'free bench' for her lifetime.
Grand Serjeantry:	Tenure of land held in return for a specified personal service to the king (or a marcher lord). Strictly, the Gower examples were 'Petit Serjeantry'.
Inquisition super visum corporis	Inquest upon view of a body.
In exigent:	Writ used where a defendant could not be found. If unsuccessfully 'called' on five successive court days, he was outlawed and his possessions forfeited.
Infangthefe:	The right of a lord to judge any felon taken in his lordship.
Inspeximus:	Confirmation of a charter.
Iur(e) Ux(or):	Land held by a husband in right of his wife's ownership.
Jetsam:	Goods washed ashore.
Lagan:	Wreckage or goods lying on the sea-bed.

Levaris:	A writ requiring a levy on a person who had forfeited a recognisance.
Mulctures:	Mill tolls, paid for grinding corn.
Non omittas:	A writ requiring and authorising the initiation of legal action by a superior authority, where the immediate authority has failed serve the required writ.
Outfangthefe:	The right of a lord to pursue a felon beyond the boundaries of his lordship and to bring him to trial within the lordship.
Pro licentia concordandi }	Money due to the king (in Gower, the lord) on a court's approval of a settlement or transaction.
Replevin:	A writ to recover distrained goods, alleged to have been wrongfully distrained.
Resiants:	Persons who constantly dwelt in one manor, not necessarily as tenants there.
Soccage:	A common form of freehold tenure, requiring payment of a fixed 'chief rent' to the lord and attendance at his courts.
Venire facias:	A writ to convene a jury.
Waifs:	Abandoned goods. After being 'cried' in nearby churches and markets, they became the property of the king (in Gower, the lord) after a year and a day.
Writ:	A written command of a court to do, or to refrain from doing, a specified act.

ii. SOME OTHER TERMS

Acre:	This apparently straight-forward unit of area measurement could vary considerably. The statute (or English) acre was 4840 square yards (0.4 ha.). The Welsh, or customary, acre could also vary but in the Lordship of Gower it was twice the area of a statute acre. It is not always clear which is being used in the various manors included in the Survey (or other surveys), but Welsh measure is usually applied in Sub and Supraboscus and in Kilvey.
Chief rent:	Rent due to the lord from a freehold tenement. Usually fixed and small.
Cover:	A measure of land, equivalent to half a Welsh acre, used in some Welsh holdings mentioned in the Survey. From 'Cyfar', a parcel of land. The word also has associations with the communal tillage of arable land.
Culm:	Coal dust and small coal.
Improved value:	The rent at which it was estimated that a holding could be let if it were back in the hands of the landlord.
Lattermath:	Grass growing after the main hay crop has been cut.
Perch:	One fortieth of an acre.
Rood:	One quarter of an acre.
Tenement:	A tenanted or tenantable landholding.
Wears/Weirs:	These were placed across rivers to divert water into leets, thus providing power for mills. Fishing weirs were set out on a tidal beach or in a river. Those on a beach were V-shaped in plan, the point towards the sea.
Wey/Weigh:	A measure of coal by volume. In the Swansea area in the eighteenth century it was estimated to be equivalent to five tons.

A

SURVEY

OF THE

Seigniories of Gower and Kilvey
with the several Members of which the most Noble
Henry Duke of Beaufort is Lord
Made in the Year 1764

By
Gabriel Powell the present Steward, Coroner,
Bayliff of the Liberties, and Recorder of the Courts of
the said Seigniories; from several antient and
authentick Papers, and the observations and Experience
of Gabriel Powell his late Father deceased and Himself
for above Sixty three Years

At the Desire of the most Noble Elizabeth
Dutchess Dowager of Beaufort (Mother and
Guardian of the said Duke) to whom this Survey
is most humbly presented by

Her Grace's
most faithful and Obedient
Servant
Gab: Powell

The Seigniory of Gower

A Survey of the Seigniory of Gower in the County of Glamorgan with the Several Members made the *[blank]* Day of November in the year of our Lord One Thousand Seven Hundred and Sixty four[1].

The said Seigniory was an Ancient Lordship Marcher of Wales, and had all Royal Jurisdictions in as large and extensive a manner as Gilbert de Clare, Earl of Gloucester and Hereford, had enjoyed within his County of Glamorgan or Morgannwg, until taken away by the Statute of the 27th Henry 8th[2], which annexed it to, and made it part of, the County of Glamorgan. Before which time Gower (in ancient times called Gŵyr) was reckoned as part of Cantref Eginoc, in the County of Carmarthen.

The Seigniory or Lordship Royal of Gower was conquered [at] the beginning of the reign of Henry the First by Henry de Beaumont, Earl of Warwick. He built the Castle of Swansea[3].

After him succeeded his son, Roger Beaumont, Earl of Warwick.

After him succeeded his son, William, Earl of Warwick, and died 3rd of Henry 2nd.

After him succeeded his brother, Walfranus, Earl of Warwick.

After him succeeded his son, Henry, Earl of Warwick.

After him succeeded his son, Thomas Beaumont, Earl of Warwick. He conveyed Gower to King Henry the Second (and died the sixth of Henry the Third).

After him succeeded King Henry the Second.

After him succeeded his son, King Richard the First.

After him succeeded his brother, King John, who gave it to William de Brewse by Charter. See the Charter which was afterwards confirmed by Edward the First, Edward the Second and Edward the Third. See the Charter of Edward the Third with an *Inspeximus* of the former Charters.

William de Brewse, Lord [of] Brecknock, Burgavenny and Brember who, by the gift of King John, was Lord of Gower, married Matilda de St Vallery, and by her had three sons: William; Giles, Bishop of Hereford; and Reynald; and a daughter called Maud, married to Prince Griffith, son to the Lord Rees. This William fled into France, [but] his wife and eldest son, William, were famished[4] in the Castle of Windsor, and the Lordships of Brecknock and Burgavenny were given to Giles. After whose decease, Reynold *[Reginald]* had the said Lordships. And Gower only [was] left to John Brewse, son to William the eldest brother who was famished at Windsor.

---

1. This heading is in Sa but not in Bn. The 'four' has been inserted.
2. The first 'Act of Union of England and Wales', 1536.
3. This account of the descent of the lordship is helpful but must be treated with caution. It omits the later Warwicks, who wrested it from the Mowbrays for a period. In places it is at variance with other sources, such as W.H.J. *History.* and *GCH.* III. Some of the regnal years quoted are incorrect.
4. Starved to death.

John de Brewse, son to the last-named William, and grandson to the first William de Brewse, was Lord of Gower. He married the daughter of Prince Llewelyn ap Jenkin. He, by the consent of the said Llewelyn, forfeited the Town and Castle of Swansea. He died by a fall off ['off' in Sa; 'of' in Bn] his horse in the fourth of Henry the Third.

Then succeeded William de Brewse his son, Lord of Gower and Brember. He died at Findon, 18th Edward 1st.

After him succeeded his son, William de Brewse, Lord of Brember and Gower. He granted the Charter of Swansea. He did grant the said Lordship of Gower to his son in law, John, Lord Mowbrey, and afterwards sold it to Hugh Spencer, Lord of Glamorgan, which occasioned a great dispute between the great Barons who took up arms against the Spencers, and the King took the Spencers' part against the Barons.

John, Lord Mowbrey, married Elinor, daughter and heiress to the said William de Brewse. He was Lord of Gower by the grant of his father in law, and held it a long time in opposition to the Spencers. And rising in arms with Thomas, Earl of Warwick, was defeated at Borrow Bridge *[Boroughbridge, 16th March 1322]* and put to death, 14th Edward 2nd.

[Folio 1/2]

Elinor, daughter and heiress to the Lord William de Brewse had a son, John, Lord Mowbrey. She died Anno Dom. 1360[5] and lies buried in Swansea. She founded the Hospital of St David's for twelve poor people, and did impropriate thereunto the Parsonage of Swansea, and gave unto it the Lordship of Brinavel and several tenements of lands in Skettie and about the Town of Swansea, and appointed a Warden of the same.

John, Lord Mowbrey, after the decease of his mother, was Lord of Gower. He was by the King restored to the Seigniory of Gower. He married Joan, daughter to Henry, Earl of Lancaster. After him succeeded his son, John.

John, Lord Mowbrey of Ephelme, Lord of Gower and Brember. He married Elizabeth, daughter to John, Lord Seagrave. He was slain at Constantinople in Anno 1368 in the third of Edward 3rd[6]. After him succeeded his son:

Thomas, Earl Mowbrey, Lord Marshal of England, so made by King Richard the Second, and also by him made Duke of Norfolk. He had a difference with Henry of Bolingbrook, Duke of Hereford, and was banished. He died in Venice Anno Domine 1398. After him succeeded his son:

Thomas, Earl of Nottingham, in whose time Swansea was burnt by Owen Glendwr. He was beheaded by Henry the 4th. After him succeeded his brother:

John, made Earl Marshal, and [Earl] of Nottingham by King Henry 5th. And in a Parliament [in the] 3rd of Henry the Sixth, this John, brother and heir to Thomas, Duke of Norfolk, was made Duke of Norfolk. And after him succeeded his son:

5. Although accepted in the past, 1360 is wrong. She died in 1331 or 32. See WHJ. *History* II, p.10, and *GCH*. III, p.247.
6. But 1368 was the forty-second year of Edward III, not the third.

John, Duke of Norfolk, who died [in the] 1st of Edward 4th. After him succeeded his son:

John, Duke of Norfolk, who in his father's lifetime, was by King Henry the 6th created Earl of Surry and Warren. And in Anno 17th. Edward 4th this John did convey Gower to the Lord William Herbert, Earl of Pembroke, in exchange for other lands in England. William Herbert, Earl of Pembroke, was Lord of Gower in the 17th of Edward 4th, as it appeared by a Deed of Confirmation, under his Chancery Seal, of certain lands in Kellibion to Henry Treharne, the son of Thomas Treharne, which was in the hands of Evan Thomas of Kellibion, bearing date 22nd of June in the above year. He was taken prisoner in Edge Cot Fields [1469] and beheaded at Banbury, in the time of Edward the 4th. After whom succeeded his son:

William, son to the said William Earl of Pembroke, was created Earl of Huntingdon and Lord of Gower, and had issue one only daughter:

Elizabeth, daughter and sole heir to William, Earl of Huntingdon, was after the death of her father, Lady of Gower, Raglan and Chepstow. She was married to Sir Charles Somerset, Knight, son to John, Duke of Somerset, who in her right was Lord of Gower. He was afterwards created Earl of Worcester.

Henry, Earl of Worcester (the son of Charles and Elizabeth), was Lord of Gower. He first married Isabella, daughter to Sir Anthony Brown, Knight, and [took] to his second wife, Isabella, daughter to John, Marquess of Montacute.

William, the son of Henry, was, after the death of his father, Earl of Worcester and Lord of Gower. He married Christian, daughter to Edward, Lord North.

Edward, the son of William, was after the death of his father, Earl of Worcester and Lord of Gower. He married Elizabeth, daughter of Francis, Earl of Huntingdon.

[Folio 2/3]

Henry, the son of Edward, was created Marquiss of Worcester by King Charles the First, and by Anne, his wife, daughter of John Lord Russell – son to Francis, Earl of Bedford – had issue Edward, who in his father's lifetime was created Earl of Glamorgan. And by Elizabeth, his wife, sister to Robert, Earl of Carnarvon, had issue Henry, who by King Charles the Second was created Duke of Beaufort, and by Mary his wife, daughter to Arthur, Lord Capel, had issue Charles, Marquiss of Worcester, who died in his father's lifetime, leaving issue by Rebecca his wife, daughter to Sir Josiah Child, Knight:

Henry, Duke of Beaufort, who by Rachael his wife, daughter to Wriothsly Baptist, Earl of Gains-borough, had issue:

Henry, Duke of Beaufort, Lord of Gower, who dying without issue in March 1745 was succeeded by his brother:

Charles Noel, Duke of Beaufort and Lord of Gower, who died in October 1756 leaving issue by Elizabeth, his wife, daughter of John Sims Berkley of Stoke in the County of Gloucester, esquire (sister to Norbourne, Lord Botetourt):

Henry, Duke of Beaufort, the present Lord of Gower.

Survey of the Seigniory[7]

The general boundary of the said Seigniory, beginning at the Town of Swansea, goes along the sea side to the Mumble Head, from thence to Pwll duy, thence to the Three Cliffs, thence to Oxwich Point, thence to Port Eynon Point, thence to Wormshead. Thence to the Holms, thence to Whitford Point, thence up the River Burry or Loughour to the place where Cathan Water discharges itself into the same. Thence up the said water or brook till you come to a place called Penllyr Castell, thence along a small path under Penllyr Castell which divides the Counties of Glamorgan and Carmarthen, and then keeping along the boundaries of the said Counties till you come to the River Twrch. And then down along the said river till it discharges itself into the River Tawy (the whole river being within the Seigniory) until it empties itself into the sea at the Town of Swansea.

The Seigniory is divided into two large Commotes called Gower Anglicana, or English Gower; and Gower Supraboscus and Subboscus, or Welsh Gower. It also contains the two Hundreds of Swansea and Llangyfelach. The Hundred of Swansea comprehends the several Parishes of Swansea, Oystermouth, Bishopston, Pennard, Penmaen, Nicholaston, Penrice, Oxwich, Port Eynon, Roscilly, Langennith, Llanmaddock, Cheriton, Lanridian, Loughour, Landilotalybont, Ilston, Knelston, Landewy, Reynoldston, and St Johns near Swansea.

And the Hundred of Langevelach [comprehends] the whole Parish of Langevelach, Languick, Lansamlet, so much of the Parish of Swansea as lies on the east side of Swansea River (and which is in the Manor of Kilvey), and so much of the Parish of Lanridian, Ilston, Bishopston, and Loughour, as constitute Gower Subboscus or Parcel Iscoed. And the said Seigniory is coextensive with the Deanery of Gower, which lies within the Diocese of Saint David's, whereas the rest of the County of Glamorgan is within the Diocese of Landaff.

The Seigniory consists of several Freehold tenants who hold their lands in Common Soccage immediately of the Lord of the Seigniory, by Rent, Fealty, Suit of Court, and Heriots; and of several Mesne Manors, some whereof are held in Demesne. Others were formerly held by Knight's Service, but since the Statute 12th of Charles 2nd *[1660-61]* Chap: 24, for taking away the Court of Wards and Liveries, Tenures *in Capite,* and by Knight's Service and Purveyance, are now held by Fealty, Suit of Court, Reliefs or Heriots. And others are held in *Libera Eleemosyna*[8].

[Folio 3/4]

Those [Manors] held in Demesne are:

The Borough and Manor of Swansea;

The Borough and Manor of Loughour *[sic]*;

---

7.   No heading in the originals, but a marginal note: 'Survey of the Seigniory'.
8.   Free Alms.

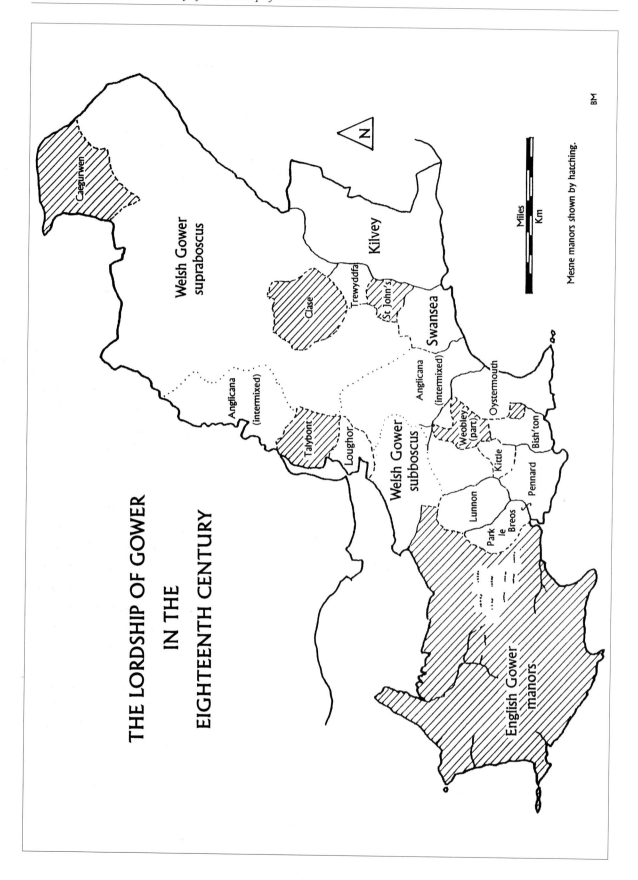

THE LORDSHIP OF GOWER
IN THE
EIGHTEENTH CENTURY

Caegurwen

Welsh Gower
supraboscus

Clase

Trewyddfa

Kilvey

St John's

Swansea

Anglicana
(intermixed)

Anglicana
(intermixed)

Talybont

Loughor

Welsh Gower
subboscus

Weobley
(part)

Oystermouth

Bish'ton

Kittle

Pennard

Lunnon

Park
le
Breos

English Gower
manors

N

Miles
Km

Mesne manors shown by hatching.

BM

The Manor of Oystermouth;

The Manor of Pennard with the Fiefs or Fees of Kittle, Lunnon and Trewyddva;

The Manor of Bishopston, which was formerly held by the Bishops of Landaff in Free Alms, and was conveyed by one of them to the Mathews; and of [by?]George Mathews late of Thurles, in the County of Tipperary in the Kingdom of Ireland esq., was sold and conveyed in or about the year 1702 to Gabriel Powell, gentleman, who immediately sold it to the Most Noble Henry, then Duke of Beaufort, for the same money he purchased it.

Manors formerly held by Knight's Service

The several Manors hereinafter mentioned were formerly held of the Seigniory by Knight's Service, but are now held in Tenure of Fealty, Suit of Court, Reliefs or Heriots[9].

Oxwich: Thomas Mansel Talbot esq., infant, holds the Manor of Oxwich by Fealty, Suit of Court and Heriot. This Manor comprehends the whole Parish of Oxwich and consists of Freehold tenants who hold their lands in Common Soccage, and several tenements held in Demesne. The Lord holds a Leet and a Baron Court for this Manor, Port Eynon, and Pitton, alias Pilton, twice a year at May and Michaelmas. And this Manor and Port Eynon bordering on the sea, the Lord claims Wreck de Mer and all wastes within the same, but all Royalties which lie in Grant belong to the Lord of the Seigniory.

Penrice: The same holds the Manor of Penrice, of which the Manor of Horton is held, by Fealty, Suit of Court and Heriot. This Manor, as well as Horton, consists wholly of lands held in Demesne. The Lord holds Leet and Baron Courts twice a year for this Manor and Horton, and [for] the Manors hereinafter mentioned, called: Stembridge, otherwise Burry; Walterston; Nicholaston; and Scurlage. There are four tenants within the Duke of Beaufort's Manor of Pennard to wit: Robert Jone; Jenkin Taylor; William Atkins; and Phillip William, who, being obliged by their leases to appear at this Court, are called over here. Penrice bordering on the sea, the Lord claims Wreck de Mer, wastes etc. but all Royalties lying in Grant are claimed and enjoyed by the Lord of Gower.

Porteynon: The same holds the Manor of Port Eynon by Fealty, Suit of Court and Heriot; of which the Manor of Pitton, otherwise Pilton, is held. The Manor of Porteynon lies in the Parish of Porteynon and consists of Freehold tenants who hold their lands in Common Soccage. And several tenements are held in Demesne which are let out by leases to several persons. And the Manor of Pitton, otherwise Pilton, lies in the Parish of Roscilly, and consists of several Freehold tenants holding their lands in Common Soccage, and several tenements held in Demesne. Vide Oxwich.

---

9.   The names of the manors appear in the Sa version merely as marginal notes, in G.P.'s own rough script, with sometimes the date of the earlier surveys from which he quotes the boundaries. He has updated the names of tenants quoted in those surveys.

'The great rock by the Tile House Barn', marking the boundary between the two manors of Llangennith.

*Three Gower manors, seen from Harding's Down. The open hillside on the left is in Rhossili manor (a part of Landimore).
The sloping fields below the houses and the flat lands by the sea are in West Town Llangennith,
and the foreground fields are in Priors Town.*

Westown of Langennith:

Copy [of a] Survey [dated] 25 Oct. 1642. *[Tenants' names updated to the 1760s.]:*

The Right Honble Earl of Warwick, the Right Honble Earl of Ashburnham, and George Venables Vernon esq., and the Honble Louisa Barbara his wife, in her Right, hold the Manor of Westown of Langennith: which is bounded by the Manor of Eastown, otherwise Priorstown, on the east till you come to Roscilly Down. From thence you go westward, leaving Roscilly Down on the south and the three tenements called Barreston on the north, till you come to a certain house called Hillend, formerly William Beynon's House. From thence due west by a certain lake which divides the both Hillends from Llangennith Moor, till you come to the sea side. Thence you go northward by the sea shore till you come to a certain lake called Moor Lake, which divideth the Parishes of Langennith and Lanmaddock. From the fall of the said Lake you go due east till you come to a very large rock on the west end of Lanmadock Hill From the said rock you go eastward along the middle of Lanmaddock Hill till you come to the east end thereof, to a certain path leading from a certain lane called Kifts Lane to the village of Lanmaddock. From thence south, or south-eastward, till you come to Taylor's Parks. From thence west, till you come to a place called Hoar Rocks, and so down the lane that divides the east and west Town Lordships till you come to the great rock by the end of the Tile House Barn.

N.B. There are some other scattered tenements which belong to the west Town Lordship *viz.* One in Landewy Parish, the lands of John Lucas esq.; the lands of Robert Batcock; the lands of Herbert Gibb; all known by the name of Cathan. All the Druids Moor; and two tenements called Harden's Down, the Estate of the Earl of Warwick, in the Parish of Landewy. And two other tenements in the said Parish of Langennith, the Estate of the Earl of Ashburnham, near Roscilly Down, called by the several names of Ruggart and the Hen's Nest. And one other tenement near Coyty Green, called the Foot lands, the Estate of the Earl of Warwick aforesaid.   *[Folio 4/5]*

Stembridge:

Thomas Mansel Talbot esq., infant, holds the Manor of Stembridge otherwise Burry, which is situate in the Parish of Langennith, and consists of about seven Freehold tenants and several tenants holding in Demesne.

Llyn y bough [10]:

The same holds the reputed Manor of Llyn y bough, otherwise Lan y bough, which is situated in the Parish of Lanridian and consists only of one tenement of lands now in the possession of Mr Thomas Gorton.

Scurlage:

Copy [of a] Survey [dated] 26th September 1632. *[Tenants' names updated to the 1760s.]:*

The same holds the Manor of Scurlage Castle by Fealty, Suit of Court and Heriot. This Manor is situated in the Parishes of Landewy and Knelston, and is bounded as followeth: beginning at the lane's end which leadeth from Port Eynons Moor unto the house of Wm Gamon, infant, at Munkenland, as the hedge leadeth eastward between the lands of Earl Talbot belonging unto the said house, called the Butts, and a close of the land in the tenure of the said William Gamon

10. Llwyn y bwch.

called the white Layes, and from thence westward as the hedge leadeth at the north side of the said Butts. And thence westward as the hedge leadeth at the south end of the close called Battlestone, being part of the said Wm Gamon's tenement, and as the hedge leadeth north-west about the said close unto the hedge of a close called Bennet's Park. And as the hedge leadeth on the west side of it and so about the said close between it and the lands late of Maysod Dawkin, widow, and the Earl of Warwick unto a close called Robin's Torrs, being the said Lord's land, and as the hedge leadeth round about the said close, bordering the land late of the said Maysod Dawkin, widow, and the said Thomas Mansel Talbot on the south-west parts. And as the hedge leadeth from the said Robin's Torrs at the north-east corner unto the Earl of Warwick's lands again, and thence north as the hedge leadeth at the west part of the said Earl of Warwick's land unto the lane which leadeth from Newton unto Johan's Crosse. And thence east unto the lands of Lady Charlotte Edwin, being the Manor of Knelston, as the hedge leadeth south between a field of Scurladge *[Folio 5/6]* called the Butters and the said Lordship of Knelston, unto a field called the Northern Demesne of Scurlage. And thence eastwards as the hedge (on the north side of the Demesne) leadeth unto a meadow containing about three acres, being part of the farm of Scurlage, [and] as the hedge leadeth on the north side of the said meadow, dividing it from the said Lordship of Knelston, unto the east end of the said meadow. And from the north hedge thereof southward as the hedge leadeth between it and Knelston Meadow, unto the northern end of a close called the Nine Acres, being part of Berry Farm. And as the hedge leadeth eastward at the north end of the said Nine Acres to a close called the little Woodland and another close called the great Woodland, bordering Knelston Meadow, Bullen Mead and the Bryndyland, being in the Parish and Lordship of Knelston, unto the hedge on the east corner of the said woodland. And as the hedge (between it and the broad Mead) leadeth southwards, dividing the Parishes of Penrice and Landewy and the Lordships of Penrice, unto Port Eynon's Moor, and thence westwards as the hedge leadeth of the farms of Berry and Scurlage, and the tenement in the tenure of Daniel Curtis, unto the Lane's End which leadeth from the said Moor unto the house at Munkenland.

There lieth within the said circuit one messuage and tenement containing about three acres which Edward Hancorne gent., holdeth freely of the Manor of west Millwood (called the Berrie in the Parish of Landewy). There is also within the said circuit one messuage and tenement of land containing about forty-two acres lying within itself, called Scurlage Castle, which the Earl of Warwick holdeth freely of the Manor of Oystermouth, and is now in the possession of John Clement paying the yearly rent of 8d, and the same also pays a yearly rent of 3d in Gower Anglicana (see Rent Roll, folio 24 *[p.74]*). Also there lieth within the said Manor one messuage and tenement of lands containing about half an acre, which the late Maysod Dawkin, widow, holds freely of the Manor of Oxwich and oweth Suit of Court, and Rent – a red rose at Midsummer.

Walterston & Kellibion:

[Copy of a] Survey [dated] 10th December 1689. *[Tenants' names updated to the 1760s.]*:
The same holds the Manor of Walterston, situate in the Parish of Lanridian, which with Kellibion formerly made one Manor and had been part of the dissolved Monastery of Neath, but was lately separated from Kellibion by being sold by Mathew Pryce esq. to Thomas, late Lord Mansel.

Joseph Pryce esq., son of the said Mathew Pryce, still holds the Manor of Kellibion which had been also part of the dissolved Monastery of Neath.

Walterston and Kellibion are adjoining and situate in the Parish of Lanridian and are included under one general boundary, as followeth: It extendeth on the east side from the Common belonging to the Seigniory of Gower called Kevenbrin along the Park Wall or Ditch that leadeth to a tenement of land called the Lodge (being the land of his Grace the Duke of Beaufort, Lord of the said Seigniory of Gower). And from thence along the said Park Wall or Ditch to another tenement of the said Duke called Letherid, and from thence it extendeth on the north-east side, along the side of a brook called Letherids Water to a place called the Forest, and from thence it extends along the side of the said brook to the meadows called the Queen's Meadows, otherwise the great Meads. And along the north hedge of those meadows *[Folio 6/7]* it extendeth to the western hedge of a parcel of ground late of Maysod Dawkin, widow, called the Well acre, and from thence crossing over the highway there leading from Swansea towards Lanridian it extendeth to the western hedge of another close of the said Maysod Dawkin, called also the Well acre. And from thence it extends southwardly to the house wherein one John Bynon doth now ['now' *deleted and* 'did formerly' *substituted*] inhabit ['but is now in ruins' *inserted*] which house is ['is' *deleted and* 'was' *substituted*] part of a tenement ['now belonging to David Long' *inserted*] called Park yr rhedin and from thence it extendeth along the southern hedge of the said tenement called Park yr rhedin joining with the Common there westwardly, as the highway leadeth from Kellibion towards Lanridian to the eastern corner of a certain close called Kae main. And from thence crossing over the highway there, it extendeth along the eastern hedge of a close called Kae Howell to the Common called Broadmoor, which is part of Kevenbryn, and so along the ditch of the inclosures, leaving the Common on the south and west, to the place the boundary was begun.

Paviland: The Right Honble Earl Talbot holds the Manor of Paviland, which had been part of the dissolved Monastery of Neath. It is a part of the Parish of Penmaen but at some distance from it, being almost surrounded by the Parish of Porteynon and the Manor of Pilton. A small part borders the sea and the Lord claims Wreck de Mer thereon, but no Court either Leet or Baron are or have been in the memory of man held for it. And [it] consists of six tenements of land which are held in Demesne.

Nicholaston: Thomas Mansel Talbot esq., infant, holds the Manor of Nicholaston of which Manselfield is a part. This Manor is situate in the Parish of Nicholaston, having Penrice on the west, Kevenbryn on the north, Penmaen on the east, and the sea on the south – on which part the Lord claims Wreck de Mer. Manselfield lies at a distance from the rest of this Parish and Manor, being surrounded by the Manors of Oystermouth and Bishopton, and is bounded as follows: Beginning at Jackshoesland near Bishop's wood along a hedge which runs straight up to the back part of Thomas Parry's house, leaving Murton on the north-west side, to Murton Common and thence to the eastern ditch of Mr Thomas Watkins's lands. And thence along the water course near to the landshare stone standing on the Common, and thence to the old ditch which separates Clyne Moor and thence to the Corner Hedge, and thence along the hedge of Furze Parks – leaving the fields belonging to Bradley on the north between it and the Common –

till you come to Clyne Moor on the east And along the water course which runs in or near the ditch of the inclosures till you come to the hedge of Furze Parks, belonging to William Dawkin esq. And thence along the same watercourse to Mourning Coomb where the water sinks underground, and thence along the western hedge of the lands of Robert Popkin esq. to the highway at Esperlone. And thence across the road to the western hedge of a field of William Griffith, called Broad Park, and along that hedge to Jack Shoes land where it began.

Brinaval: The Right Honble Earl of Warwick holds the Barony or Manor of Brinavel and Ilston. This Barony is situate in the Parish of Ilston, and consists of four or five tenements of lands which pay Chief Rents to the Lord of Gower. And the Tenants do Suit to the Leet and Baron Courts held for the Seigniory and a Relief is due on the death of the Earl of Warwick. See the Chief Rents paid by the said Earl in the Rent Roll of Gower Anglicana in the Parish of Ilston. Folio 25 *[p.75.]*.

[Folio 7/8]

Hospital of St Davids: William Hurst and Calvert Richard Jones esqs., the Representatives of the late Thomas Herbert esq. hold the suppressed Hospital of St Davids in Swansea. This Hospital was founded by Elinor, only daughter and heir of William de Bruce. She was married to John, Lord Mowbray. What lands were particularly granted for the support of this Hospital are not now known, but are supposed to be a great part of the Estates which the Earl of Warwick, the late Mr Herbert of the Friars near Cardiff, and the said Wm Hurst and Calvert Richard Jones now enjoy in the Seigniory.

Sketty: The Right Honble the Earl of Warwick holds the Barony of Sketty. This Barony is wholly situate in the Parish of Swansea and consists of several tenements which pay Chief Rents to the Lord of Gower, and the tenants do Suit to the Leet and Baron Courts of the Seigniory and a Heriot of five shillings [is] due on the death of the proprietor or on Alienation of it. See the Chief Rents paid by the said Earl in Gower Anglicana and Gower Supraboscus within the Parish of Swansea.

Penmaen:
Copy [of a] Deed dated 1696; ditto. 1676; ditto. 1710.
Jane Mansel, widow, holds the Manor of Penmaen, which consists only of one tenement of lands. And is bounded by the sea on the south side thereof, the Lordship and Manor of Nicholaston on the west, and the pathway leading from Nicholaston Parish over the corner of Kevenbrin unto a ditch adjoining the pale or wall of Park le Bruce which encompasseth a close called the Quabbs on the north-west, the Glebe lands and a tenement called Furzehill on the north and north-east, and Pennard's Pill on the east. Part of this Manor adjoining the sea, the Lord claims Wreck de Mer thereon.

Henllis: Thomas Mansel Talbot esq. holds the Manor of Henllis otherwise Kilvrough. This is a very scattered Lordship, consisting of several tenements of lands held by lease under the Lord and lying in five or six different Parishes. There are called in the Leet and Baron Courts kept for this Manor three Freehold tenants, to wit, the Earl of Warwick, the Right Honble Lady Charlotte

Edwin and William Dawkin of Kilvrough esq. But there are no Chief or Quit Rents paid, nor is it known what the lands are or where situate which are pretended to be held of this Manor.

Landimore:

Copy [of a] Survey [dated] 29th July 1598. Earls of Pembroke['s] Patent. *[Tenants' names updated to the 1760s.]:*

The same holds the Manor of Landimore, which was formerly held by Sir Rees ap Thomas, Knight of the Garter, and came to the Crown by his attainder in the reign of King Henry 7th, and was by Queen Elizabeth granted to William Earl of Pembroke and afterwards sold by one of his descendants to Sir Edward Mansel, Baronet. There is paid to the Lord of Gower yearly for this Manor, a pair of gilded spurs or twenty shillings. This Manor was anciently granted by John, Duke of Norfolk, Lord of Gower to Sir Hugh Johns, one of the Knights of Jerusalem, for his gallant behaviour in the Holy War against the Turks. This Manor together with the Manors of Roscilly, Lanridian, Weobley, and Reynoldstone, are held by Fealty, Suit of Court and a Relief of twenty-eight shillings on the death of every Lord. There are Leet and Baron Courts held for these several Manors *[Folio 8/9]* together, twice a year. The tenants do their Suits promiscuously and one Jury is sworn for them all There are several Freehold tenants within these Manors who hold their lands in Common Soccage, and several Demesne tenements which are held by leases under the Lord. These Manors are held of the Seigniory by the payment of a pair of gilt spurs, or twenty shillings in lieu therof, and a small rent of 7s 8½d payable at Michaelmas yearly. This Manor of Landimore is bounded as follows: Beginning at the fall of the River of Burry into the great River of Loughor, and as the same river of Burry leadeth unto a well called Dervell's Well, and from Dervell's Well southward to a place called the old Fort on Lanmadock Downe. And from thence eastward, right along a hedge being the landshare between the lands anciently of Phillip Cradock, and now of William John and John Lucas esq., and the lands of Sir Thomas Mansel called Rhyw'r hwth, leadeth eastward to the highway that leadeth unto the Stone Mill. And so as that way leadeth unto a bridge upon the River of Burry called the Stone Bridge and so eastward as the said River of Burry leadeth up to the north corner of a close, anciently Lewis John's and now in the possession of Henry Evan as tenant to Lady Charlotte Edwin. And as the east hedge of the said close leadeth up to the highway that leadeth from Stembridge towards Langennith, and as that highway leadeth eastward to the west hedge of a close called little Underhill and as that hedge leadeth northward to the west hedge of the Allyfield. And as that hedge leadeth to the west hedge of Burgwin's Park, and so as the hedge of that close leadeth northward to the way that leadeth from Landimore towards Swansea. And so crossing the said way to the eastern hedge of a close antiently in the hands of David Batcock and now of John Howell as tenant to John Lucas esq., called the three Acres. And so as that hedge, being the landshare between the Demesnes of Weobly and the Lordship aforesaid leadeth northward to the south side of the wood called Weobly's Wood. And so as that hedge leadeth westward to a hedge called the Slade, being lands anciently of William White and now of John Lucas esq., part of Towns End. And as that hedge leadeth eastward to the west hedge of the great close called the Seven Acres, anciently in the possession of Jenkin Hopkins and now of Elisha Gorton, part of Weobley Castle. And so as that hedge leadeth northward to a ditch, being the landshare between the meadows anciently in the possession of Hopkin Jenkins, and the meadows of Wm White and now in the possession of Anne Bowen, widow, as tenant to John Lucas esq. And so as that ditch leadeth to the Marshe, being the

Lord's Commons without division between the Lordship aforesaid and the Lordship of Weobly, and so northward as the great River of Loughor leadeth to the fall of the River Burry aforesaid.

Roscilly: The Manor of Roscilly is bounded as follows: Beginning at a well called Talgarth's Well and joining to the hedge of lands anciently Owen Perkin's (and now the lands of the late Maysod Dawkin, widow) called Free Land, and so as that hedge leadeth southward to Elliot's Cross. From thence crossing the lane as a hedge leadeth to a place called Brine's Torrs, and there hence as a stone wall (being the landshare between this Lordship and the lands of George Venables Vernon esq., which anciently were Wm Price esquire's) leadeth to a little creek called Mew Slade to the sea. And so westward by the sea side to the furthest or uttermost point of Wormshead, being within this Lordship. And so northward by the sea side to the fall of the Dill Lake, being the landshare between the Parish[es] of Langennith and Roscilly, and from there thence as a hedge leadeth to the north side of a house called Hill End, anciently the land of Sir Wm Herbert, knight, and now of the Earl of Warwick. And so eastward and southward as the mears lead off the Commons of Roscilly Down to Talgarth's Well aforesaid.

[Folio 9/10]

Lanridian: The said Manor of Lanridian is bounded as follows: Beginning at the fall of the River Morles into the great River of Loughor, and so as the said River of Morles cometh eastward to the west hedge of a close called Llwyn yr Aust And as that hedge leadeth southward to the highway that leadeth from Llan y newyr Chapel towards Harry Thomas Nicholas's ['Harry Thomas Nicholas's' *deleted and* 'the' *inserted*] house [*formerly of Harry Thomas Nicholas & now of Mr Gabriel Powell'* *inserted*], called Llwyn Robert, to the last hedge of Harry Gwyn's land ['formerly and now of the said Gabriel Powell' *inserted*]. And so as that hedge of Harry Gwyn's ['the said Gabriel Powell' *inserted*] land leadeth southward to the highway that leadeth towards Y newyr fould, and crossing over that way to the western hedge of Brin y gwase, and so as that hedge leadeth southward to the north hedge of a meadow called North Hills. And so as that hedge leadeth towards Tyr Coch, and as that lane leadeth to the east hedge of the waste called the Welsh Moor. And so as that hedge leadeth to Letherid's Water and so as that water runneth from the north, to the south hedge of the meadow anciently in the possession of Jenkin Franklen and now of John Ace as tenant ['to the late Maysod Dawkin, widow.' *inserted*]. And so as that hedge leadeth westward to the north hedge of the Queens Meadow called Y Wain Hyre, and so as that hedge leadeth westward to the west end of the Queen's Meadow called Y Wain Hyr aforesaid. And from thence as the hedge leadeth southward to the western end of a close called the Well Acre, and as that hedge leadeth eastward to the south hedge of a close called Park yr rhedin, and so as that hedge leadeth westward to the east hedge of a close called y Kae Mayn. And so crossing the highway that leadeth from Kellibion towards Lanridian to the east of a close called Kae Howell, and so as that hedge leadeth southward to the hedge, (being the landshare between it and the Common called Kevenbryn on the westward) to Fredow. And from thence to the eastern hedge of a close called Beat Park, and as that hedge leadeth directly northward to the highway that leadeth from Mansel's fold to Swansea. And so crossing that way to the eastern hedge of a close called Martin's Acre, and as that hedge leadeth northward to the western hedge of a close called Sickman's Hill. And so as that hedge leadeth to the eastern hedge of the Honourable George

Venables Vernon's wood called Leaston Wood, and so as that hedge leadeth to the eastern side of a close Lodgecot Park ['and now called the three acres, the lands of John Dawkin gent.' *inserted*]. And as that hedge leadeth to the Marsh being the Commons without division between the Lordship of Landimore and the Lordship of Weobly, and so westward to the great River of Loughor [and] to the fall of Morles Water aforesaid.

Weobly:

Copy [of a] Survey [dated] 28th Octr 1630. *[Tenants' names updated to the 1760s.]*:

The said Manor of Weobly is bounded as follows: Beginning at a place called Stembridge upon the River of Burry, and so southwards to the fall of a brook called Redwell Lake, and as that brook leadeth eastward through Lan y bwch to Keven bryn near to the house anciently in the possession of one John ap John ['otherwise little Hill End, but the house is now in ruins' *inserted*] and now of Margaret Thomas, widow. And from thence as the hedges and inclosures of Mary Hughes of Swansea, spinster, [lead] eastward by Kevenbryn to the highway that leadeth northward to a place called Beat Park by Keven bryn, [and] to the corner of a close anciently in the possession of Owen Bach and now of William Mudon, mariner. From thence as the said Beat Park hedge leadeth northward to the east corner of a close of the Honourable George Venables Vernon called Martin's Acre, and from thence as the eastern hedge of the close leadeth northward to the lands of the said Thos Mansel Talbot called Mansel's field. And *[Folio 10/11]* from thence as that hedge leadeth to the east Field ['formerly' *inserted*] of ['the said' *deleted*] William Dawkin ['and now of Rowland Prichard ge[nt]' *inserted*]. From thence as the way leadeth northward to a place called Harry Dare, and from thence to the salt marsh called Lanridian's Marsh without division to the said River of Loughor. The other part of the bounds of this Lordship beginneth at Stembridge upon Burry aforesaid, joining to the Parishes of Langennith and Cheriton, and from thence as the highway leadeth eastward to Swansea to a corner of a close called the little Wind Mill, and as that hedge leadeth northward to a corner of a close called the Allyfield. And as the said Allyfield hedge leadeth westward round the corner of a close called Bwrgwms Park, and as that hedge leadeth northward to the highway, by William Bach's house, that leadeth from Landymore to Swansea. And from thence as the highway leadeth eastward to the western corner of a close called the Sheephouse Park, and as that hedge leadeth westward over Weobly's Wood [and] southward to the highway by the western corner of the hedge between the Bowgrove and the Slade. And from thence northward and eastward to the hedge that leadeth under Weobly's Wood to the south and western hedge of the Seven Acres under Hill And as that hedge leadeth northward to the salt marsh called Lanridian's Marsh without division to the River of Loughor. All the bounds aforesaid are within the Parishes of Lanridian and Cheriton.

Weobly:

[The part which is within Bishopston Parish]

There are also certain parcels of land held of the Lordship of Weobly, lying and being within the Parish of Bishopston, and are bounded as follows: First of all from the north-west corner of a field of his Grace the Duke of Beaufort's called Bryncoch in the Parish of Oystermouth, adjoining a field of David Hamon's called Bryncoch in the Parish of Bishopston. Crossing the Common to the north to a well called Fynon Dwr Da, near a parcel of lands of his Grace the Duke of

Beaufort's called the new Ground, and along that well stream to a river called Reed y defed where the Parishes of Swansea, Oystermouth and Bishopston join. And up that river to a wood called Hen park, belonging to Thomas Mansel Talbot esq., and up that dingle to a lane called Hen park Lane. And crossing that lane by a hedge joining Mr Gabriel Powell's and Mrs Watkins's land called Weekland and Killay, as far as a field called Keven y maes. And from thence alongside that hedge that joins between Mr Richard Davies and Mrs Watkins, to the lands of Mr Talbot, now in the possession of Edward Clement. Crossing there to the north by the lands of Mr Richard Davies to Fairwood's Moor, and crossing to the east corner of a field called Kae Crwn on Fairwood's Moor, and from thence down a rivulet or gutter, to a place called the Ddole Lane. And from that place [it] takes the boundary of Bishopston and Lanridian Parish, crossing the Common to a place called Scotland, the lands of Mr George Bydder, in the Parish of Pennard. And down that rivulet between the Parish of Pennard and Bishopston to a field of Lord Brook's late in the possession of Roger Morgan, and from thence along the hedge which joins Littlehill, the lands of Mrs. Anne Prichard, now in the possession of William Thomas, to a field called Culverhouse, the lands of Samuel Griffith. And along the hedge that joins that field to the lands of Mr Robert Mansel called Cradocks Moor, and up that watercourse to the lands of his Grace the Duke of Beaufort called Broadlay. And up that water to a lane called Wern y llaeth lane, and crossing that lane by the corner of a field of George Ace's that joins Mr Thomas Richards and David Hammon's lands. And along the hedge that joins between the lands of Mr Thomas Richards and David Hamon, to a field of Mr George Ace's called Britus, and from thence alongside the hedge that joins David Hamon's to a field of Thos Mansel Talbot esq. called little Henpark, late in the possession of Roger Morgan. And along that hedge joining David Hammon's to a field of Thomas Richard called Sheephouse Meadow, and from thence alongside the hedge joining David Hamon's to the Common, and down that hedge to the corner of the field called Bryncoch aforesaid.
Folio 11/12)

Reynoldston:

Copy [of a] Survey [dated] 28th. Octr 1630 & 1665. *[Tenants' names updated to the 1760s.]:*
Thomas Mansel Talbot esq., infant, holds the Manor of Reynoldston which is bounded as hereinafter mentioned, that is to say: Beginning at the north-east corner of the lands called Perkins, late the Estate of Mr William Bennet and now of John Lucas esq., having the Common of Kevenbryn on the north side. And the bounds run westward to the east corner of a garden wall now of the said John Lucas, and as the said wall leads along the lands of the said John Lucas and thence westwards again by the hedge that leadeth to Tucker's Stile. And from thence northward to the east corner of the Hill park, and from thence as the hedge of the said close leads westwards to the north-east corner of the higher Church Park. And thence still northwards, having Kevenbryn on the north or right hand, to the west corner of the Hays, formerly of Thomas Jones and now of the said Thomas Mansel Talbot, and then as the hedge leadeth southward along the western hedge of the Glebe lands unto Frogmore lane, otherwise Big Pit Way. And then as the north hedge leads eastwards and the Moores, parcel of the said Common on the north and west sides, meared with hedges between it and the said Commons and the way called Big Pit Way, to a pool called Goosemear, unto the south-west side. And so as the hedge leadeth to Bullins Mead, parting it from the Lordship of Knelston, and thence as the hedge leadeth to a place called Bryndyland,

still on the south-west side. And so as the hedge leadeth to a brook or water called Mead Lake in the meadows called the Weymoors, the said ditch or brook being the landshare between the said Weymores and the lands of the said Thos Mansel Talbot. And thence as the said water or landshare leadeth eastwards to the west side of a close called Slade Acre Meadow, and so as the said landshare leadeth eastward to the west side of a close called Gladacre, formerly part of Henllis Estate and now of the said Thos Mansel Talbot. And so as the west hedge of the said close leadeth northward to a close of John Lucas esq. called Derry Slade, and as the south hedge thereof leadeth eastward to Paviland Way. And as the way leadeth to the Commons of Keven-bryn, having the said Commons on the east side, unto the north-east corner of the lands late of Mr Rees Thomas, and now of George Ace and Thomas Bowen, till you come to the north-east corner of Perkin's where we began.

Also there is a great parcel of the said Lordship or Manor within the Parish of Reynoldston separated from the former part by the Commons aforesaid called Kevenbryn, having a little brook called Redwell lake, which mears that part of Lan y bwch which is within the said Lord-ship on the north-east side, to a brook called Mellins Lake. And as the same leadeth to the river called Burry on the west side of Stackpole's Mill, and as the said river and landshare leadeth unto the south-west corner of Mr Richard Lucas's meadow called Burrys Mead. And as the south hedge thereof leadeth to Carter's Moore, and thence to a house and garden of the Lord wherein Thomas Grove anciently dwelt, and now in the possession of Robert Grove and John Eaton as his under-tenant, and then as the hedges on the east and south side lead by the Commons of Kevenbryn to Redwell Lake aforesaid.

Leaston: The same holds the Manor of Leaston, otherwise Lesanston, which came to the Crown by the attainder of Sir Rees ap Thomas, and afterwards granted with Landimore, and is included within the same boundaries.

 [Added note in G.P.'s script] Mr Franklen's letter dated 14th Sept 1761. A Grant dated anno. 1315.

Knelston: Lady Charlotte Edwin now holds the Manor of Knelston, which is situate in the Parish of Knelston. This Manor consists of a few Demesne tenements, and they claim about four shillings and six pence Quit Rent, to be paid out of eight different tenements, now the Estates of the Earl of Warwick, late Mrs. Dawkin of Kit[t]lehill; Thos Bowen Gould (John Price gent. [before him?] married the widow of Azariah Prichard[)]; and John Lucas esq. – lately sold to Mr Paul Bevan of Swansea, but for what particular tenements are not known nor can the boundaries be ascertained. No Courts are held for this Manor.

Kilvrough: William Dawkin esq., infant, holds the Manor of Kilvrough, which consists only of the Demesne lands of Kilvrough and is held by Fealty, Suit of Court and Heriot.   *[Folio 12/13]*

Priors Town:
Copy [of a] Survey [dated] 25th October 1642. *[Tenants' names updated to the 1760s.]:*
The Warden and Fellows of All Souls College in Oxford hold the Manor of Priorstown otherwise eastown of Langennith. This Manor lies in the eastern part of the Parish of Langennith and consists

of several Freehold and Customary or Copyhold tenements. And is bounded by the westown Lordship westward, beginning at a very large rock lying in the highway near the Tile House Barn, from thence southward down a certain lane leading to the eastern or Colledge Mill. From the said mill eastward by a certain hedge which divides the lands of David Long called Barrestone from John Taylor's meadow of Vicarage. From thence by a certain hedge which divides the Tile House Ground, the Estate of Richard Gorton (formerly John Rogers's) from the lands of the aforesaid David Long called Barrestone, till you come to Roscilly Downe. From thence eastward leaving the said Downe on the south, till you come to a certain lane called the Summer Lane. From thence down the said lane, till you come to a certain plain called Coyty Green, from thence eastward by a certain lake between a field called the Foot Lands (the Estate of the Right Honble the Earl of Warwick) and a field called the Six Acres, the Estate of Lewis Tucker. From thence southward by a certain hedge which divides the lands of the said Earl of Warwick from the lands of the said Lewis Tucker, till you come to Roscilly Downe aforesaid. From thence, including a certain tenement, the Estate of William David, called Smarts, you go by a certain hedge between the Six Acres aforesaid and a certain field called Ruggart, the lands of the Earl of Ashburnham. From thence eastward by a certain hedge between the three acres and the Drunkylands, so on by a certain hedge between a certain field called Brown Lays and a tenement of lands, the Estate of the said Earl of Warwick, called Snailstone, till you come to Hardens Downe. From thence you go eastward by the hedges adjoining the said hill called Harden's Downe till you come to Robert Batcock's house at Hardens Downe, the Estate of Mr Paul Bevan. From thence, including all the lands belonging to the said house, at the east side of a certain lane leading from the aforesaid house to a certain field called the three acres, thence leaving the said three acres on the east, you come to a certain lane called Coom Lane. From thence along the said lane westward, till you come to a certain house called old Muzzard, the Estate of John Lucas esq. From the said house called old Muzzard, the lands thereto belonging included, you come along the highway leading to Muzzard Cross, from thence directly up a certain lane, till you come to a cott on the side of Harden's Downe aforesaid, formerly the Estate of Margaret William of Muzzard. From thence northward along a certain footpath between the lands of John Lucas esq. and Thomas Rogers's lands. From thence westward by a certain hedge between the lands of the said John Lucas and a certain tenement, the Estate of the Earl of Warwick aforesaid, till you come to a certain field called Cross Park. From thence eastward by the hedges adjoining a certain moor called Tanky Lake Moore till you come to John Holland's house, formerly Jennet Kifts. From thence along a footpath leading eastward from the said house till you come to a certain field called Cole's Field, and from thence east or north-east till you come to the end of Taylor's Parks. From the end of Taylor's Parks aforesaid you turn westward, having Llanmaddock Hill on the north, and the parcel of Penmoneth on the south, till you come to Joseph Mathew's house, formerly Morgan Lewis's house. From thence directly west, along a broad path on the side of Lanmaddock Hill, till you come to a certain place called the Hoar Rocks, and from the said Hoar Rocks down a lane till you come to the great rock by the Tile House Barn where we begun.

N.B. There are some other parcels, scattered, belonging to this Lordship, *viz*: An island in the sea called the Holms, bearing due north from Wormshead; one meadow in the Parish of Lanridian near the three Crosses, the lands of Mathew Pryce esq.; and one cott thereabouts formerly Mr

Seys's of Killan's; and one house or garden called Priors Garden in the Town of Swansea, formerly belonging to the Herberts; and one small field or parcel of ground near Burry's head in the Parish of Knelston, the Estate of Lady Charlotte Edwin.   *[Folio 13/14]*

Tallibont: Mathew Pryce esq. and William Dawkin esq., infant, hold the Manor of Tallibont, which consists of several tenements of lands held in Demesne belonging to the said Mathew Pryce and William Dawkin, situate within the parcel of Tyr y Brennin in the Parish of Landilo-talybont. And [it] is bounded as follows: Beginning at Llyw River at the south-west corner of a close called Cae Glandwr, and up that corner to the watercourse leading to the mill, and so along the mill water to Gorse Vawr. And along the ditch between Gorse Vawr and Wain Newydd and thence to the Common called Mynnyd Llyw, and so along the ditch between the Common and Wain Newydd as the brook called Coal Brook runs, and up along the brook to Gorse Vach. And so keeping the brook across the lower end of Gorse Vach, and keeping along the brook as it runs through the ditch of Wain Newydd to the corner of Mynydd Vach. And still keeping the brook to the corner of Wain Pen y Gelly, and from thence along the said brook to Rhose Whyth. And thence across the meadows between the lands of Walter Powell of Glantowy in Carmarthenshire esq. called Caie Brynne Llwydon and Gwain Hen and the lands of the said Mathew Pryce called Cae Berth vawr, Coed Cas, Gwain ycha and Gwain yssa, till you come to Maes y Brawd fields. And then along the ditch of Maes y Brawd fields to Nant maes y Brawd, and so along the nant or brook to the River of Loughor. There are neither Leet nor Baron Courts held for this Manor. It was formerly part of the dissolved Monastery of Neath, called the Abbey, and was granted by John de Mowbray, Lord of Gower, to the monks of Neath Abbey in the year 1334.

St John's, Swansea:
Copy [of a] Survey [dated] 27th. May 1641. *[Tenants' names updated to the 1760s.]:*
The Reverend Mr Evan Seys holds the Manor of St Johns near Swansea, otherwise east and west Millwood. It was formerly the Estate of the Knights of Jerusalem in England within the Commandery of Slebbedge in Pembrokeshire. It consists of several Freehold and Copyhold Estates. The greatest part thereof lie in the Parishes of St Johns and Langevelach; but several parts of it lie scattered in the Town and Franchise of Swansea and several other Parishes in the Seigniory of Gower. The boundary of so much of the Manor as lies contiguous within the Parishes of St Johns and Langevelach are: Beginning at a place called Pill y Velin Vach, and as the said pill leadeth into the River of Tawey, and as the same river leadeth northward into the fall of the water of the brook called Nant Rhyd y Vilast into the said River Tawy. And from thence along as the same brook leadeth north-west into an old ditch near the water grist mill of William Hurst and Calvert Richard Jones esqs, now fallen down and in ruins. And from thence as the same old ditch leadeth to the higher pound of the said mill and from thence as the water course of the said mill leadeth unto a stile being on a close there called Kaerwargrach Ycha. And from thence along the western ditch of the said close to a meadow called Gwayn Rees Gryther, and from thence to another meadow called Gwayn Davydd and a place called Cwm Spyder. And from thence along by the hedges that are between the lands there, anciently of Roger Seys and Richard Seys but now of the Reverend Mr Evan Seys, and the lands of the said William Hurst and Calvert Richard Jones called Kae'r Gove, Mynydd Newydd and Tyr Kegernew, now in the tenures of Thomas Rosser; John John and

the widow of Morgan Owen, otherwise Rees. And from thence along a little lane to a place called Llechlas being in the highway leading from Cadley's Mill towards Swansea. And from thence right southward as the brook there called Nant y Fyn leadeth, until it falleth into another brook called Cwmbwrla, and from thence directly as the same brook called Cwmbwrla leadeth into the Pill aforesaid *[Folio 14/15]* called Pill y Velin Vach. All which are situate, lying, and being within the several Parishes of St Johns and Langevelach.

There is within the said circuit two parcels of ground, being the lands of his Grace the Duke of Beaufort, adjoining to the aforesaid River of Tawey, held under the Lordship of Gower and called or known by the several names of Morva Coch and the Island, now in the tenure of Mr Paul Bevan.

Also there is within the said circuit one other parcel of ground of the said William Hurst and Calvert Richard Jones called Morva Awry, belonging to the Hospital of Saint Davids, in the tenure of Elinor Jans of Biddeford, widow.

Also there are divers messuages and tenements with divers parcels of lands, being part and parcel of the said Lordship and Manor of Millwood, lying and being in several places within the Liberties of the Town and Parish of Swansea, and also in several places within the several Parishes of Langevelach, Oystermouth, Loughor, Ilston, Penmaen, Nicholaston Penrice, Reynoldston, Landewy, Lanridian, and Languick, the boundaries whereof are not known.

Lanmaddock: Thomas Awbrey esq. holds the Manor of Lanmaddock, which is situate in the Parish of Lanmadock and consists of several Freehold tenants, who hold in Common Soccage, and some lands held in Demesne of the Lord by leases. This Manor is bounded by the sea on the west, the Manor of westown Langennith on the south, Priorstown or eastown to Dervins Well situate on Llanmaddock Downe on the east, and the pill or brook of water running to Cheriton Pill and along the said pill to the sea on the north part thereof.

Caegurwen:
Copy [of] Surveys [dated] 19th April 1610.
Herbert Mackworth esq. holds the Manor of Caegurwen which is situate in the Parish of Languick and consists entirely of Copyhold lands of Inheritance. This Manor is held of the Seigniory by Fealty, Suit of Court, Heriot, and the payment at Michaelmas yearly of one shilling, and is bounded as follows: It beginneth in the north-east at a place there which divideth between this Lordship and the Commons called y Mynnydd Ddu, called Kenol y Gorse Healig, where the water there naturally taketh its course eastwards, and butteth upon and with the running of the same water to the River of Llyfnel. And passeth along the side of the said River of Llyfnel southward about a quarter of a mile, till the same meeteth with an old ditch there, called Clawdd Tomen Wen, and by and with the same ditch passeth between east and south to the river called Twrch. And along the side of the said River of Twrch it passeth southward till the same boundeth upon the lands of the Reverend Mr James Gough Aubrey of Yniskedwin, called Gors Brin y Graynod and Gelly warreg, being part of the lands of the Lordship of Gower very nigh unto the ways called y Rhiwye gwnion, otherwise y Rhyw Granod, otherwise Heol y Rhiwye gwnion, where it is to be noted that the County of Brecon was always of the east side of the said River Twrch against the said Lordship of Kaegurwen till this place, and here the mear runneth westward and passeth from the said River of Twrch to a place called Bryn y Twyn, thence to Bryn y Fulberd, then to Nant y Pompren to a place or heap of stones called y Garn ar ben y Rhiw Vawr.

Then it passeth by a pathway leading westward, till the same way passeth to a place called y Garn Llwyd, which Garn Llwyd lies on the north side of the said way. Then it passeth as the way leadeth to a place called y Foshalog, then to a place called y Rhyd Garregos somewhat near to a place called Carn y redydd, and on the south side of the said Carn y redydd to a place called Brin y Maen. Then to a brook called Nant y Gasseg, and then the said Lordship butteth upon the same brook called Nant y Gasseg always westward, till the same brook cometh to a place there called Corse y Veisach. At which place it runneth northward and butteth upon the water called Nant y Gorse till the water of the same brook called Nant y Gorse begins its natural course towards the south. Till which place it had always on the other side of the same mear *[Folio 15/16]* the Lordship of Gower, from the said River of Twrch. Then it butteth in Corse y Veisach aforesaid along the brook there which taketh its course northward called y Garnant, which divideth there between the same Lordship and the Parish of Bettws in the County of Carmarthen. And having passed northward about half a mile along that brook side, then the same Lordship again turneth along that brook side westward and followeth that brook till the same falleth in the west unto the River Ammon. Then it turneth upwards between north and east along the side of the said River of Ammon, and as the same water heretofor ran and now runneth, till it cometh nigh unto a place called y Rhyd Wen ar Ammon. There it standeth and passeth eastward along the water side that runneth westward in a place called y Gorse Helig, till the same taketh its beginning to run. So westward and there joineth with the beginning of the said mear. There is a large Common within this Manor called Gwayn Kaegurwen which is entirely surrounded by the Copyhold tenements, and the tenants of this Manor claim the sole right of depasturing it. And there is also another large Common called Mynydd Blanegal which adjoins to, and part of it is within, this Manor. But the boundaries here are unsettled, the tenants of the Seigniory and of this Manor not agreeing upon the places which are called by particular names, so that they here intercommon and very often disputes arise between them.

It appears by the E[arl] of Pembroke's Pat[ent] temp. Eliz. that the Lord of Caegurwen should pay one shilling annually to the Lord of the Seigniory.

Lands at Pilton: The late Mrs Dawkin of Kittlehill and one Daniel Curtis held several parcels of lands at Pilton, by Fealty, Suit of Court, Heriot, and the payment at Michaelmas yearly of six swallow-tailed arrows, or six pence.

Vernhill: The late Mrs Dawkin and Richard Bydder hold the Manor of Vernhill by Fealty, Suit of Court, Heriot, and the payment at Michaelmas yearly of six swallow-tailed arrows, or six pence.

Culverhouse Meadow: Samuel Griffith holds a meadow at Wernllaeth in the Parish of Bishopston, called Culverhouse, in Grand Sergeantry and the paying at Michaelmas yearly of a bow and halbert.

Wernllaeth: Anne Prichard, widow, holds ten acres of lands at Wernllaeth in the parish of Bishopston, called Littlehill, in Grand Serjeantry and the paying at Michaelmas yearly [of] a bow and halbert.

Landewy: The Bishop of St David's, in the Right of his Bishopric, holds the Manor and Castle of Landwey in Free Alms. This Manor consists of only three or four tenements, which are held by lease from the Bishop and are situate in the Parish of Landewy. The Bishop keeps neither a Leet or Baron Court within this Manor.

Clase Langevelach:

The Bishop of Saint David's also holds in the Right of his Bishopric the Manor of Clase Langevelach in Free Alms. This Manor consists entirely of Copyhold lands and is situate within the Parish of Langevelach, and bounded as herein after mentioned: From the large mearstone at Pant y lasse, through the lane leading to Maes Eglwys it turns into a field belonging to Pompren Llwyd. Thence it goes along a gutter between Coed Kae Dorgllwyd and Coedkae Pompren Llwyd to the river, and goes up the river till it turns up the brook *[Folio 16/17]* called Nant Keven y Bettingva between Wain y Car and Kae Tew. And so along the said brook till you come between Cae newydd, belonging to Keven y Bettingva, and Wain Pwll, and then turns along the ditch between the meadow belonging to Maes Eglwys and Abergelly Vawr. And then between Maes Eglwys and Abergelly Vach and Brynllwyd, and thence to Pen y Wain and Lletty'r Scilp, and then adjoining to Gellyvethan it goes to the highway leading from Swansea to Velindre, at a brook called Nant y Krimp. And crossing the said highway it goes to a highway leading towards Keven y Forest and then turns between the lands of Pen y Wain and Keven y Forrest, along a brook called Nant y Funon, alias Nant y Keven Forrest, till it discharges itself into the river a little below Velin y Bau. And along the said river till it turns up below Glyn Sillin, and goes up along a lane between the lands called Cadle, in the possession of Llewelyn David, and the lands called Tyr Morgan Bevan, in possession of Wm John. And thence to Heol Ddee and along the north side to Mynydd Carn Llwyd and down the brook to Clyndee, and then quitting the brook between Pentrepoth and Tuy Genol, alias Cae Glandwr, leading from Swansea to Forrest Bridge. And thence to the brook called Cwm rhyd y Cwrw till you come to the house of James Evan, then quitting the brook you go through a window in the said house and then turning to the brook again, and then along the brook to Bryndorrian Fields, thence to the highway leading from Pant lasse to Forrest Bridge and up the said highway to the mearstone on Pant y lasse.

The Lord of the Seigniory till very lately exercised every Act of Jurisdiction over the tenants and inhabitants of this Manor, they constantly brought actions and were sued in the Seigniory Courts, the Processes of the said Courts were always executed within it, they were Summoned and did appear on Juries before the Coroner of the liberty of Gower who held Inquisitions, *Super Visum Corporis*, within the same. The Bailiff of the Liberty of Gower executed all Writs (Except *non Omittas* Writs) within the said Manor. All Forfeitures, Fines and Amerciaments in any of the Courts at Westminster or at the Great or Quarter Sessions have been always claimed and allowed at the King's Audit to the Lord of the Seigniory. And the Jurisdiction of the Seigniory over this Manor was never disputed, till about six years ago an Information in the nature of a *Qua Warranto* was moved for in the Court of King's Bench against the Coroner of the Liberty for taking an Inquisition within the said Manor. Upon which a feigned issue was directed to be tried [as to] whether the said Manor was within the Precincts and Jurisdiction of the Coroner of the Seigniory. Upon the trial of which a verdict being given against the Coroner; since which all other Acts of Juridiction have been suspended.

The Officers of the Seigniory

The Steward: The Lord by Patent under his hand and seal appoints a Steward for the Seigniory and his other Manors, whose office is to hold all the Courts and superintend all the Officers and business of the Seigniory and the other Manors. He ought to be a person of fortune and consequence in the country, to support the dignity and respect due to his office. He has no salary, it being considered a place of honour and trust rather than profit. No fees or perquisites belong to it, but two pence for every Action entered in the Court, and four pence every Judgment; except in *Replevin,* where the fees are double. And in the Copyhold Manors he receives three shillings upon every Surrender, and [for] signing every Copy of Surrender – six pence.   *[Folio 17/18]*

The Recorder: The Lord also appoints by Patent under his hand and seal an officer called the Recorder. He is under the immediate direction of the Steward, and his duty is to make out all Warrants and Processes of the Courts, to keep all the Books and Rolls, to draw all Surrenders and Admittances in the Copyhold Manors, and to transact all other businesses whatever relating to the Courts. He has no salary, but his place is worth about twelve pounds a year arising from several fees within the Courts, and in the Seigniory Courts are paid the following:

	£	s	d
Swearing every Tenant to his Fealty	–	1	–
Swearing every Constable in Court, or for the Warrant in case he does not appear to be sworn in Court	–	–	6
Swearing every witness to give evidence to the Jury at the Leet or to discharge a Presentment	–	–	6
For discharging every Presentment	–	–	4
For every Summons (out of which 2d is paid to the Steward)	–	–	6
For every Appearance	–	–	2
For every Rule	–	–	2
For entering every Judgment by Default (out of which is paid 4d to the Steward and 2d to ye Crier)	–	1	5
For Filing every Declaration	–	–	4
Filing Plea, Replication, Rejoinder &c (being 4d for filing & 4d for Copy of Declaration) & also 4d for Copy of every other pleading	–	–	8
– every *Distringas*	–	–	6
– every Warrant for Witnesses to attend a trial	–	–	6
– every *Venire facias*	–	–	6
Swearing every Witness or administering an Oath on all occasions	–	–	6
Swearing every Jury (out of which 6d is paid the Jury)	–	1	6
Taxing every Bill of Costs	–	–	4
Every Verdict (out of which 4d is paid the Steward, and 2d to the Crier)	–	–	11
In *Replevin* all the Fees are double			

The Bailiffs: There are four Bailiffs, appointed by the Steward, who live in different parts of the Seigniory. They are constantly to attend the Courts to execute all the Warrants and Processes issued from thence, to seize and collect all Heriots and Alienations, to assist the Heywards in driving the Commons and taking up Estrays, to look over all the Commons and wastes and to bring an account to the Steward of all trespasses done on them, to levy all Fines and Amerciaments, to distrain for any Chief or Enchroachment Rents that may be in arrear, and do all other business directed by the Steward relating to the affairs of the Seigniory.

They each receive a yearly salary of forty shillings payable every Lady Day, and they have been usually paid the following perquisites or fees, to wit:

	s	d
For every Heriot of the best beast, seized by either of them, paid by the Lord	2	6
For levying or distraining for any Chief, or Encroachment Rents, paid by the Tenants	1	–
For executing every *Replevin*	2	6
For serving every Summons in Actions defending in the Courts	–	4
For summoning juries to try Actions	–	6
Serving witnesses to attend Trials	–	6
For executing all *levaris* for debt or damages	–	6
[Folio 18/19]		

Courts Leet and Courts Baron: The tenants within the Seigniory at large hold their lands in Soccage Tenure by certain Chief or Quit Rents payable at Michaelmas yearly, Fealty, Suit of Court to the two general Baron Courts, which are held together with the Leet Courts upon Summons within a month of Easter Day and Saint Michael the Archangel, yearly, which Summons or Notice is by custom to be proclaimed on a Market Day in the Town of Swansea and at the Churches of Landilotal y bont, Langevelach, and Languick, at least eight days before the Courts are held, which by custom are to be held on Tuesday at the Guildhall of Swansea, at which Courts all the tenants and resiants are to attend on pain of Amerciaments. And the tenants also owe Suit of Court to the Courts Baron held at the said Guild Hall every three weeks, upon adjournments from three weeks to three weeks, for the trial of all Actions under forty shillings, being specially summoned. Which Courts are to be held by the Statutes of 27th Henry 8th *[1535-36]*, Chapter 26th, Sections 30th, 34th & 35th; Henry 8th *[1543-44]*, Chapter 26th, Section 23rd; 1st & 2nd of Phillip and Mary *[1554-55]*, Chapter 15, Section 6; and by the Patent granted the 5th of James the First *[1607-08]* to Edward, Earl of Worcester; before the Steward only. And every tenant making default may be amerced by the Court, which Amerciament is to be Affeered by two of the tenants sworn for that purpose, and may afterwards be levied by Distress if the Tenant refuses payment, by virtue of a Warrant for that purpose under the hand and seal of the Steward.

The Constables: Constables are appointed and sworn at Michelmas Leet for the following Parishes and Hamlets.

Gower Anglicana

Containing the several Parishes and Hamlets following –

Swansea Parish

Higher Division	1
Lower Division	1

Loughor Parish

	2

Landilotalybont Parish

Priskedwin	1
Glyn Loughor	1
Ynis Loughor	1
Gwyn lais	1

Heywards are appointed and sworn at every May Leet for the following Parishes and Hamlets.

Gower Anglicana

Containing the several places hereunder named.

Morva Mawr & Mynnydd Lluw	2
Fairwoods Moor	2
Graig Vawr	2

Heriot, which by the custom of the said Seigniory is a best beast on the death of every Free tenant dying within the said Manor, or in the occupation of their own Freehold lands, but for want of a beast, five shillings. And in case any tenant dies seized of any Free lands within the Manors of *[Folio 19/20]* Gower Anglicana, Gower Supraboscus and Gower Subboscus, then a best beast is to be paid for the lands within which he died, and five shillings in each of the others. And there is also five shillings for every Alienation or sale of their Freehold lands within each or either of the said Manors.

A Rental of the Chief or Quit Rents within Gower Anglicana

No.	Freeholders Names	Names of tenements	Names of Tenants	Rent p Annum		
				£	s	d

Langevelach Parcel Clase

No.	Freeholders Names	Names of tenements	Names of Tenants	£	s	d
1	Mr Edwd Thomas	Dorglwyd	Wm Jenkin John	–	–	9
2	The same	Tyr Enghared alias Dorglwyd Vach	The same	–	–	4
3	Gryffydd Pryce esq.	Keven y Velindre	John Rees	–	–	6
4	The same	Pant yr Ychedith Ycha	Rees John	–	–	3
5	The same	Pant yr Ychedith Ycha *(sic)*	Daniel Gregory	–	–	4
6	Thos Popkin esq.	Tyr Evan Llwyd	Rees Owen & Joseph Hopkin	–	–	9
7	The same	Two tenements called Gelly deg	Morgan Howell	–	1	–
8	Mr Wm Roberts	Penrhwyr Gwisfa	David Daniel ['Hopkin Evan' in Bn]	–	–	6

Langevelach Parcel Mawr

No.	Freeholders Names	Names of tenements	Names of Tenants	£	s	d
9	G.V. Vernon esq.	Llwyn y Domen	John Beynon	–	–	8
10	The same	Blaen yr Olchva	Catherine Jenkin, widow	–	–	4
11	The same	Bryn y Maen	William David	–	–	7
12	Thos Morgan gent. ['Mary Morgan' in Bn]	Mothvay alias Letty Thomas	Henry William	–	1	2
13	The same Keven Mothway	Gwayn Gwynion alias	David Bowen ['David Bevan' in Bn]	–	–	2
14	The same	Keven Mothvay alias Tuy Ycha	Henry William	–	–	2
15	Gryff. Price esq.	Pant y fa alias Bwlch Pant y fa	William Morris	–	–	8
16	Thos Price esq. ['The same' (i.e. G.P.) in Bn]	Tuy Mawr	David Rees	–	–	1

No.	Freeholders Names	Names of tenements	Names of Tenants	Rent p Annum		
				£	s	d
17	Griffith Morgan	Pen y Veedy Ucha	Henry William	–	–	4
18	Griffydd Price esq.	Peny Vedow	Hopkin William	–	–	8
19	John Walter	Bwlch pant y fa alias Pant y fa ['alias Twyn' in Bn]	Thomas Clement	–	–	6
20	Mr Thos Jones	Letty Vrane alias Maes dir Ycha alias Maes dir Mawr	Thomas Robert, ['widow' added in Bn]	–	1	–
21	The same	Maesdir Ysha alias Cwm Kille Vawr	Thomas Robert, ['widow' added in Bn]	–	–	1
22	Catherine Rees spinster and Thos Price esq. ['Gryffydd P.' in Bn]	Pen yr heol	David Rees	–	–	6
23	Isaac Morgan Tylle Bach	Maesdir alias Cwm	William Morgan	–	–	2
24	John Bevan	Keynant	John William	–	1	–
25	Mary Powell widow.	Coed Kae Iswell	John Powell	–	–	1

Langevelach Parcel Pentherry

No.	Freeholders Names	Names of tenements	Names of Tenants	Rent p Annum		
26	Sarah Prichard, infant ['spinster' in Bn]	Lands near Rheedy Mairdy called Tuy Yssha	David Daniel's widow	–	–	6
27	The same [Folio 20/21]	Gelly Organs	Charles Robert	–	–	6

Languick

No.	Freeholders Names	Names of tenements	Names of Tenants	Rent p Annum		
28	James Gough Aubrey clerk ['Revd JGA' in Bn]	Two tenements called Kilmangwin Ycha & Kilmangwin Bach	John Thomas	–	1	–
			Thomas John [sic]	–	–	6
29	The same	Tyr Glan Tawy near Ynismedw	Margaret Morgan	–	–	7
30	Elizth. Evan spinster	Ynis parcell	Hopkin William	–	–	7

No.	Freeholders Names	Names of tenements	Names of Tenants	Rent p Annum		
				£	s	d
31	The same ['David Morgan' in Bn]	Kilmangwyn Yssha	David Morgan ['Isaac John' in Bn]	–	1	2
32	James Gough Aubrey clerk ['Revd.' in Bn]	Kilmangwyn Genol	David Harry	–	–	6

Loughor

No.	Freeholders Names	Names of tenements	Names of Tenants	£	s	d
33	Lady Charlotte Edwin	Lands called Cwm y Trolle	William Atkins	–	–	6
34	The same	Gelly Eythrim	David Morgan	–	–	6
35	The same	Altwen and Cobs Bridge	Thos Gamage & Jno. Richard	–	13	4
36	Joseph Pryce esq.	Tyr yr Eydon alias Bevexy Vawr	William Bevan	–	1	–
37	The same	Lands at Berth Llwyd	William Morgan	–	–	6
38	Mr Thomas Jones	Kevenstylle	His own possession	–	1	–
39	Thomas Pryce esq. ['Gryffydd Price esq.' in Bn]	Pen y Vode Vawr	David Jones	–	4	2
40	John Bassett clerk ['Revd. Mr' in Bn]	Kevengole	Llewelin John	–	–	6
41	The same	Lands called Y Velin Vach	John William's widow	–	–	4
42	Thomas Popkin esq.	Brin Mawr	John Hopkin	–	–	10
43	Matthew Pryce esq.	Bryn gwyn	Edward Bevan ['Rees Bevan' in Bn]	–	4	5
44	William Phillips	Penyvode vach	His own possession	–	2	–
45	Anne Lewis widow	Travlle	John Cornelius	–	4	–
46	Mr Richard Sey's widow ['Jane Seys, widow' in Bn]	Kae Newidd	Catherine Howell widow	–	–	4

| No. | Freeholders Names | Names of tenements | Names of Tenants | Rent p Annum | | |
|-----|-------------------|--------------------|------------------| £ | s | d |

Lanridian

47	G. Venables Vernon esq. ['Thomas Mansel Talbot esq.' in Bn]	Berthy Newir	Jeremiah Morgan	–	–	3
48	Robert Popkin esq. ['Thomas P. esq.' in Bn]	Wimblewood	Thomas Parry	–	–	2
49	Mathew Pryce esq.	A meadow called Gwain, or Prior Garw	Thomas Bowen	–	–	3
50	Maysod Dawkins widow	Cwym y Newir	William Howell	–	2	6
51	Wm Richard, Thos Dorset & Mathew Pryce esq.	Kevendraw	George William	–	–	8
52	The same	Lands called Caer Eithin	Harry Humphrey's widow ['Ann Richards widow' in Bn]	–	–	1
53	George Bydder	One tenement at Wimblewood	His own possession ['Henry Jenkin' in Bn]	–	–	5
54	The same	Another tenement at Wimblewood	The same	–	–	5
55	David Bowen (*Iur. ux.*)	House & lands near Yslys yr Rhyan ['called Penywerne' in Bn]	David Bowen	–	–	2

Swansea Parish

56	Rt. Honble Earl of Warwick	Tenement at Goytre	Phillip Bowen	–	1	–
57	The same	Several tenements called Rheed y Devid and Wern Dee	Wm Rosser ['John Lewis' added in Bn]	–	2	–
58	The same	Llwyn Dderry alias Pen y bank	Mathew Virley	–	1	–
59	The same [Folio 21/22]	New Mills	William Rosser	–	–	8
60	The same	Carn Glase	David Williams	–	–	4

No.	Freeholders Names	Names of tenements	Names of Tenants	Rent p Annum		
				£	s	d
61	The same	A tenement at Sketty called Tuy yr Coed	Richard David	–	1	–
62	Gabriel Powell gent.	Lands at Cocket, late Uriah Jenkins	David Owen	–	–	2
63	Earl of Warwick	Hendee	William Thomas ['and Mansel Mansel esq.' in Bn]	–	1	4
64	The same	A tenement at Sketty	Thomas Rosser	–	–	2
65	The same	Gellydowill	John William	–	–	2
66	The same	Weeg Vach alias Cwmbach	Llewelyn William	–	–	3
67	The same	Lands at Sketty call'd Wern Ivith ['near Singleton called Gwern Evith' in Bn]	Roger David	–	1	–
68	The same	Lands at Weeg	Owen Morgan's widow	–	–	3
69	The same	Tyr Coch	William Thomas	–	1	4
70	The same	Lloyn Mawr Dd. Jno. *[sic]*	Thomas Robert John Rosser ['David John's Wid. & John Rosser' in Bn]	–	1	1
71	The same	A tenement at Sketty called Wern Eynon	William Rosser	–	–	11
72	The same	A tenement at Llanerch	John Griffith	–	2	–
73	The same	Tenement at Sketty	Samuel Hugh	–	–	9
74	Sir Wm Mansel Bart.	Goytre	David Bennet ['William Thomas' in Bn]	–	–	8
75	Evan Seys, clerk ['Revd Mr E.S.' in Bn]	Cwmbwrla	Evan Jenkin	–	1	–
76	Richard Jenkin	Ystradllawen Nant	Richard Jenkins	–	1	–
77	Joseph Pryce esq.	A tenement at Dynvant	Thomas William	–	–	1

No.	Freeholders Names	Names of tenements	Names of Tenants	Rent p Annum		
				£	s	d
78	The same	A tenement near Llanerch called Sych Clawdd	Thomas Hugh	–	–	3
79	Sir Thomas Stepney Baronet	Cregennith	William Mathew	–	–	4½
80	The same	Craig y Bulden	Thos Habbakuk	–	–	2½
81	The same	A tenement at Cockett	Thos Habbakuk	–	–	2
82	Robert Popkin esq. ['Thomas P.' in Bn]	Cwm Llwyd	William David	–	–	11
83	The same ['Thomas Popkin esq.' in Bn]	Lanerth Vawr	John Humphrey	–	2	–
84	Gabriel Powell gent.	west Kefncoed	John Morgan	–	–	4
85	The same	east Kefncoed	John Morgan	–	–	2½
86	Franklen Mathews's widow	Cregennith Vach	John Thomas Evan	–	–	2
87	Gabriel Powell gent.	A tenement at Sketty	David Franklen	–	–	11
88	Henry Simmons	A tenement called Lanerch	Elizabeth Davies	–	–	2
89	Sir Thos Stepney, Bart.	Ano'r tenement at Cocket	Thos Habbakuk	–	–	2
90	Mr William Roberts	A tenement called Kergenith	William Harry	–	–	4
91	Robert Popkin esq. ['Thomas P.' in Bn]	Weig Vach	John Hopkin William	–	–	4
92	The same	Kae Crwn, Cae Llidiad Weeg and Kae Llethir	His own possession & John David Rees	–	–	4
93	The same	A tenement called Kevencoed	John Knoyl	–	–	3
94	Gabriel Powell gent.	A tenement called Kevencoed	Elinor Knowles ['John Rytherch' in Bn]	–	–	2½

No.	Freeholders Names	Names of tenements	Names of Tenants	Rent p Annum		
				£	s	d
95	Richard Bydder (*Iur. ux.*) and Elizabeth Bowen spinster ['Richard Bydder and Eliz. Bowen spinster' in Bn] [Folio 22/23]	A tenement called Kevencoed	Joseph John alias. Mathew	–	–	1
96	Gabriel Powell gent.	Tuy Gwyn	David Harry	–	–	9
97	William Thomas	Goytre	William Thomas	–	–	3
98	Thomas Popkin esq.	Tuy yn Cae	John David	–	–	2
99	John Gorton	Tenement called Goytre	John Gorton	–	–	1
100	Mr Hugh Powell	Ystraed Yssha	His own possession	–	1	–
101	John David	Brinkenol	John Harry	–	–	2
102	Sarah Harry, widow ['John Harry' in Bn]	Ynis	Her own possession ['His' in Bn]	–	–	3
103	Mrs. Jane Phillips	Keven Llanerch	David Bennett	–	–	3
104	John Thomas	House and garden at Cocket	John Thomas	–	–	2
105	Richard David	Cregennith Vach	Richard David	–	–	1
106	John Thomas (of Gellyorllan) ['J.T. infant' in Bn].	Pen y lan ['His own possession' in Bn].	Thomas Kneath	–	–	5
107	Owen Morgan Rees's widow	Weeg Vach	Owen Morgan Rees's widow	–	–	2
108	John Harry	A tenement called Cwmbach	Edward Thomas	–	–	1
109	Wm Robert (son of Jno. Robert)	Another tenement called Cwmbach	William Robert	–	–	1

Landilo tal y bont

110	Geo. Venables Vernon esq.	Landremore Vach	Anne Hopkin	–	1	–

No.	Freeholders Names	Names of tenements	Names of Tenants	Rent p Annum		
				£	s	d
111	The same	Landremore Ycha or Vawr	James Bottin	–	1	–
112	The same	Tyr Edward	The same	–	–	8
113	The same	Gellywerne	John Bevan	–	–	2
114	The same	Tall y Van Vach	David Williams	–	–	4
115	The same	Pen y bont	Jonathan William	–	–	4
116	The same	Kaer kerrig	John Hopkin	–	–	4
117	The same	Gwinlais Ycha alias Gwinlais Vach	John Harry	–	–	8
118	The same	Tyr ychyr lawr Heol	The same	–	–	4
119	The Rt Honble Lord Talbot	Llwyn Court Howell Vach alias Tuy Rush	Rees William	–	–	1
120	The same	Clyn hyr	Griffith Morgan	–	–	9
121	Edward Evans esq., infant	A tenement at Ynis Loughor	David William	–	–	6
122	The same	Y Pandy bach	Griffith William	–	–	4
123	The same	A tenement near the Pound at Bolgoed	Rees William	–	–	4
124	Mary Morgan ['Thomas Morgan esq.' in Bn]	A Croft called Croft y Pant near Coppa Vach	Mary Lewis	–	–	2
125	The same	Tyr y Gove at Glyn Loughor	Thomas Jenkin	–	–	4
126	The same	Tenement at Pen y lan called *[blank]* ['called y lan' in Bn]	John Gronow	–	–	4
127	The same	Ano'r tenement called Pen y lan	The same	–	–	4
128	The same	A tenement called Brinbach alias Tyr Rennall	Thos Hopkin Evan	–	–	6

No.	Freeholders Names	Names of tenements	Names of Tenants	Rent p Annum		
				£	s	d
129	Wm Lloyd gent.	Priskedwin	William David	–	–	7
130	The same	Hendrebedlem	The same	–	–	4
131	The same	Tyr yr Ellin	William Jenkin	–	–	6
132	The same	Tally Clyn Llwyn	Mary Hopkin, widow	–	–	2
133	Walter Powell esq.	Llwyn Adam	David Davies	–	2	8
134	Thomas Price esq. ['Griffydd P.' in Bn]	Bolgod Ycha	David Thomas	–	–	8
135	Gryffydd Price esq. ['The same' in Bn]	Pant y ffa	William Morris	–	–	4
136	Richard Price gent. [Folio 23/24]	Tuy yn y Werne	William Evan	–	–	3
137	Mr Wm Morgan's widow ['Thomas Morgan gent.' in Bn]	Gwin Lais vawr ['vawr' omitted in Bn]	Richard John	–	1	–
138	The same	Brintelech Vach	William Jones	–	–	4
139	Sarah Pritchard, infant	Melin Llyw	Richard Lewis	–	–	4
140	The same	A tenement near Melin Llyw	The same	–	–	4
141	John Knaeth *(Iur. ux..)*	Allt Graben Vawr	John Knaeth	–	–	4
142	Walter Powell esq.	Glyn Loughor Yssha	Griffith Lott	–	–	4
143	Edwd David Jno. Hugh ['David William' in Bn]	Hendrewen Yssha	David William ['His own possession' in Bn]	–	–	2
144	*[blank]* ['Mary Watkins & others' in Bn]	Foes yr Evel	Thomas John	–	–	6
145	Rachael Mansel, widow.	Alt yago	David William	–	1	–
146	Gryffydd Price esq.	Abergwynlais	William Gronow	–	–	8
147	The same	Part of said lands called Gwain llean Wen	William Gronow	–	–	2
148	Walter Powell esq.	Ynis Lletty	Christopher Gregory	–	–	3

No.	Freeholders Names	Names of tenements	Names of Tenants	Rent p Annum		
				£	s	d
149	Thomas Mathews	A tenement late the lands of Edwd Robert and Tyr Llwyd near the pound	Thomas Matthews	–	–	4
150	Joseph Pryce esq.	Hendrewen	Evan David Hopkin	–	–	2
151	Jacob William	A tenement at Glyn Loughor called Ty yn y Coed Ysha	Griffith Morgan	–	–	4
152	Edward Snead & Austin Loyd ['John Price clerk and A.L. in Bn]	Coyd Saison	Ellis Hugh	–	–	2
153	Benjamin Davies *(Iur. ux.)* ['Christopher Gregory' in Bn]	Glan Llyw alias y Tyr Bach	Edward Griffith	–	–	2
154	The same	Tuy Yssha alias ycha	William Thomas	–	–	6
155	William Llewellin *(Iur. ux.)* ['Catherine Evan' named as his wife in Bn]	Allt y Graban Vach	William Mathew	–	–	1
156	John Walter	Kaer Pistill or Gwin Lais Ysha	John Walter	–	–	4
157	Thos Clement	Brinbach alias Caer ddeentye	Sarah John widow ['widow' not in Bn]	–	–	2
158	Thomas Mathew	Croft Gwenllian	David Rees	–	–	4
159	John Griffith	Glyn Loughor	His own possession	–	–	4

Langennith

No.	Freeholders Names	Names of tenements	Names of Tenants	Rent p Annum		
160	Geo. Venables Vernon esq.	Tankillake	John Stote	–	–	2
161	Gabriel Powell gent.	A tenement at Burryshead	Shadrach David ['Joseph Walker' in Bn]	–	13	4
162	Wm Price, clerk. *(Iur. ux.)* ['Iur. ux.' not in Bn]	A tenement at Burryshead	John Eynon	–	13	4

No.	Freeholders Names	Names of tenements	Names of Tenants	Rent p Annum		
				£	s	d
163	The same	Lands there called the Coomes	The same	–	6	8

Knelstone

| 164 | Gabriel Powell gent. | Bristow | Shadrach Davies ['Joseph Walker' in Bn] | – | 1 | – |

Landewy

165	Earl of Warwick	Scurla Castle	John Clement	–	–	3
166	Mrs Dawkins	Lower Newton	Nathaniel Eynon	–	–	2
167 [Folio 24/25]	John Taylor	Pile Well	Daniel Curtis	–	–	2

Pennard

168	Geo. Venables Vernon esq.	Part of a tenement called Heal	Thomas David	–	–	8
169	The same	Lands at Wydiat called Mansel's lands	The same	–	–	4
170	The same	A tenement at Wydiat	Thomas Kneath	–	–	4
171	Mrs. Dawkins	A tenement at Hunts	Edward Lloyd	–	6	8
172	William Thomas, gent.	A tenement at Wydiat	Phillip Knaeth	–	–	4
173	Theophilus Davies (*Iur. ux.*) and Thomas Watkins	Highway	Mrs Watkins	–	–	4
174	George Bydder	Lands late Hugh Griffiths alias Scotland	Richard Gwyn	–	–	3
175	Peter Meyrick	A tenement at Wydiat	His own possession	–	–	2
176	Rowland Dawkin esq.	Lands at Norton	Morgan Thomas	–	1	6½

No.	Freeholders Names	Names of tenements	Names of Tenants	Rent p Annum		
				£	s	d

Ilston

No.	Freeholders Names	Names of tenements	Names of Tenants	£	s	d
177	Earl of Warwick	Tenement at Ilston	Richd Bowen & Jno. Knaeth	–	2	–
178	The same	Another tenement	John Kneath	–	1	4
179	The same	Brinavel	Samuel Dunn	–	1	8
180	The same	A tenement by the Church	William Atkins	–	1	8
181	Joseph Pryce esq.	Gellyhyr	Joseph Pryce, esq.	–	2	8
182	The same	John Brown's lands	David Jones	–	–	4
183	The same	A tenement called Fairwood	William Morgan	–	–	4
184	Mrs. Dawkins	Courthouse	Phillip Bevan	–	–	9
185	William Harry (*Iur. ux*)	Hills ['alias wester Hills' added in Bn]	David Bowen	–	–	2½
186	Mrs. Dawkins	Another tenement called Hills	Henry Harry	–	–	2½
187	David Hugh	Tenement called Gelly Eylin ['alias Hills' added in Bn]	David William	–	–	2
188	Richard Bowen	Moorehouse	William Atkins	–	–	4

Bishopston

No.	Freeholders Names	Names of tenements	Names of Tenants	£	s	d
189	Rachel Mansel, widow ['Richard Mansel Talbot' in Bn].	Cradocks Moor	Richard Bydder	–	3	–
190	Thos Richards gent.	Three tenements at Wern llaeth	Elizabeth Hammon, widow	–	2	3
191	Curate of Landewy	Blackhills	Thos Griffith	–	–	7½
192	Gabriel Powell gent.	Week's lands	Thomas David	–	–	4
193	David Maddocks ['Elizth Maddock Spinster.' in Bn]	Gwaindraw	Ellen Eaton, widow	–	–	6
194	Mr Richard Davies	Killay	His own possession	–	4	3

No.	Freeholders Names	Names of tenements	Names of Tenants	Rent p Annum		
				£	s	d
195	Thomas David ['Gabriel Powell, Gent [and] Morgan Thomas, clerk, Rector of Oxwich.' in Bn]	Two tenements at Killay	His own possession ['Thomas David [and] Evan Howell' in Bn]	–	–	8
196	Samuel Griffith, infant	Culverhouse in the Parish of Bishopston	Mary Griffiths, widow	Bow & Halbert & Suit of Court		
197	Anne Pritchard, widow ['Ann Richard, widow.' in Bn]	A tenement called Littlehill in the Parish of Bishopston	William Thomas	Bow & Halbert & Suit of Court		
198	Maysod Dawkin and Daniel Curtis	Several parcels of land at Pilton, in the Parish of Roscilly	Matthew Button & William Hoskin	Six Swallow- tailed Arrows or Sixpence		
199	Maysod Dawkin and Richard Bydder	The Manor of Vernhill, in the Parish of Roscilly	Matthew Bynon	Six Swallow- tailed Arrows or Sixpence		

[Folio 25/26]

[*The following two paragraphs are in the Bn version in this position, but not in the Sa version, where they now appear in the Miscellanea volume.*]

There is within this Manor a large Common called Fairwood Moor, lying within the Parishes of Ilston, Lanridian, and Bishopstone, and having Pennard's Moor on the south, for which the neighbouring tenants who graze it pay the yearly rent of 20s.

There is another Common called Long Mead and Welsh Moor, lying in the Parish of Lanridian, for which the neighbouring tenants who graze it pay the yearly rent of 6s 8d.

[Folio 26 continues]

Customary Payments

Toll Pixie

There is also within the said Seigniory a customary yearly payment of fifty shillings called Toll Pixie, that is to say, one pound six shillings and eight pence on the western side of Pennard's Pill, to be rated on all Artificers, Handy Craftsmen, Buyers, and Sellers, within the several Parishes of

Penmaen, Nicholaston, Penrice, Oxwich, Port Eynon, Knelston, Landewy and Langennith, and within the Hamlet of Pitton otherwise Pilton. And one pound three shillings and four pence on the eastern side of Pennard's Pill to be rated on all Artificers, Handy Craftsmen, Buyers and Sellers within the Parishes of Oystermouth, Pennard, Ilston and that part or Hamlet of Nicholaston called Manselfield.

Ferry Corn

There is another customary payment called Ferry Corn, which is to be made by all the inhabitants of the several Parishes of Swansea, Oystermouth, Bishopston, Pennard, Penmaen, Ilston, Nicholaston, Penrice, Oxwich, Port Eynon, Roscilly, Langennith, Cheriton, Lanmaddock, Lanridian, Reynoldston, Knelston, Landewy, Lansamlet, the Borough of Swansea, and the Borough and Parish of Loughor. The payments within these Parishes differ according to their respective customs, but are all payable at Michaelmas yearly, and are as follows:

Swansea Parish:

The inhabitants who sow corn pay twenty-five sheaves of oats, or a customary peck containing five gallons and a half, and all cottagers or persons keeping house and not sowing corn, – two pence each.

Oystermouth, Bishopston, Pennard, Penmaen, Ilston, Nicholaston, Penrice, Oxwich, Port Eynon, Roscilly, Langennith, Cheriton, Lanmaddock, Lanridian, Reynoldston, Knelston and Landewy.

The inhabitants of these several Parishes pay three sheaves of each sort of corn they sow, or fourpence at the Lord's choice; and every cottager, or person keeping house and not sowing corn, – two pence a piece.

Borough and Parish of Loughor.

The inhabitants sowing corn pay twenty-five sheaves of Oats or four pence at the Lord's election, and all cottagers and other housekeepers pay two pence each.

Borough of Swansea:

All married housekeepers pay four pence each, and all unmarried housekeepers, two pence each.

Manor of Kilvey:

which contains the whole Parish of Lansamlet and that part of Swansea Parish which lies on the eastern side of the river. All the housekeepers and cottagers within the Lower Division pay four pence each, and those within the Higher Division, two pence each.

In consideration of these several payments all the inhabitants and their respective families are to pass over Swansea Ferry without any other payment, and the Lord is to keep a ferry boat.

Mises:

Which is a customary payment due to the Lord upon his becoming seized of the Seigniory upon the death of the former Lord, of the sum of £200, to be made up by the Freeholders, tenants and occupiers of lands within the whole Seigniory, the Manor of Kilvey, the Borough and Manor of Swansea, the Borough and Manor of *[Folio 26/27]* Loughor, and by the Freeholders, Copyholders, tenants, and occupiers of lands within the Manors of Oystermouth, Pennard and the Fees of Kittle, Lunnon and Trewyddva in the proportions following:

	£	s	d
Gower Anglicana	18	18	10
Supraboscus	60	0	0
Subboscus	7	14	6
Manor of Kilvey	20	0	0
Borough and Manor of Swansea	26	13	4
Borough and Manor of Loughor	6	13	4
Manor of Oystermouth	19	12	0
Manor of Pennard and Fee of Kittle	23	1	0
Fee of Lunnon	15	7	0
Fee of Trewyddva	2	0	0
	£200	0	0

According to the ancient custom, the Lord is by a commission under his hand and seal to appoint Commissioners, two or more of whom are to call Courts for the respective Manors. At those Courts the Commissioners issue out Warrants under their hands and seals, appointing two or more of the tenants or inhabitants within the several Divisions of the said respective Manors, who are directed to make equal Assessments within the same, to be returned at subsequent Courts appointed by adjournments to particular days. On which days the respective Assessors are to bring in their Assessments, and all Appeals heard. The Commissioners are then to issue out Warrants under their hands and seals appointing one or more Collectors who are to collect the same. And if any person refuses to pay the sum on him rated, the Collectors may by the custom Distrain for the same on the goods, cattle and chattels of the person so refusing, and such Distress keep until the money be paid, with reasonable charges for distraining and detaining such Distress.

The Lord is by immemorial custom, confirmed by the Statute of Wales[11], as well as by the Charter of the 5th James the First, intituled to all Waifs, Estrays, Infangthefe, Outfangthefe, Treasure Trove, Deodands, Goods and Chattles of Felons, and of persons condemned or outlawed for Felony or Murder, put in Exigent for Felony or Murder, and Wrecks of the Sea, Tolls, Keelage, Anchorage, and Customs of Strangers[12].

The Lord is by the said Charter of James the First authorized to appoint a **Bayliff** or Bayliffs of the Liberty of Gower, who is to execute all Writs (*Non Omittas* Writs excepted) within the same, and to make returns thereof. His fees are two shillings each Warrant on a Mandate, and Poundage

---

11. The Act of Union.
12. For explanation of some of the more obscure terms, see the Glossary above on p.37 & 38.

for each Writ executed. The profits of this Office one year with another for twenty-five years past have not been twenty shillings per annum. And for that he is obliged to be at the expense and risk of the execution of Writs, delivering them to the Sheriff by Indenture, and attending the two Great Sessions.

The Lord is intituled to all the Fine *Pro Licentia Concordandi* or Composition money paid upon the levying of Fines upon lands within the Seigniory of Gower at large, and all the Fines, Amerciaments, Penalties and Forfeitures whatsoever in any of the Courts at Westminster, Great Sessions or Quarter Sessions. And those are constantly claimed and allowed at the *[Folio 27/28]* King's Audit held at Brecon upon passing of the Sheriff of Glamorganshire's Account, for which the Auditor is paid a fee of 6s. 8d, but if a *Constat* be granted, then 21s. But the Fines *pro Licentia Concordandi* are received by John Vaughan of Golden Grove esq., heir to the late Earl of Carberry, who claims by a Prior Grant, but his right is not clear and a dispute was begun by Henry, late Duke of Beaufort, about the year 1710 against the then Earl of Carberry, which was never determined.

The Lord is also empowered to appoint a **Coroner** within the said Seigniory who is to execute that Office through the whole Seigniory. And always did so without interruption, till it was lately insisted on that the Manor of Clase Langevelach was not within the precincts of the Seigniory. Which upon a Feigned Issue being tried at Hereford [in] August 1755, was determined against the Coroner of the Seigniory. This Office was a burden and expense to the Coroner, till the late Act of Parliament for allowing Coroners twenty shillings for every Inquisition, and nine pence a mile for every mile they were obliged to travel to view the body and take the Inquisition. But since that Act the Coroner of the Seigniory or liberty of Gower receives one year with another about six or seven pounds, out of which he pays to the Bailiff who summons the Juries 2s. 6d. [for] each Inquisition. He is at the trouble and expense of journeys to take the Inquisitions, making out the Warrants for summoning the Juries and Witnesses, drawing the Depositions of the Witnesses and Inquisitions. He pays five shillings to the Judges' clerks each Great Sessions in lieu of a Purse, and is obliged to attend the both Great Sessions, and four Quarter Sessions.

The Lord is to appoint a **Clerk of the Market**. Swansea is the only Market Town within the Seigniory, in which there is a Market held every Saturday, and it is said there might be a weekly Market on Tuesdays, but it is scarce ever held. The Portreeve has immemorially been and acted as Clerk of the Market, for which he receives no fee whatever.

The Lord is **Vice Admiral of the Seigniory**, and as such intituled to all the profits and advantages belonging to the Office of Admiral, to the holding of an Admiralty Court for the trying of all offences on the sea within the Precincts of the Seigniory; but that has never been done within my memory. He is intituled also to all Wrecks, Flotsam, Jetsam, and Lagan. In virtue of his said Office as Vice Admiral the Lord appoints an Officer called a **Water Bailiff**, who receives a fee of *[blank]* from every vessel, which might amount one year with another to about the sum of *[blank]*.

The Lord is also intituled to the **Prisage and Butlerage of Wines**. Prisage is an ancient Duty which the Kings of England have time out of mind received and had. The manner has been by taking of every ship or vessel that should come into the realm with wine – if ten tons, to have for Prisage one ton, and if it contains twenty tons or more to have two tons, paying 20s for each ton.

Butlerage is a Custom due from merchant strangers, of two shillings of every ton of wine brought into this realm by them, but Englishmen pay it not.

The Prisage and Butlerage of Wines within the Seigniory are demised to His Grace the Duke of Cleveland, who has a Grant from the *[Folio 28/29]* Crown of all the Prisage and Butlerage of Wines in England.

Demesne Tenements in Gower Anglicana

The Lord is also intituled to the several Demesne tenements hereinafter mentioned which are situate within the Manor[13]:

Griffith Thomas rents four parcels of meadow ground part of **Wain Arglwydd** in the Parish of Swansea, having the highway leading from Swansea to Pont y Cobb on the south, the parts rented by William George on the east and west, [and] the brook dividing it from the lands of Mr Hugh Powell called Ustrad on the north, to wit:

	Customary		
	Acres	Qrs	
The great Meadow	10	1	
The lower Meadow	4	–	
The middle Meadow	3	2	
The higher Meadow	3	2	
	21	1	£12 – –

There are several parcels of coppice wood scattered in them which might contain about an acre.

John Evan rents part of **Wain Arglwydd** late in the possession of John Rees, and is bounded by Mrs. Mathew's lands called Cregynnith on the east, the Common on the north, the highway on the south, and that part of Wain Arglwydd in the possession of William George on the west. It contains two parcels of ground, to wit:

	Acres	Qrs	
Three Acres above the Wood	3	0	
Six Acres below the Wood	6	0	
Customary measure	9	0	£4 10 –

['£5 10 -' in Bn]

Some timber was cut here by Mr Gardiner[14] and there is now about an acre of scattered coppice on it, and three or four veins of coal run through it.

---

13. There are columns against the following entries for 'Number of Customary Acres' and 'Improved Yearly Rent' . There is usually only one entry in these columns for each holding listed, so the column format has not been followed here. Customary acres were approximately twice the area of statute acres. 'Improved rent' was the rent a holding might be expected to re-let for if it came into the lord's possession.
14. The Duke's Receiver (accountant) for the Gower Estate.

William George rents a house, barn and two stables or beast houses, and another part of **Wain Arglwydd** containing in the whole about sixteen acres, to wit:

	Acres	Qrs
The large Piece next the House called Wain Ycha	7	0
Cae Ycha	2	2
Cae Kenol	2	0
Cae Yssha yn Hyn	2	2
Cae Yssha	2	0
A meadow called Wain Yssha	2	0

£18　0　–

This part is bounded on the south by the highway, on the east by Mr Popkin's part of Wain Arglwydd, on the north by the brook dividing it from the lands of Thomas Price of Penllergare esq., and on the west by Mr Price as far as the brook called Nant y Gorse, and then by the said brook and Lady Charlotte Edwin's lands to the highway. There are a few oak trees growing on the hedges round the meadows.

William George rents another part of **Wain Arglwyd**. It consists of an old ruinous cottage and a meadow containing about an acre, and two small crofts on the south side thereof and *[Folio 30/31]* now in the possession of Griffith Hosea. He also holds a potato garden taken from the highway together with a field and two meadows, part of Wain Arglwydd, having the lane on the east, the Common and the lands of Mr Hugh Powell called Ystrad on the north, the brook running between them, the highway on the south and that part of Wain Arllwydd held by Mr Popkin on the west:

	Acres	Qrs
The Field contains about one Cover	0	2
The Upper Meadow	2	0
The lower Meadow	4	0
	6	2

These are also held by Griffith Hosea who lives in a small house adjoining to the west of the field, having a beast house and two small gardens belonging to it.

The rent of the whole　　£8　17　–

Mary Davies of Oystermouth, widow, holds a messuage, tenement and lands in the Parish of Swansea, called **Singleton,** by Lease dated 20th of December 1734, for the lives of John Davies, Mary Davies and Elizabeth Davies, son and daughters of the said Mary Davies, at the yearly rent of five shillings payable [at] Michaelmas and Lady Day, two fat pullets or one shilling in lieu thereof. Heriot or Alienation – five shillings. Suit of Mill and Suit of Court – or three shillings and four pence. It consists of a messuage, barn stable and stall and several parcels of land, to wit:

		Acres	Qrs
Coed Cae	Arable lands	1	0
Caer Skibor	Arable	3	0
Caer Kenol	Arable	2	2
Wain Vawr	Meadow	3	0
Cae Tair Erw	Arable	3	0
Cae Newydd	Arable	2	0
Cae Mawr	Arable	6	0
Wain Velen	Meadow	2	0
The Wood		3	0
		25	2	£16	—	—

The timber has been lately cut. There are several young oak trees in the wood, meadows and hedge rows.   *[Folio 30/31]*

Nicholas Ball holds a messuage, tenement and lands situate at **Burry's head** in the Parish of Langennith by Lease dated 6th day of September 1743, for the lives of the said Nicholas, Mary the wife of John Ball, and Sarah the wife of the said Nicholas, at the yearly rent of ten shillings payable Lady Day and Michaelmas[15], two fat pullets or one shilling in lieu thereof, five shillings in lieu of a Heriot or Alienation, Suit of Mill and Suit of Court or two shillings on default of either of the said suits. It consists of a good house, barn and stall, a garden and orchard below the road, two small meadows by the river side.

	Acres	Qrs
Two small meadows by the river side	1	0
Half an acre of land above the road	—	2
Half an acre below the road	—	2
One field	3	0
One other field	3	0
One field of	2	0
One other field	2	0
	12	0

All arable lands and worth at the utmost improved value per annum   £6   —   —

David Long holds a messuage and tenement of lands, being three several parcels (mearing to Sir Edward Mansel's lands on the west, the lands of Thomas Gamage on the east, the highway leading from Swansea to Lanridian village on the south, and the Common on the north sides thereof) commonly called Leeston Wick, situate in the Parish of Lanridian, by Lease dated 10th December 1705, for the life of David Long senr, at the yearly rent of three pounds and ten shillings payable at Lady Day and Michaelmas, two fat capons or one shilling in lieu thereof, and six shillings and eight pence in lieu of a Heriot.

It consists of a house, barn, stall, stable and garden.

---

15. 24th March and 29th September.

	Acres	Qrs			
Two small fields adjoining the highway called Leeston Wick	2	0			
A field called Green Close	1	2			
A field above the Wood called Splot	–	2			
A field called Lay Close (Arable)	1	2			
The Wood containing about	30	2			
	35	2			
The improved value of this may amount to			£5	–	–

John Thomas holds a messuage and tenement of lands called **Gurnoss**, situate in the Parish of Loughor, by Lease dated 17th of September 1751 for the lives of Anne, the wife of Joseph Morgan of the Parish of Bishopston, the said John Thomas, and Mary Kneath, spinster, daughter of Phillip Knaeth of the Parish of Pennard, at the yearly rent of ten shillings, payable at Lady Day and Michaelmas, two fat pullets or one shilling in lieu thereof, five shillings in lieu of a Heriot or Alienation. It consists of four pieces of rough ground and a small meadow under the wood, and two fields and three small meadows above the wood. There is a house, small barn, stable, and stall, and two small gardens. There are several old trees as oaks standils and a few young oaks growing. It is bounded on the east by Heol y Crwse, *[Folio 31/32]* on the north by the highway leading from Gorse Velin to Cobbs Bridge, and on the south by Mr Talbot's lands called Kevengorwidd, and a field called Kae Davidd belonging to Keven Corwidd on the west:

Improved rent per annum	£16 – –

Joseph Pryce esq. has, by Lease granted him the 18th October 1755, full and free liberty power and authority to make, lay down, and erect all and every **wagon-way or wagon-ways** or other devices, upon and over all that Common or waste of the said Duke's called Mynnydd Bach, otherwise **Mynnydd Bach y Cocks**, situate in the Parish of Lanridian, to the upper corner of a certain meadow of Jane Mathews called Wain Vawr, in the possession of Mary Morgan, widow, or to a certain close or parcel of ground of the said Joseph Pryce called *[blank]* adjoining or near to the said meadow, and in, upon, over and across any other waste, open or uninclosed lands of the said Duke's, or any highway or highways which he or they shall have occasion to cross, pass, or go over, from the said meadow or close to the River of Burry.

To hold to the said Joseph Pryce for the term of twenty-one years at and under the yearly rent of two pounds and two shillings, payable at Lady Day and Michaelmas:

	£2 2 –

William Thomas holds a messuage and tenement of lands called Carn Garw and Gorse Llan situate in the Parish of Landilotalybont by Lease bearing date the 6th day of September 1743, at the yearly rent of £4 6s. It consists of a dwelling house and old barn, stable and stall, and a potato garden round the pound and stable in the middle of the waste, and the several closes following, to wit:

	Acres	Qrs
A Croft behind the House, two covers	1	0
Cae Glase, arable	1	0

Gorse lase, meadow	3	0
Cae Garw Ycha, arable	2	0
Cae Garw Kenol, arable	2	0
Cae Garw Yssha, arable	2	0
	11	0

£5   –   –

[Folio 32/33]

The Croft behind the House, and the meadow called Gorse Lase, are bounded as follows: having Cwm Nant Llech on the north, the lands of Gryffydd Price esq. called Bolgod and the lands of Mr Edward Evans of Eagle's Bush on the west, and the lane leading to Mynnydd Llyw on the south and east sides. The said closes called Cae Garw Ycha, Cae Garw Kenol and Cae Garw Yssha are bounded by the lands of Thomas Mathew, alias Joseph, called Tuy Llwyd on the north and east, the lane on the west and the lands of John Thomas and Evan Powell called Allt y graban Vach on the south.

Mr Paul Bevan holds by Lease dated the 15th day of July 1735 ['1753' in Bn and in folio 37, p.87, below], for the life of the said Mr Bevan: **Portmead**, situate in the Parishes of Swansea and Langevelach, which is bounded by the Commons called Forrest Vach, Bryn y dyon and Gorse Llawenna on the south, the lane leading from Cadley to Gorse Llawenna and a cot, garden and three small crofts called Bryn y dyon on the west, the highway leading from Swansea to Carmarthen on the north, and the lane leading from Llydiad yr Odin Calch to Pentilabrain on the east. It consists of the following particulars:

A cottage and garden called **Tyr Helig** in the possession of David John who holds:

	Acres	Qrs
Two small fields containing about	2	2
And a meadow containing about	6	2

A cottage and garden called **Tuy Funnon Crwk Bona** and a large croft and meadow in possession of Jennet John, widow, containing about *[blank]*.

A cottage and garden in possession of Lewellin Jenkin, adjoining to **Forrest Vach** *[blank]*.

A cottage and garden at **Pentilabrain** in possession of John David, who also holds the three following fields, to wit:

	Acres	Qrs
Kae Pella	1	2
Kae Kenol	1	3
Kae Bach	1	1

Which three fields are bounded by the highway leading from Swansea to Loughor on the north, Heol y Weig on the east, and the lands of Messrs. Hurst and Jones called Pentilabrain on the south and west.

A cott and garden at **Pentilabrain** in possession of William Owen.

	Acres	Qrs
A meadow in posesssion of Robert Terry containing	6	2
Three fields in his possession containing 18 covers – or	9	0
A meadow in possession of Thomas Evan	8	0
Four arable fields in the possession of Thos Evan	6	0
Six acres of rough ground in Thomas Evan's possession	6	0
A meadow in possession of Thomas Benjamin	5	0

The improved yearly value of the whole may amount to	£20	–	–

Mr James Griffiths lately held ['holds' in Bn, 'lately held' inserted in Sa] by Lease dated the 10th of July 1741 all that small piece of ground containing by estimation half quarter *[sic]* of an acre formerly part of **Loughor Marsh**, adjoining to Sluice Pill and lately inclosed by the said James Griffiths, together with the Dock Pond, at the yearly rent of 10 shillings which Lease expired 15th July 1762.   £– 10 –

[Folio 33/34]

Richard David holds by Lease dated the 2nd day of October, 6th Queen Anne *[1707]*, for the life of the said Richard David, at the yearly rent of seven pounds, six shillings and eight pence, a large piece of **salt marsh near Cobbs Bridge** containing about forty acres, having the lands of Lady Charlotte Edwin on the east and the Rivers Llyw and Llyw Ytha surrounding it on all other parts thereof. He holds by the same Lease a parcel of lands called **Graig y Buldan** containing a field called Kae Newydd, about three acres, having the lands of Joseph Pryce esq. on the south, east and west, and Kae Mawr and Sir Thomas Stepney's lands on the north. Kae-mawr contains eight acres, having the lands of Sir Thomas Stepney on the east, Trawstir and Talduy on the north and west, and the lands of Joseph Pryce esq. and Kaenewydd on the south. Trawstir contains about two acres and a half, and Talduy one acre and a half. A field under the road with some rough ground under, it to the brook, about one acre and half; and the wood and wet ground under it, about fifteen acres. The out bounds are the lands of Mr Roberts on the west, Sir Thomas Stepney's lands on the north and east, and the lands of Joseph Pryce esq. on the south. The timber and wood are only fit for coal pit timber and charcoal, except some pieces.

The improved yearly value of this tenement together with the marsh may amount to the sum of: £10 – –

David Harry holds by Lease dated 10th July 1741 for the term of 21 years, at the yearly rent of three pounds, and one shilling duties: All those several closes or parcels of lands, containing by estimation six customary acres, called or known by the name of **Pentyr Arlwydd**, situate in the Parish of Langevelach, having the lands of William Phillips of Penyvoda on the north part thereof, and the Lord's Common called Mynnydd Carn Goch on all other sides thereof. This Lease is now expired and is now let out at the yearly rent of: £4 – –

[Folio 34/35]

Alexander Trotter holds the **Keelage** of ships at Penclawdd.

Joseph Pryce of Gellyhyr [esq.] holds land on [the] east side of **Mynnydd bach y Cocks**.

John George holds a smith's shop on the side of the highway at **Dyfnant** in the Parish of Lanridian, at the yearly rent of   £–   –   6

Griffith Eaton holds [a] piece of land by [the] side of [the] highway in Lanrhidian [at a] place called **San Kerrig**.   Vide Subboscus – Folio 41. *[p.94.]*
[*These last three appear in Sa only.*]

William Jones holds a garden near the **Pentre** in the Parish of Swansea
    at the yearly rent of: £–   1   –

Jenkin Thomas holds a cottage, garden and croft near the **Olchfa** in the Parish of Swansea at the yearly rent of: £–   7   –

Morgan John holds a cottage, garden and orchard in **Heol y Marchog** in the Parish of Swansea at the yearly rent of: £–   10   –

Catherine Terry holds a garden on the side of the highway near **Sketty** in the Parish of Swansea at the yearly rent of: £–   –   6

David Robert holds a cottage and garden at **Pentilbrain** in the Parish of Swansea at the yearly rent of: £–   –   6

John Harry holds a small court before his house on **the Bryn at Sketty**, in the Parish of Swansea, at the yearly rent of: £–   –   6

Ellis Hugh holds a cottage (now in ruins) and garden near **Waingron** in the Parish of Landilo talybont at the yearly rent of: £–   –   6

David Bowen holds a house, garden and three crofts on **Kevendrim** in the Parish of Landilo talybont, at the yearly rent of: £1   10   –

Morgan Hopkin's widow holds a cottage, garden and croft on **Graig Vawr** in the Parish of Landilo talybont, at the yearly rent of: £–   12   6
[Folio 35/36]

David William holds a ruinous cottage and croft on **Graig Vawr** in the Parish of Landilo talybont, at the yearly rent of: £–   1   –

Anne William holds a cottage, garden and croft on **Graig Vawr** in the Parish of Landilo talybont, at the yearly rent of: £–   8   –

William John holds a cottage, garden and three crofts on **Mynnydd Llyw** in Landeilo talybont, at the yearly rent of: £1   10   0

William Hugh holds a cottage and garden on **Mynnydd Rhose y Bishwell** in the Parish of Loughor at the yearly rent of: £–   1   –

David William holds a croft near **Kellibion**, encroached on the Lord's Common called Kevenbryn, at the yearly rent of: £–   1   –
[Folio 36/37]

Robert Jone holds a croft near **Walterston**, encroached on Kevenbryn,
at the yearly rent of: £–   –   2

Anne Tale, widow, holds a small court before her house at **Walterston**, encroached on the Lord's Common called Kevenbryn, at the yearly rent of: £–   –   1

John Williams holds a garden at **Walterston**, encroached on the Lord's Common called Kevenbryn, at the yearly rent of: £–   –   2

John Jones holds a court or garden before his house at **Walterston**
at the yearly rent of: £–   –   1
[Folio 37/38]

Mr Paul Bevan also holds by this Lease dated the 15th of July 1753 (see Folio 33 *[p.84]*) two large parcels of marsh land surrounded by the Manor of east and west Millwood, called **the Red Marsh, alias Morva Coch,** and **the Ishland** *[sic]*, having the River Tawy on the east; the marsh of William Hurst and Calvert Richard Jones, called Morva Awry, and the lands of George Venables Vernon esq., part of Havod Farm, on the south; the lands of Thomas Bennett, gentleman, on the west; and the lands of the said Thomas Bennett and the said river on the north. It is overflowed on spring tides; and contains about 15 acres, and may be worth per annum, about: £12   –   –

There is included in the said Lease an old ruinous building called the **Old Salt House**, lying under the cliffs in the Parish of **Oystermouth**, which has been lately built and erected into a dwelling and outhouses, and is now in the possession of Anne Bowen, widow, and worth per annum: £5   –   –

The whole rent reserved by Lease is £5 5, payable at Michaelmas and Lady Day, two capons or two shillings in lieu thereof at the Lord's choice on the Feast Day of Saint Thomas the Apostle yearly, and the sum of 5s in lieu of a Heriot and for every Alienation. Doing Suit of Mill, and Suit of Court upon every reasonable Summons, or 3s 4d for every default.

*Typical Gower Subboscus scenery. Looking north across the Morlais Valley from Cilonen,
showing the intermixed fields and woodlands.*

*Mynydd Bach y Cocs common, near Three Crosses.
Although it was not the best agricultural land, Gower Subboscus was rich in coal. See page 19.*

Gower Subboscus

This Manor, which constitutes part of the Seigniory, is a part of Gower Wallicana or Welsh Gower, and is commonly called Parcel Iscoyd and sometimes west Gower. It takes in part of the Parishes of Lanridian, Ilston, Bishopston, and Loughor. It makes a part of the Hundred of Langevelach, though detached from it, and surrounded entirely by the Hundred of Swansea. It is bounded on the west by the River Loughor, taking half of the said river; on the south by Morlais, otherwise Salt House Pill, and part of the Manor of Lanridian, parcel of the Manor of Landimore, belonging to Thomas Mansel Talbot esq.; on the east by part of the Parishes of Ilston, Bishopston and Swansea; and on the north by part of the Parishes of Swansea and Loughor.

The tenants of this Manor hold their lands in Common Soccage by Rents, Fealty, Suit of Court and Heriot; and they appear and do their Suits and Services, and serve on Juries promiscuously[16] with the tenants of Anglicana.

The Lord is intituled to all the same rights and jurisdictions within this Manor as in Gower Anglicana.

There are two **Constables** appointed and sworn at Michaelmas Leet, yearly.

A Rental of the Chief Rents within Gower Subboscus

No.	Freeholders Names	Names of Tenements	Names of Tenants	Rents p Ann. £	s	d
1	The Earl of Warwick ['Lord Brook' in Bn]	Killay	William Landeg	–	7	3
2	The same	Gellyor llwyn	John Thomas' widow	–	3	–
3	The same	Tenement at Kevenbuchen	John David	–	1	6
4	Thos Mansel Talbot esq.	Keelonen Vawr	John Bowen	–	1	–
5	Sir William Mansel Bart.	A meadow called Gwain draw	David Bennet ['William Thomas' in Bn]	–	–	7
6	Lady Charlotte Edwin	Killan Vach	Henry William	–	–	10
7	The same	Kevengorvid	Owen William	–	3	–

16. i.e. 'amongst' or 'mixed in with'.

No.	Freeholders Names	Names of Tenements	Names of Tenants	Rents p Ann.		
				£	s	d
8	Earl Talbot ['Lord Talbot in Bn]	Gellyon	Phillip Gwyn	–	–	8
9	Thomas Mansel Talbot esq.	Llodrog	Owen Howell	–	–	6
10	Robert Popkin esq. ['Thomas P.' in Bn]	Part of Wimblewood	David Lewis	–	–	2
11	Robert Morris esq.	Pencaer Venny	John Bowen	–	2	–
12	Mathew Pryce esq.	A tenement called Melinhavod	John William	–	–	11
13	The same	A tenement called Kae Garw alias Gwarda	Evan Evan	–	–	2
14	Mrs. Dawkin	Llanmorlais	William Evan	–	1	–
15	The same	A tenement called Doycae	William Howell	–	1	–
16	The same	A tenement called Penllech	Nicholas David	–	1	–
17	The same	A tenement at Crofte called Penllech	Hopkin Long ['Samuel L' in Bn]	–	1	–
18	The same	Pen yr heol	David Hugh	–	–	2
19	The same	Lower Wimblewood	Maysod Lucas, widow	–	3	4
20	Thomas Popkin esq.	Erw Vawr at Kevenbuchan	Samuel Morris	–	–	3
21	The same	Voylant	Thomas Jones	–	–	3
22	Catherine Seys, widow	Killan Vawr	Her own possession	–	2	–
23	Joseph Pryce esq.	Pantglase & Kilonnen Vach	Griffith Jeffrey & Jas David	–	2	–
24	The same	Tyrkethen	David Lewis	–	–	10
25	Priscilla Jones, widow	Part of Cwm Mawr	Her own possession	–	–	10

[Folio 38/39]

No.	Freeholders Names	Names of Tenements	Names of Tenants	Rents p Ann.		
-----	-------------------	--------------------	--------------------	£	s	d
26	Mathew Price esq.	Ryan Vawr & Tyr Wilcock	Samuel Griffith	–	4	10
27	The same	Ryan Vach	The same	–	1	–
28	Gabriel Powell gent.	Tenement at Berthllwy<u>dd</u>	William Bowen	–	1	8
29	Mr Paul Bevan & Jno. Harry	Tenement at Berthllwyd	John Webber and William Wilkin ['W.W.' not in Bn]	–	–	4
30	Mr Thomas Jones	Lands at Berthllwyd called Tyr Prudence Morgan	His own possession	–	–	2
31	Mrs Richards, Mr Dorset & Mathew Pryce esq,	Tenement at Pen y lan	John Atkins	–	–	2
32	Thomas Price esq. ['Gryffidd Pryce Esq'. in Bn]	Kaer Velin	David Jones	–	–	10
33	The same	Tyr y Bryn	David Jones	–	–	2
34	Mr Rowland Prichard's widow ['Ann Pritchard, widow' in Bn]	Hendy alias Yslys y Ryan	Mathew Coleman ['Eliz: Coleman, widow in Bn]	–	2	–
35	The same	Tenement at Aberkedy called Dan y Lan	William Morgan	–	1	10
36	The same	Another tenement there	William Morgan	–	–	5
37	The same	Cwmynewir	William Atkins	–	1	8
38	The same	Pant Glase	William Jenkin	–	–	4
39	Mr Franklen Mathew's widow ['Jane Matthews, widow' in Bn]	Pen y cae near Penylan	John Morgan's widow	–	1	6
40	The same	Tenement near Killan	Isaac David	–	–	8
41	Mr Geo. Bydder	Tay Keed	David John	–	–	8
42	John Bassett, clerk	Cwm yr Rhyan	John Llewelyn	–	–	5

No.	Freeholders Names	Names of Tenements	Names of Tenants	Rents p Ann.		
				£	s	d
43	The same	Kevenhole	Llewellin John	–	1	–
44	Mathew Pryce esq.	Hendy or Aberkedy	John William	–	1	–
45	Mr Franklen Mathew's widow ['Jane Matthews, widow' in Bn]	Hendy or Aberkedy alias Penylan	Mary Morgan	–	1	–
46	Mr Silvanus Bevan	Lands called Tyr Dulast	John Davies	–	1	–
47	David John of Tay Keed & Mr Paul Bevan	Lands at Berthllwyd called Berthllwyd Ysha	John Jones	–	–	3
48	Mr Silvanus Bevan	Higher & Lower Penclawdd	Mary David and Thos Thomas	–	–	10
49	Geo. Thomas, William Givelin & Saml Morris	Lands at Kevenbuchan	Their own possession	–	1	4½
50	Phillip David	Lands at Kevenbuchan called Cold Harbour	His own possession	–	1	4½
51	Mrs. Dawkins	Lands called Duglast	Nicholas David	–	1	–
52	Matthew Pryce esq. Rosser & two Mysidd	Llwyn y Aust, Tyr Will	John Atkins	–	1	–
53	Richard Pryce gent. Kevenbuchan	A tenement at	John Atkins	–	1	–
54	John Rowland	Tyr y Wilcock near Tyrkethin	Henry Thomas	–	–	4
55	Evan Howell ['Griffith Howell' in Bn]	Lands at Berthllwyd ['Griff. Howell' in Bn]	Griffith William	–	1	–
56	William Matthew [blank in Bn]	Lands near Killan	John Hugh	–	–	4½
57	Mathew Pryce esq. [Folio 39/40]	Lands called Aberkedy	Daniel Evan	–	–	11
58	Mr Gamaliel Hughes	Brin Mawr	William Thomas of 3 Crosses	–	–	8

No.	Freeholders Names	Names of Tenements	Names of Tenants	Rents p Ann.		
				£	s	d
59	John David, infant	Land at Bevexey	David Robert	–	1	8
60	John David (*Iur. ux.*)	Cwm y Glo	John Jeffrey	–	–	4
61	Mathew Pryce esq.	Yslys y Rhyan	Hopkin Long	–	–	10
62	William Griffith	Lands at Pen y lan	Roger Griffiths	–	2	–
63	John John near Cadle	Kae Croft	Thomas Clement	–	–	5
64	Robert Popkin esq. ['Thomas Popkin esq.' in Bn]	Blaenkedy	John Harry	–	1	8
65	Mr Paul Bevan	Lands at Penylan	Jenkin Hoskin	–	–	4
66	The same	Keven mawr & Kae Krwn	The same	–	–	10
67	Mrs. Pritchard ['Margaret P.' in Bn]	Tyr y Gill near Llanmorlais	Samuel Morris	–	1	–
68	Mathew Pryce esq.	A tenement at Kevenbuchan	John Atkins	–	–	5
69	Thomas Clement	Llodrog alias St Wall	Thomas Clement	–	1	–
70	John Lucas esq.	Part of Llodrog	John Griffith	–	–	4
71	Mr Thomas Jones	Cwm yr Hooch near Killan	Thomas Benjamin	–	–	1
72	John Howell	Lands at Berthllwyd	Robert Morris	–	–	5
73	Mathew Pryce esq.	Gwain Davychan alias Cwm y Nant	Rees Evan	–	–	3
74	Mrs. Dawkin	Kae Morgan near Krickton	David Long [plus 'John Ace, & Hezekiah Lane' in Bn]	–	–	4
75	Anne Eaton, widow ['Henry Eaton' in Bn]	Lands near Pumfald	Her own possession ['Griffith Eaton' in Bn]	–	–	4
76	John Gorton	Land called Tyr draw	His own possession	–	–	1
77	Mrs. Dawkin	Llan y newir or Cwm y Nant	David Hugh	–	–	10

Demesne Lands in Subboscus

The Lord is intituled to the several Demesne lands hereafter mentioned within the said Manor of Subboscus:

William Morgan holds by Lease dated 11th February 1731 for the lives of William, Evan and John, sons of the said William Morgan and the life of the survivor, at the yearly rent of 2s 6d, and 6d Duties and 2s 6d Heriot or Alienation, a piece of ground called **the Lord's Hill, otherwise Graig Hene Castell**, in the Parish of Lanridian lying above Aberkedy, containing about two acres, of which one acre is cleared and the other furze, having the lands of the late Mr Pritchard of Bach y Greiddin, called Tyr Dan y lan, in the possession of William Morgan, on the south, east and north sides thereof and the lands of Joseph Price esq. called Aberkedy on the west.

The improved yearly rent of	£–	5	–

[Folio 41/42]

David Hugh holds by Lease dated 28th October 1735, for the lives of David Hugh David and Mary, his son and daughter and the life of the survivor, at the yearly rent of 2s 6d and two pullets or one shilling Duties, and 5s. Heriot or Alienation: two meadows in the Parish of Lanridian called **Gwain Phillip** containing about seven acres having the lands of Joseph Pryce esq. called Kaenewydd on the north and the Common called Mynnydd Bach on all other sides thereof. He also holds by the same Lease two fields near the three Crosses containing seven customary acres, having the lands of Lady Charlotte Edwin now in the possession of Anne Eaton, widow, on the north; the road leading from the three Crosses to the Lord's Common called Fairwoods Moor on the west; the said Common on the south; and the lands of Lady Charlotte Edwin in the possession of Anne Eaton, widow, on the east. He, by the same Lease, holds a landshare of land in Kaemaen-llwyd at Kevenbuchen, lying on the east side of the said close and containing by estimation three covers, having the lane on the south, Mr Paul Bevan's landshare on the west and north, and the hedge on the east.

The improved yearly value of these lands may amount to	£6	–	–

Alexander Trotter holds the **Keelage and Moorage of ships at Penclawdd**, from Salt House Pill to Sluice Pill, at the yearly rent of

	£1	–	–

Joseph Pryce esq. holds a piece of land on the east side of **Mynnydd Bach y Cocks** in the Parish of Lanridian containing about two acres, which has been lately divided into two parcels.

	£–	1	–

Griffith Eaton holds a piece of land on the side of the highway at a place called **San Kerrig** in the Parish of Lanridian, at the yearly rent of

	£–	1	–

[Folio 41/42]

Gower Supraboscus

This Manor constitutes a great part of the Seigniory [and] is frequently called Gower Wallicana or Welsh Gower; and what is now considered as comprehending the whole of this Manor are the entire Parishes of Langevelach and Languick (though it must be observed by the rent roll of the Chief Rents that the Englishery and Welshery were in ancient times greatly intermixed). And what are now considered as the general boundaries of this Manor are: On the east the River Tawe dividing it from the Manor of Herbert Mackworth esq. called Neath Ultra and Killebebill; the Manor of Cadoxton belonging to Geo. Price esq., Hans Stanley esq. and Henry Willis Compton esq. and part of the Lord's Manor of Kilvey, quite from the County of Brecon to the south end of the Parish of Langevelach. On the south by the Parishes of Saint John's, Swansea, Loughor and Landilotal y bont. On the north by the brook called Cathan; the small brook called Nant Melin, running by the Lord's Demesne lands called Cwm y Gorse; and the Rivers Amman and Twrch dividing it from the Counties of Carmarthen and Brecon.

There are Leet and Baron Courts held twice a year for this Manor within a month of May and Michaelmas, and a Baron Court every three weeks at the Guild Hall of Swansea by immemorial custom, for the trial of all small actions, and recovery of debts under forty shillings. These Courts are held at one and the same time with the Courts for Gower Anglicana, and although there are different Juries sworn and different rolls and books kept, they may be considered as one Court for the whole Seigniory, but kept thus separate only for the more convenient dispatch of business.

There are several **Constables** appointed and sworn at Michaelmas Leet yearly, for the following parcels:

Langevelach Parcel Mawr
Higher Division ... 1
Lower Division ... 1
Middle Division ... 1

Parcel Rhwyndwyclydach
Higher Division ... 1
Lower Division ... 1

Parcel Penderry
Higher Division ... 1
Lower Division ... 1

Parcel Clase ... 1

Languick
Parcel Mawr ... 1
Parcel Blaenegal ... 1
Parcel Altgrug ... 1

There are **Heywards** appointed and sworn at May Leet yearly, for the parcels following –

Parcel Mawr Llangevelach ... 2
Parcel Rhwyndwyclydach ... 2
Parcel Clase ... 2
Parcel Penderry ... 2
Languick Parcel Mawr ... 2
[Ditto] Parcel Blanegal ... 2

The Lord is intituled within this Manor to all the same Rights and Jurisdictions and the tenants hold their respective Estates by the same tenure and are subject to the same Suits, Services, and Heriots as the tenants of Gower Anglicana. Vide Folio 19 *[p.62.]*   *[Folio 42/43]*

There are within the circuit of this Manor: the Fee of Trewyddva, the Bishops Manor of Clase Llangevelach, and Kaegurwen. And the tenants within these Manors bring actions, are sued, and serve on Juries for the trial of actions and Suits in the Courts held for Supraboscus in the same manner as the tenants of the other mesne Manors do in the Courts of Gower Anglicana[17].

There are within the circuit of this Manor several very large and extensive Commons and wastes, all which belong to the Lord. And the Lord is intituled to the soil of the same and to all veins and mines of Coal and Culm and other mines and minerals, all quarries of stone and slate and all other profits arising from or growing on the same.

There are under the Commons and wastes within this Manor several valuable mines of coal and culm belonging to the Lord, but being at a distance from navigation the tenants have licence granted them to work coal for their own use during the Lord's pleasure.

The Lord is intituled to the water, soil and sole fishery of the River Tawy, [and] one half of the River Loughor, from Morlais alias Salthouse Pill upwards.

A Rental of the Chief Rent within Gower Supraboscus

No.	Freeholders	Tenements	Tenants	Rent per Annum		
				£	s	d

Llangevelach Parcel Clase

No.	Freeholders	Tenements	Tenants	£	s	d
1	Geo. Venables Vernon, esq.	Keven y Bettingva Genol alias Penyvedw	David Thomas & John Beynon ['Matthew Thomas, Phillip Jones & John Beynon' in Bn]	–	2	–
2	The same	Bettingva Yssha	Evan John	–	–	7
3	The same	Bettingva Ycha	Rees Wm Hopkin	–	–	6
4	The same	Ynisvorgan	Thomas Popkin esq.	–	1	6
5	The same	Glyn Collen	John Thomas	–	1	–
6	The same	Tyr David William	John Thomas alias Mathew	–	1	2
7	The same	Twy Mawr, alias Tuy Main, alias Pant Caedraw	John Hopkin David	–	–	7
8	The same	Two tenements called Pant y Milwr	Jenkin Griffiths and Rees Hopkin David	–	–	8

17. This statement seems to overlook that the tenants of Trewyddva owed suit to the court of Pennard.

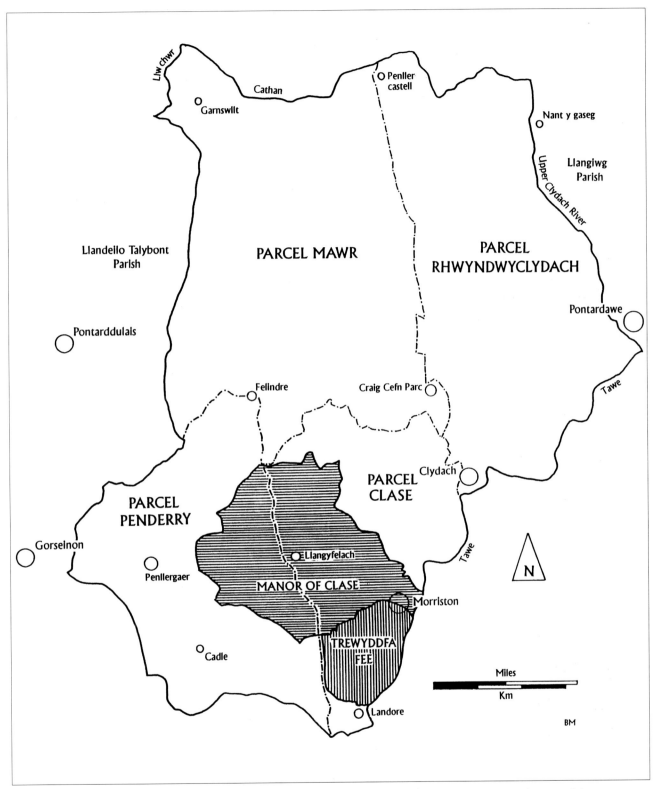

Gower Supraboscus (excluding Llangiwg) and its subdivisions as mentioned in the Survey. The 'Parcels' were subdivisions of the parish of Llangyfelach, which had been adopted for the more convenient handling of manorial affairs. Their boundaries overlap those of the two manors of Clase and Trewyddfa.

No.	Freeholders	Tenements	Tenants	Rent per Annum		
				£	s	d
9	The same	Tuy Duy	Thomas John	–	–	4
10	Thomas Popkin esq.	Tyr y Velin alias Tuy Kenol	Mathew Isaac	–	–	6
11	The same	Kae Glandwr	David Isaac	–	–	6
12	The same	Tyr Glandwr alias Tyr y bont	Mathew Isaac and William William	–	–	4
13	The same	Tyr Penry Williams	Elizabeth Jeremiah widow	–	–	6
14	John Bowen of Gurrey[sic] esq. ['and Richard Lucas gent.' in Bn]	Cwndwm Cady	Evan Hopkin	–	–	2
15	Gryffydd Pryce esq.	Pant yr Echedith Yssha alias Pant lassa Ycha alias Cawsey	William John	–	–	– ['- - 10' in Bn]
16	Mr Geo. Ace and Mr Thomas Bowen	Tyr Tanglwst alias Cwm y dwr	Morgan Lewis	–	–	6
17	William Jones, Surgeon (Iur. ux.)	Tyr yn y Bulla & Tyr y Velin	Thomas William	–	–	6
18	Geo. Ace & Thomas Bowen	Tyr y Mynnydd alias Tyr Banwen	Evan Thomas	–	–	4
19	Thos Popkin esq. ['William Jones (Iur. ux.)' in Bn]	Gwernvadock	William Thomas, collier	–	–	6
20	The same	Tyr Evan Llwyd	Jos. Hopkin & Rees Owen	–	–	6
21	Mr George Ace	Tyr David Goch Vach	Rees Owen	–	–	6
22	John Knaeth	Abergelly Ycha or Mawr	John Thomas	–	–	9
23	Phillip Knaeth	Abergelly Ysha or Vach & Brin Mawr	Griffith David & Griff Thomas	–	–	9

[Folio 43/44]

No.	Freeholders	Tenements	Tenants	Rent per Annum		
24	Thomas Popkin esq.	Lletty'r Scilp	Griffith William	–	–	4
25	The same	Maesgarney alias Maesgwernen	William George	–	–	6
26	The same	Brin Barddory	John Rees	–	–	3

No.	Freeholders	Tenements	Tenants	Rent per Annum £	s	d

Langavelach Parcel Mawr

No.	Freeholders	Tenements	Tenants	£	s	d
27	Geo. Venables Vernon esq.	Tuy Mawr & Tyr y Velin	John Prees	–	–	10
28	The same	Maes Meyrick	John Prees	–	1	–
29	The same	Llwyn y Domen	John Beynon	–	–	8
30	The same	Vagorwen	Hopkin John	–	–	4
31	The same	Pant Cadwgan	Zephania David	–	1	2
32[18]	The same	Tyr pen yr heol	Hopkin Llewelyn	–	1	2
33	The same	Another tenement called Tyr pen yr heol	The same	–	–	4
34	The same	Keven y Park	David Robert, and Jno. Evan Hopkin	–	1	1½
35	The same	Cynhordy Ycha	Jenkin John	–	–	9
36	The same	Blaen yr Olchva Ycha	Cath Jenkin	–	–	6
37	The same	Funnon Mydow	Henry William's widow	–	–	3
38	The same	Brin y Maen	William David	–	–	5
39	The same	Kae Ycha at Pen yr heol	Hopkin Lewelyn	–	–	2
40	Jane Matthews, widow Thomas Morgan gent ['esq.' in Bn]	Tenement called Skiach	David Hopkin	–	–	8
41	Thomas Morgan gent. ['esq.' in Bn]	Tenement at Blaen Nant Dy Vawr	Richard Hopkin	–	1	2
42	The same, and Jane Matthews, widow	Tenement called Keven Skiach or Bayly Glase ['Skiach or Bayly Glase' in Bn]	Thomas Jenkins ['William David' in Bn]	–	–	8
43	Thomas Morgan gent. ['esq.' in Bn]	Blaen Nant dy Vach	Richard Hopkin	–	–	2
44	The same	Kae Llwyd	Mary Rees, widow	–	–	2
45	The same	Tyr Funnon Wen	William Harry	–	–	3½

18. '31' appears again instead of '32' in Sa , so subsequent numbering is too low. Bn numbers are therefore used here.

No.	Freeholders	Tenements	Tenants	Rent per Annum		
				£	s	d
46	The same	Pentwyn	The same	–	–	3
47	The same	Blaen Mothvay[19]	Evan Bevan	–	–	3
48	The same	Keven Mothvay alias Cwmbrin Llefrith	Anne Powell	–	1	–
49	The same	Yr Hendy Vawr at Keven Mothvay	David Bowen	–	1	2
50	The same	Tenement called Keven Mothvay	David Bowen	–	1	9
51	The same	Tenement there called Keven Mothvay	Mary Rees, widow	–	1	–
52	The same	Lletty John	Richard Hopkin	–	–	4
53	The same & Jane Mathews, widow	Mothvay alias Pant Funnon Wicknos	Rees Bowen	–	–	1
54	Thomas Morgan gent. ['esq.' in Bn]	Gelly gron	Llewelyn Howell	–	1	2
55	The same	Tyr Pen y Twyn	John Rees	–	1	1
56	Richard Williams	Pen y Veedy Yssha alias Tuy yn y Cwm	Henry William ['Elizth. Williams, widow' in Bn]	–	–	6
57	The same	Cwm Dylais	His own possession ['Henry Davies' in Bn]	–	–	7
58	Thomas Popkin esq.	Funnon Sant	William Isaac	–	–	8
59	Evan Bevan alias Lewelin	Ky Nant Vach	John William	–	–	6
60	William Dawkin esq. ['infant' in Bn]	Ynistawlog	William John	–	2	7

[Folio 44/45]

No.	Freeholders	Tenements	Tenants	Rent per Annum		
61	William Dawkin esq. ['The same' in Bn]	Aberkathan alias Pen y Garn	John Morgan's widow	–	–	7
62	The same ['Willm. Dawkin esq. infant' in Bn]	Carne Swlt	David William John	–	–	4
63	The same	Esgirgathan	John Morgan's widow	–	–	6

19. i.e. Myddfai.

No.	Freeholders	Tenements	Tenants	Rent per Annum		
				£	s	d
64	Jane Jeffreys widow ['Mrs. Jane Jeffries' in Bn]	Cynhorde	David Lewis	–	–	4½
65	Cath. Roberts, widow, & others	Blaen y Cwm	Evan David	–	–	6
66	Jane Jeffreys, widow ['Mrs. Jane Jeffries' in Bn]	Brynhire	David Lewis	–	–	2
67	Joseph Pryce esq.	Troed Rhiw Velin	Rees Bevan	–	–	3
68	Richard Walter	Havod Lase	John Mathew	–	–	2
69	Mary Morgan widow ['Thomas Morgan, Esq' in Bn]	Tenement in Cwmdylais	David Edward ['alias Hopkin' in Bn]	–	–	5
70	Thomas Price esq. ['Gryffyd P.' in Bn]	Tenement at Gelly Gwm called Trwyn Tylle	David Hopkin	–	3	6
71	Mr Chas. Morgan	Tenement at Gelly gwm	Evan Thomas	–	–	4
72	Mr Walter Vaughan ['Margt Vaughan, widow' in Bn]	Knwffe y Bongam	Davd. John & Jno. Thomas	–	–	4
73	Robt. Morris esq.	Tylle Coch	Thos David John	–	–	4
74	Robt. Morris Jones esq.	Two tenements at Skiach	Davld Morgan & Thos Jones	–	– ['- - 4' in Bn]	8
75	Richard Price gent.	Hendrevawr	David Bevan ['Mary Lloyd, widow' in Bn]	–	–	3
76	The same	Y Garnant Ycha	Mary Lloyd, widow ['The same' in Bn]	–	–	6
77	Thos Price esq. ['Gryffydd P.' in Bn]	Glyncasnog	Hugh Wm Griffith	–	–	8
78	The same	Gerdinen	Thomas William Griffith	–	1	4
79	Mr John Collins	A tenement at Gelly gwm	Evan Thomas	–	–	4
80	Phillip Williams esq.	Court Mawr	Edward Rees	–	1	–
81	John Powell	Yr House Mawr	Morgan Dd. Lewis	–	–	10
82	The same	Place bach	The same	–	–	4

No.	Freeholders	Tenements	Tenants	Rent per Annum		
				£	s	d
83	Thomas Popkin esq.	Gellyvethan	Thomas Jenkin	–	–	6
84	Isaac Morgan	Llwyn Gwenno Ycha	Thomas Harry	–	–	5
85	The same	Tenement called Skiach or Tuy Llwyd	Jno. Bowen & Owen Bowen	–	–	8
86	Richard William	Tuy yn y Cwm	William Morgan Lewis	–	–	3
87	Mr Isaac Morgan	Llwyn Gwenno Yssha alias Carreg Llwyd	His own possession	–	–	3
88	Morgan John	Court Ycha alias Mawr	Morgan John ['Morgan Lewis' in Bn]	–	–	8
89	Owen Bevan ['Martha Bowen, widow.' in Bn]	Blaen Skiach	Davd. Morgan Lewis	–	1	1
90	Catherine Rees	Llyr Vedwin	William Thomas	–	–	10
91	Lewelyn Bevan's widow	Tenement at Gardinnen called Sythin y Tuy Ycha & Sythin y Tuy Yssha	Evan Llewelyn ['Evan Lewis' in Bn]	–	1	1
92	The same	Lands called Blaen Gardinen & Kae Newydd	The same	–	–	9
93	Thomas Pryce esq.	Tenement at Gardinen Yssha	John Jones	–	–	9
94	David Bevan	Blaen y Cuffon	David Bevan	–	–	7
95	John Bevan	Kynant Vawr	John William John	–	1	–
96	William Dawkin esq.	Blaen Cathan alias Cwm alias Kilvach Llyddon	William Morgan	–	–	6
97	Morgan Matthew	Blaen yr Olchfa Yssha	His own possession	–	–	2
98	The same	Blaen yr Olchfa Ycha	The same	–	–	8
99	William Phillip	Bullva Ddy	Evan Thomas alias William	–	–	4
100	Mr Thomas Jones [Folio 45/46]	Maesdir Mawr	Thomas Robert	–	1	–
101	John Powell	Tenement called Pen yr heol	Morgan David Lewis	–	–	4

No.	Freeholders	Tenements	Tenants	Rent per Annum		
				£	s	d
102	Cathn. Roberts, widow & others	Tenement at Blaen Cathan alias Cwm	Evan David	–	–	3
103	John William John	Tenement called Garnant Genol	John Rees	–	–	2

Langevelach Parcel Penderry

No.	Freeholders	Tenements	Tenants	Rent per Annum		
104	Sir William Mansel Bart	Nydvwch Vach	John Williams	–	2	7
105	The same	Park Mawr	Thomas William	–	4	–
106	Lady Charlotte Edwin	Tenement called Tuy Ycha yn y Gorse	John George	–	–	4
107	Thomas Popkin esq.	Gellywran Yssha	John Wm Lewis	–	–	8
108	Thos Price esq. ['Gryffydd P.' in Bn]	Penllergare	His own possession	–	7	1
109	The same	Kaye Davychan	The same	–	1	6
110	The same	Keven y Forrest & Bryn Rhose	The same	–	3	9
111	The same	Penllwynaydden	Hopkin John	–	–	8
112	Gryffydd Price esq. ['The same', i.e. Thos P., in Bn]	Nydvwych & Bryn David	Richard Jenkin & William David	–	11	–
113	The same	Gellyhill	Enoch Bowen	–	3	6
114	The same	Llysnyny	Morgan David ['Lewellyn John' in Bn]	–	–	6
115	Mr Charles Morgans	Cadle Vawr	Evan Thomas Lewis and Thomas Richard	–	3	4
116	The same	Cadle Ycha	Llewellyn David	–	1	10
117	Gryffydd Price esq. ['The same' in Bn]	Cadle Vach & Tyr Rosser	The same	–	3	4
118	Gryffydd Price esq.	Cadle Yssha	Thomas Morgan	–	1	–
119	The same	Cadle Yssha [sic]	William Thomas	–	1	–
120	Sarah Prichard, spinster, infant	Bach y Greiddin	Rees Morgan	–	1	7

No.	Freeholders	Tenements	Tenants	Rent per Annum		
				£	s	d
121	The same	Llanllyw	The same	–	–	7½
122	Mr Thomas Morgan	Pentherry	Rees Thomas	–	4	10
123	The same	Havodty	His own possession	–	–	8
124	Robt Morris Jones esq.	Clyn Coch	Thomas Price	–	–	2
125	Thos Price esq. ['Gryffydd P.' in Bn]	Llwyn Cadwgan	William Owen	–	1	6
126	Robert Morris esq.	Part of Llettybach called Brinlleffridd	Thomas William	–	–	1½
127	Thos Price esq. ['Gryffydd P.' in Bn]	Tyle Duy	His own possession	–	4	8
128	Joseph Lord	Pentherry Vach	William Morgan	–	–	8
129	Thos Price esq. ['Gryffydd P.' in Bn]	Coed Trenning	His own possession	–	2	–
130	The same	Clyn Brich	David Gronow	–	–	4
131	Mr Thomas Morgan	Coed Bach	Rees Thomas	–	–	4
132	Gryffydd Price esq.	Gorse Eynon	William Jenkin	–	–	7½
133	The same	Tyr y Gorse	The same & Amy Atho *[sic]*	–	–	3
134	Catherine Hughes & Margaret Thomas, widow	Tenement called Cadle	Hopkin Habbacuck	–	–	10
135	Anne Powell, widow	Two tenements called Keven y Forrest and Gelly Lwydwen	John Powell	–	1	6
136	Henry William *[Folio 46/47]*	Gelly wran Genol	His own possession	–	1	–
137	Rachel Llewellyn, widow, & William Rosser	Tenement called Llanlluw alias Bach y Greyddin Ycha	Their own possession	–	–	6
138	William Thomas widow ['Thos Morgan (*Iur. ux.*)' in Bn]	Tenement at Cadle	Phillip Bevan	–	–	10

No.	Freeholders	Tenements	Tenants	Rent per Annum		
				£	s	d
139	Thomas Mathew	Two tenements called Penrhiw & Kilsant	His own possession	–	–	8
140	John Rosser ['Edwd William (*Iur. ux.*)' in Bn]	Tenement called Glanlluw & Letty Bach	His own possession	–	–	7½
141	David Harry	Gellygynorog	John Harry	–	–	6
142	David Howell	Tenement called Gorse Eynon	John Llewelyn	–	–	8
143	Thos Price esq. ['Gryffydd P.' in Bn]	Pen y Quare	William Lewis	–	–	2
144	Christopher Gregory	Gorse y Coed	Thomas Robert	–	–	8
145	Mr Hurst & Mr Jones ['Edward Hurst esq. & Calvert Richd Jones esq.' in Bn]	Lands called Wain y kydie	Thos Hopkin David's widow	–	–	3
146	Sarah Prichard, infant	Tenement called Glanllyw	Thomas John	–	–	2
147	David Jones	Part of Lletty Bach	William Francis	–	–	1½

Langevelach Parcel Rhwyndwyclydach

No.	Freeholders	Tenements	Tenants	Rent per Annum		
148	Herbert Mackworth, esq.	Ynis Penllwch Wear & Fishery	Mr Thomas Lewis	–	8	4
149	The same	Craig Trebannoes	Jenkin Lewis	–	1	–
150	The same	Kellyonen Yssha	William David	–	1	8
151	The same	Kellyonen Genol	Lewis William	–	1	8
152	The same	Kellyonen Ycha	Willm Evan Hopkin	–	–	10
153	The same	Tuy yn y Cae	John Thomas	–	–	6
154	The same	Tuy Gwyn	William Evan Griffith	–	1	8
155	The same	Tuy yn y Coed & Tuy yn Vard[r]e	William Roberts	–	1	8
156	The same	Eythrim Genol	David Hopkin	–	–	6
157	The same	Tuy yn y Coed	John Floyd	–	1	8

No.	Freeholders	Tenements	Tenants	Rent per Annum		
				£	s	d
158	The same	Gwrach Lynna	Jenkin lewis	–	–	4
159	The same	Eythrim Yssha	David Robert	–	–	10
160	George Venables Vernon esq.	Penllynne	William John	–	1	6
161	The same	Wyll Gwythill	William James ['Willm James' widow.' in Bn]	–	1	10
162	The same	Gwain yr Eyrol ['Gwain yr Eyrsh' in Bn]	Thomas Rees	–	2	–
163	The same	Eythrim Ycha	Richard William	–	1	8
164	The same	Tenement by Cwm Clydach Mill	John Walter	–	–	4
165	The same	Tenement near Aberclydach called Gellyvelin	David Eynon ['William D. E.' in Bn]	–	–	6
166	The same	Tenement in Cwm Clydach [called] Clyn Coch	Anne Bevan, widow	–	1	–
167	The same	Tenement in Cwm Clydach called Tyr y Berllan	The same	–	–	5
168	The same	Tenement there called Clyn Eithrim Yssha	The same	–	1	8
169	The same	Tenement near Aber Clydach	Thomas Beynon ['Jenkin Jenkin' in Bn]	–	–	6
170	The same	Cottage near Aberclydach	Jenkin Richard's widow	–	–	6
171	The same	Llychart Vawr	John David	–	1	–
172	The Revd Mr Williams, Curate of Britonferry ['Mr Thomas' in Bn]	Tenement at Gellyonnen	Lewis Rytherch ['Willm R.' in Bn]	–	1	–
[Folio 47/48]						
173	Geo. V. Vernon esq.	Allt y Vannog	Griffith Jenkin	–	1	–
174	The same	Keven y Park	Edward Freestone and Jno. Evan Hopkin	–	1	1½

The landscape of Gower Supraboscus. The Lower Clydach valley, seen from Tor Clawdd.
Open high moorland, and fields carved out from the ancient woodlands.

Lygos farm, south-east of Penlle'rcastell. See No. 181, p.108 ("Llygoes").

No.	Freeholders	Tenements	Tenants	Rent per Annum		
				£	s	d
175	The same	Gwernllwyn	William Evan	–	–	8
176	The same	Lletty or Llwyn Evan at Nantmole	David Bowen	–	–	6
177	Arthur Davies (*Iur. ux.*)	Llychart Vach	Henry Phillip	–	1	3
178	Richard Awbrey ['Gryffydd Pryce esq.' in Bn]	Tyr Pen y lan	William Llewelyn	–	1	–
179	Gryffydd Price esq. ['The same' in Bn]	Alt y Trebannoes alias Clyn y March	David Llewelyn & David Samuel	–	1	–
180	Richd Turberville esq.	Ynisdderw	James Jervis	–	–	4
181	Robert Morris Jones esq.	Llygoes	John Llewelyn ['William John' in Bn]	–	–	10
182	The same	Pen yr Esgirne	David Phillip	–	–	4
183	The same	Tenement at Nant mole called Tyr y llan	Thomas Eynon	–	–	6
184	The same	Tenement there called Tuy yn y Berth	John Wm Rytherch	–	–	4
185	The same	Tenement near Pwllva Watkin called Nant y Gaviley	Jenkin Thomas	–	–	6
186	Thos Price esq. ['Thomas Popkin esq.' in Bn]	Two tenements called Hendy Ycha and Hendy Yssha	Evan David	–	–	10
187	Jno. Wm Rytherch & Howell Roger	Blaen Nant Mole Ycha	Their own possession	–	–	8
188	John Morgan ['Mr Isaac Morgan' in Bn]	Blaen Nant Mole Yssha	John David Bowen	–	–	6
189	Henry William ['The same' in Bn]	Gellylyog alias Kae yr Weren	William Morgan	–	1	3
190	John Morgan ['The same' in Bn]	Another tenement called Gellylyog	Evan William Thos Prees	–	1	–
191	Thos Popkin esq.	Gellylyog Ycha	Thomas Harry	–	–	4

No.	Freeholders	Tenements	Tenants	Rent per Annum		
				£	s	d
192	Watkin Howel & his wife and Roger Howell	Tenement called Gellylyog	Richard Jenkin	–	1	8
193	Mr David Thomas & his wife	Cathelid Ycha	Lewis Howell ['Lewis David' in Bn]	–	1	3
194	The same	Tuy Llwydin	The same	–	–	8
195	Nehemiah Thos widow & Thos Popkin Esq ['Mr Arthur Davis & T.P.' in Bn]	Two tenements called Cathelid Genol & Cathelid	William Morgan & Hopkin Evan Yssha	–	1	4½
196	Geo. Ven. Vernon esq.	Keven Eithrim Ycha	William Hopkin	–	–	6
197	Robt. Morris Jones esq.	Pwllva Watkin	David Thos Bevan	–	–	6
198	Thos Popkin esq.	Lands at Trescyrch	Richard John	–	1	5
199	Robert Popkin esq. ['The same' in Bn]	Keven Gellyonnen	David John Jenkin	–	–	8
200	William Evan Hopkin	Keven Eithrim Yssha	John Hopkin David ['Phillip William' in Bn]	–	–	4
201	Thomas Phillip	Tenement called Tuy yn y pant	John Morgan	–	–	6
202	Gabriel Powell gent. ['Mr G.P.' in Bn]	Coed Kae Mawr	Griffith Simon ['John Richards' in Bn]	–	–	4
203	The Lord's Land	Bwlch y Gwybedin	Davd John & Willm David	–	–	2
204	Robt Morris Jones esq.	Nant y Gweene	Thomas Eynon	–	–	7
205	The same	Tyr bach, alias Penllwyn Vedwen	Rachel Lewis	–	–	6
206	Geo. Ven. Vernon esq. *[Folio 48/49]*	Llean Ycha	William David Eynon	–	–	4

Languick

No.	Freeholders	Tenements	Tenants			
207	George Ven. Vernon esq.	Ynis y medw Ycha	Maud Morgan	–	1	–
208	Mr Wm Shewen & Mr Jos. Shewen & wives	Two tenements called Prees Gellyllwk	Evan Thomas	–	1	–

No.	Freeholders	Tenements	Tenants	Rent per Annum		
				£	s	d
209	Richd Turberville esq.	Pen y Garne	William David	–	1	–
210	The same	Llwyn y Medw	Thomas Phillip	–	1	6
211	The same	Two tenements called Betting & Keven y Grych	Isaac John ['John Richard' in Bn]	–	1	8
212	James Gough Aubrey, clerk	Keven y Llan Ycha	David Gibbs	–	1	2
213	The same	Y Dderry	William Rees	–	–	4
214	The same	Another tenement called Y Ddery	Eliz. David, widow	–	–	3
215	The same	Brin y Granod	Watkin John ['William J.' in Bn]	–	–	3
216	The same	Tenement at Alltgreeg called Maesgunrig	Richard John	–	–	10
217	The same	Y Gilvach Goch	William Evan	–	–	4
218	The same	Clyn Gwin	Eynon Awbrey	–	–	4
219	The same	Tenement at Alltgreeg called Tyr Coed Kae Mawr	Richard John & Saml Llewellyn ['& Llewelyn Thomas' in Bn]	–	–	6
220	The same	Tuy Gwyn	Richard Jones	–	–	6
221	The same	Tenement at Alltgreeg	David Howell	–	–	8
222	The same	Tenement at Glan Twrch	William Williams	–	–	1½
223	The same	Tenement at Altgrug called Stallferry	David Prees	–	–	3
224	The same	Tenement there called Tyr y Funnon	Llewelyn Thomas	–	–	4
225	The same	Tenement there called Tyr Cwm Tawy	The same	–	–	6
226	The same	Tenement there called Stall y Ferry Yssha	Mary Thos Rowland	–	–	4
227	The same	Tenement there called Cwm Tawy	William Hopkin	–	–	6

No.	Freeholders	Tenements	Tenants	Rent per Annum £	s	d
228	The same	Two tenements there called Tyr yr Onnen	Lewelyn Thomas	–	1	–
229	The same	Pen y Wain	David Thomas ['William Rees' in Bn]	–	–	4
230	The same	Tenement at Alltgreeg called Pen y Wain	John Watkin	–	–	4
231	The same	Tenement there called Gilvach yr Haidd	William David	–	–	4
232	The same	Pant y Gwannyd	Thos William & Anne Watkin	–	–	6
233	The same	Betting Yssha	David Thomas	–	–	7
234	The same	Gellyvowy Vawr	David Hopkin	–	–	1
235	The same	Gellyvowy Vach	William Harry	–	–	1
236	The same	Cwm Nant Lliky	William Bowen	–	–	8
237	The same	Tenement at Alltgreeg called Llwyn y Kelin	Watkin John	–	–	4
238	The same	Ynismedw Yssha	Thomas John Jenkin	–	–	7
239	Gryffydd Pryce esq.	Gelly Gron	Robert Elias ['David Hopkin' in Bn]	–	–	4
240	The same	Tenement at Keven y Llan	Jennet Hopkin	–	–	6
241	The same	Alt y cham	Lewis William	–	1	–
242	Richard Jones	Crach llwyn	Jennett Harry, widow	–	1	6
243	Mr William Shewen & Joseph Shewen ['Mr J.S.' in Bn]	Ynis medw Genol	Jenkin Thomas	–	–	9
244	The same	Gellyvowy Genol	Grace Bowen, widow	–	–	5
245	Phillip Williams esq.	Tenement at Blanegel, called Court y Barrions	Owen Bowen	–	–	3

[Folio 49/50]

No.	Freeholders	Tenements	Tenants	Rent per Annum		
				£	s	d
246	The same	Tenement there called Blanegal	The same	–	–	3
247	The same	Another tenement there	The same	–	–	4
248	The same	Tenement there called Nant y Stavell	Rees John Morgan	–	–	8
249	The same	Tenement at Rhyd y Vro	Eliz. William alias Jenkin	–	–	3
250	The same	Llwyn y Pryfaid	David John	–	–	7
251	The same	Tyr y Gwrid Yssha alias Llwyn Gwin alias Pistyll Gwin	William Evan	–	–	3½
252	Catherine Rees widow ['Evan William' in Bn]	Pant y Gwrid Ycha ['His own possession' in Bn]	Isaac John	–	–	6
253	Maud Morgan, widow	Y Gwrid Yssha	John Timothy	–	–	4
254	Maud James, widow	Tyr y Gwrid Ycha alias Tuy yn y Pant	Morgan Jenkin	–	–	3½
255	David Bowen	Nant y Gasseg	Evan John	–	1	2
256	The same	Ynis y Gelynen alias y Garth	John Evan Hopkin	–	–	6
257	Mr Willm & Jos. Shewen	Tenement called Melin Rhyd y vro	Wm Rees Henry ['Jenkin William' in Bn]	–	–	6
258	Richd Turberville esq.	Tyr y Bont	James Jervis	–	–	4
259	Thos Pryce esq. ['Gryffydd P.' in Bn]	Tenements at Blaenegel	Thomas William	–	–	2
260	David Samuel (*Iur. ux.*)	Tenement there called Forch Egel	William Roger	–	–	8
261	Hopkin Lewelyn	Tenement there called Perth y Gwynnon	John Thomas	–	–	3
262	Mr William & Jos. Shewen	Two tenements there called Bogel Egel	Thomas William	–	1	3
263	Llewelyn Bevan	Garth Ycha	Thomas Richard	–	–	6

No.	Freeholders	Tenements	Tenants	Rent per Annum		
				£	s	d
264	Llewelyn Richard [L.R's. widow in Bn]	Godre Garth Yssha	His own possession ['Her ...' in Bn]	–	–	1
265	John Llewelyn	Godre Garth Ycha	William John	–	–	4
266	James Gough Awbrey, clerk	Tenement at Godre Garth Genol	Rees Richard Prees	–	–	4
267	The same	Gellyvarrog	Morgan Thomas	–	1	2
268	Phillip Williams esq.	Crach Llwyn	Phillip William	–	–	4
269	Thomas Phillip	Maes y ago	His own possession	–	1	–
270	James Gough Aubrey, clerk	Tenement called Melin Dwrch	John Gwillim	–	–	6
271	Richard Turberville esq. [Folio 50/51]	Ynis y Gellynen	James Jervis	–	–	4

Swansea Parish

No.	Freeholders	Tenements	Tenants	Rent per Annum		
272	Geo. Ven. Vernon esq.	Lands near Weeg Vach called Wain Avis	Mr Mansel ['John Thomas' in Bn]	–	–	2
273	Sir Thos Stepney, Bart.	Cregennith Vawr	William Mathew	–	1	8
274	Robert Popkin esq. ['Thos.P' in Bn]	Weeg Vach	John Hopkin William	–	–	6
275	Thos Price esq. ['Gryffydd P.' in Bn]	Penllwyn ayddon	Thomas Evan ['John Terry' in Bn]	–	1	9
276	The same	The Weeg alias Penllwynayddon Ycha	Thomas Benjamin	–	2	–
277	Mrs. Phillips	Llodrybryth	John Knoyle	–	2	–
278	Thos Popkin esq.	Tal y frewe	John William	–	–	6
279	Mrs. Phillips	Paradws Vach	William Richard	–	–	4
280	Mr William Roberts	Cregennith Yssha	William Harry	–	–	4
281	John David	Sketty Llwyd alias Brinkenol	John Harry	–	1	1

No.	Freeholders	Tenements	Tenants	Rent per Annum		
				£	s	d
282	Mr Gabriel Powell	Part of Brinmiskil called Pantgwin	David Harry	–	–	2
283	Mr Hugh Powell	Brynmiskill	His own possession	–	–	6
284	John Harry	Part of Brynmiskil-Caiewilw	His own possession	–	–	3
285	William Rosser (and 'Jno.lewis' in WGRO)	A tenement at lower Sketty	His own possession	–	1	–
286	Owen Morgan's widow	Y Weeg Vach	Her own possession	–	–	7
287	Thos John (*Iur. ux.*)	A tenement at Cockett	His own possession	–	1	–
288	Earl of Warwick	Lands at Weeg	Thomas Owen	–	–	6
289	Henry Simmonds ['Simons' in Bn]	Tyr y Bryn	His own possession ['Mr John Morgans' in Bn]	–	–	2
290	Thomas Price esq. ['Gryffydd P.' in Bn]	Tal y frewe Vach	Joseph Bowen	–	–	2
291	Mr Gabriel Powell	Hendrevoylan	John Evan ['William Rytherch' in Bn]	–	1	–

Landilotalybont

No.	Freeholders	Tenements	Tenants	Rent per Annum		
292	Lady Charlotte Edwin	Tuy yn y Coed	Samuel William	–	–	2
293	Geo. Venables Vernon esq.	Part of Bolgod Yssha	Wm Jenkin & Jno. Lewis	–	–	7
294	The same	Other part of Bolgod Yssha	Evan Morgan	–	–	6
295	Earl Talbot	Llwyn Court Howell	Richard William	–	–	3½
296	Catherine Walters, widow	Tenement called Priskedwin alias Tuy kenol	Thomas David	–	–	6
297	John Meyrick's widow	Tyn y Coed Yssha	Evan John	–	–	6
298	Mr Gamaliel Hughes	Tenement, near Mynnydd Lluw called Pen y Gelly	John Morgan	–	–	6
299	Walter Powell esq.	Drayn Pen y Gelly	John Mathew's widow	–	–	6

No.	Freeholders	Tenements	Tenants	Rent per Annum		
				£	s	d
300	The same	Tenement near Mynnydd Lluw	John Evan	–	–	6
301	The same	Tyr pen y Carn	Matthew David	–	–	4
302	The same	Tyr Pen y Twyn	Christopher Gregory	–	–	6
303	The same	Two tenements, Tyr Llwyn Gwin & Tyr y Bone	David Rees	–	1	4
304	William Hopkin	Tyr y Bedw	Thomas James	–	–	5
305	Mr William Lloyd	Twy yn y Coed	Mary Hopkins, widow	–	–	4
306	Mr Richard Price ['R.P. gent' in Bn]	Llwyn Evan Ddee	John Morgan	–	–	6
307	The same	Pistill Gwyn	David Hopkin	–	–	2
308	William John & his motherLodowick	Tyr Dan y Twyne	Griffith John	–	–	6

[Folio 51/52]

No.	Freeholders	Tenements	Tenants	Rent per Annum		
309	Howell David & his mother	Tenement near Pen y Twyn	Rees David	–	–	4
310	Mr Isaac Morgan	Gwern Sweedach	John Walter	–	–	3
311	Richard Walter	Tuy yn yr Heol	Morgan Morgan	–	–	11
312	Joseph Price esq.	Pen y Gelly	John Timothy	–	1	3
313	The same	Tyngharney	John Timothy	–	–	4
314	Catherine Thomas & Wm Llewelyn	Tuy yn y Box	Evan Powell	–	–	4
315	William Maddocks	Coed Bach	Richard Henry	–	–	4
316	Thos Rennett's widow	Two tenements at Ynis Loughor	Her own possession	–	–	8
317	Thos Morgan	Clyn y Veed	Morgan John	–	–	6
318	Thomas Botting (*Iur. ux.*) Morgan John and Thomas Morgan ['James B' etc. in Bn]	Lands at Landremore	Their own possession	–	1	–

No.	Freeholders	Tenements	Tenants	Rent per Annum		
				£	s	d
319	John David Hopkin	Two tenements called Pont y Chappell & Garn't ['& Garnett' in Bn]	John Hugh	–	1	–
320	Thos Popkin esq.	Cae Garrw, alias Kaer Pistill	Morgan John	–	–	2
321	Walter Powell esq. ['Griffith Thomas' in Bn]	Tal y Van Vawr	William David	–	–	4
322	The same	Lands called Llwyn Bean Goch	Christopher Gregory	–	–	6
323	Henry William	Bryn Arrad near Mynnydd Llyw	His own possession	–	–	3
324	Ruth Morris, widow	Tuy Gwyn	Anne John	–	–	4

[Folio 52/53]

Demesne Lands in Supraboscus

The Lord is intituled to the several Demesne tenements hereinafter mentioned within the said Manor of Gower Supraboscus:

Elinor Evans holds from year to year a tenement of lands called **Cwm Clydach**, situate in the Parish of Langevelach, at the yearly rent of three pounds and one shilling. It consists of the following particulars, to wit: a messuage, barn and stall, and the several closes following: Cae wrth y Tuy containing two covers[20] of arable land; Quarter Clyne, four covers; Traustir, two covers; Kae Pren, Hene Pren, three covers; Cae Newydd, two covers and a half; Cae Newydd Yssha, two covers; Cae Bach, two covers and a half; Caer Odin, one cover and a half; Cae Melin Vach, half a cover; Enherrag, two covers; Meadow Wern Vach Dan y Tuy, one cover of meadow; Croft y Gorse Vawr, one cover; Croften Vach by the river, one cover; two small pieces of rough ground; Twyn Mawr by the river, containing one cover of rough ground. The outward bounds of this tenement are: Clyn Eithrim Yssha on the west and south, Clyn Eithrim Ycha on the north, and the river on the east, ['and a small Piece on the east side of the River.' in Bn]

Improved yearly rent	£3	1	–

Thomas Pryce esq. holds by Lease dated the 24th November 1740 and granted to Thomas Popkin esq., his grandfather: All that water corn grist mill commonly called Clydach and known by the name of **Clydach Mill**, and all buildings, streams, mill ponds, waters, mill dams, flood-

---

20. A 'cover' in this area, was, from the evidence in the Survey, half a Welsh acre, so it approximated to one statute acre. From Welsh 'cyfar' – a portion of land. The term is also connected with communal ploughing. See *A Dictionary of the Welsh Language* (University of Wales, Cardiff, 1950 onwards).

gates, tolls, mulctures, profits and commodities whatsoever *[Folio 53/54]* to the said mill belonging or in any wise appertaining, situate and being in the Parish of Langevelach in the said County of Glamorgan. To hold to the said Thomas Popkin for the lives of Thomas Popkins gent. (since deceased), the said Thomas Price and Grace Lewis, the daughter of Gabriel Lewis late of Lanishen esq., deceased, and the life of the survivor of them. At and under the yearly rent of twenty shillings payable half yearly, to wit: at Lady Day and Michaelmas, clear of all deductions. Together with two fat pullets or one shilling in lieu thereof on St Thomas's Day yearly, a Heriot of five shillings on the decease of every tenant dying in possession of the said premises, and five shillings upon every Alienation or Assignment.

['The improved value about': but the words are in Bn only.]   £9   –   –

David John holds by Lease dated the 11th of February 1731 for the life of the said David John, Margaret his wife and William David his son, and the life of the survivor of them, at the yearly rent of eight pounds, payable half yearly, to wit: at Lady Day and Michaelmas, clear of all deductions; together with two fat pullets, or two shillings in lieu thereof, on St Thomas's Day yearly; a Heriot of ten shillings on the decease of every tenant dying in possession of the said premises; Suit of Court, or one shilling in lieu thereof, ten shillings upon every Alienation or Assignment, Suit of Mill, and Suit of Court, or one shilling in lieu thereof: All that messuage or tenement called or known by the names of **Bwlch y Gwybedin** and **Graig y Trebannoes**, situate in the Parish of Langevelach in the County of Glamorgan.

Graig y Trebannoes consists of a house, barn, stable, stall, and two gardens, and the several closes following: Caer Eithrim Mawr, containing ten covers; Caer Kerrig, two covers; Caer Bedw, four covers; Caer Crwn, five covers; Caer dan y Crwn by the river [Tawe] side, three covers; a small field called Carreg yr Avon, [on] the east side of the river. Kae Dan yr Heol above the river, three covers; Caer Odin, four covers; Kaer Skybor, four covers; a meadow on the hill, about 1¾ acres. And a large piece of waste containing about fifty acres. There is on the said waste a cott and garden which belongs to Roger Howell of Lanerch. There is also a cott and garden on the said tenement which is now let out by the tenant at the yearly rent of ten shillings. This tenement is bounded on the south by the lands of Herbert Mackworth esq. called *[blank]*; the river on the east; Bwlch y Gwebedin on the west; lands on the Graig – claimed by Thomas Phillip, Gryffydd ['Griffith' in Bn] Pryce esq. and Richard Turberville esq. – on the north. On this piece of waste Thomas Phillip claims from his hedge by the cottage in a line down to about the middle of the waste towards the east, Gryffydd Pryce claims from his hedge to Cwm Kenol, and Richard Turberville claims to the same, Cwm Kenol being on the south, and Ynis Medw is his boundary on the east and north. There is a gate kept by him on the north.

Bwlch y Gwybedin consists of a house and stable, and an old house some time since converted into a barn and beast house, and the several closes following: Arable – Kaer Fald, four covers; Caer Odin, four covers; Cae Mawr, eight covers; The Three Quarters, three covers; Kae Dan y Tuy, five covers; Crachllwyn four covers, on which there are a few scrubbed trees; Kaer Pant, two covers. Meadow: Gwain Crochlen Ycha, two acres; Gwain Genol, one acre and three quarters; Cwm-bach, two covers; half an acre on the south side of a meadow called Wain y Carreg, alias *[Folio 54/55]* Enherrag Carreg, between the part of Herbert Mackworth esq. and Robert ['Thomas' in Bn]

Popkin esq. Mr Popkin's share of this meadow has a gutter on the south, three stones to the east, [and] the hedge on the north and west. Mr Mackworth has a narrow strip adjoining Mr Popkin's part, having the gutter on the north, a bush of scrubbed oaks on the east, and – in a line to the west between two stones lying a yard asunder – to the hedge on the west. The rest of the meadow is the Duke's; and half an acre of meadow called Wain Vach Dan y Tuy. This tenement is bounded by the lands of Herbert Mackworth esq. called Gellyonnen Yssha on the south, the Graig on the east and the mountain called Gellyonnen on all other parts thereof. There are a few young oaks and ashes growing on the tenement.

And the improved yearly value of this tenement and Graig Trebannoes may amount to   £14   –   –

William Hopkin holds by Lease dated 16th of August 1740: All that messuage and tenement called **Cwm y Gorse**, situate and being in the Parish of Langevelach. To hold to the said William Hopkin for the lives of the said William Hopkin, luce, his wife, and Jennet Hopkin, his daughter, and the life of the survivor of them. At and under the yearly rent of three pounds payable half yearly, clear of all deductions, to wit: at Lady Day and Michaelmas. One couple of fat pullets, or a shilling in lieu thereof. Five shillings on the decease of every tenant dying in possession. Five shillings upon every Assignment or Alienation, and doing Suit of Mill and Suit of Court, on pain of two shillings and six pence for every default. It consists of a house, stall and barn, and the several closes following:

			Acres.	Qrs.
Henga, a rushy Piece of Ground, about 5 covers			2	2
Arable lands	Kae Kenol	four covers	2	0
Kae Quar	four covers		2	–
Kae Yssha	four covers		2	–
Kae Bach	two covers		1	–
Meadow Wain Dan Tuy	one acre and a half		1	2
Gwerlled Ycha	one acre and a half		1	2
& Gwerlled Yssha	Wain Yssha	four acres	4	–
			16	2

There are about ten oaks on this tenement. It is bounded on the south by Nant y Gavila, on the east by the river dividing it from Kaegurwen, on the west by Mynnydd Ycha, on the north the boundary between this County and Carmarthenshire.

The improved yearly value of this tenement may amount to   £7   –   –

[Folio 55/56]

William Penry holds by Lease dated the 6th day of December 1755, all that messuage or tenement of lands with the appurtenances called **Gellywren Ycha**, situate and being in the Parish of Langefelach. To hold to the said William Penry for and during his natural life, the lives of Catherine, his wife and Richard Penry, son of Thomas Penry of the Parish of Langevelach aforesaid, and the life of the survivor of them. At and under the yearly rent of ten pounds, payable half yearly on every 25th day of March and 29th September, clear of all repairs and deductions whatsoever. Two fat pullets, or one shilling in lieu thereof, on the Feast of St Thomas yearly. The sum of five shillings in lieu of a Heriot upon the decease of every tenant dying in possession, and also the sum of five shillings upon every Assignment or Alienation, and doing Suit of Mill and Suit of Court, upon pain of five shillings for every default.

It consists of a house, barn, stables and stalls, and the several closes following, to wit: Two meadows called Gwain Gwair, containing four acres and a half, with several young trees growing thereon, the greatest part thereof meadow ground, and some patches arable; a close called Forrest Clovers, twelve covers of arable land and two covers meadow; a coarse piece of ground called Forrest Robbin, containing one acre and a quarter; another piece of wet ground called Forrest John David, now divided into two parcels, containing three acres; a coarse boggy piece of ground called Forrest Pobbill, containing ten acres; a meadow called Gwain Newydd, containing one acre and three quarters, and half an acre of arable; Coed Kae Newydd, a rough piece of ground [containing] three acres; Coed Kae Havod, a rough piece of ground containing two acres; Coedkae Bach, one acre of wood; Coed Ivor, about four acres of timber; Cae Coed Ivor, three covers arable; Gwain Coed Ivor, three acres and a half; Gwain Dan y Tuy, containing five acres and a half, the hay of one acre of which meadow belongs to Henry William of Gellywran Genol, about which there is a landshare mark on all sides, except on the south-west where a parcel of wood joins it; Kae Coed Kae, containing two acres of arable ground; Cae Garw Ycha, four acres arable; Kae Davatty, four acres arable; Cae Garw Yssha, three acres arable; Kae Funnon Wernos, one acre and a quarter arable; Kae Skibor, two acres arable; Kae Dryscol, three acres arable; Kae Berkin, two acres arable; Kaer odin, one acre arable.

This tenement is bounded on the east by the lands of Thomas Popkin esq. called Gellyvethan, and the lane called Heol Tyleddee, on the south by Keven y Forrest, on the west by part of Gellywran Yssha and Gellywran Genol, and on the north by part of Kilvane and Gelly Vethan. There is also a piece of land on the east of Heol Tyle ddee, called Forrest Vach, containing four covers and a half of meadow, and one cover and a half of arable ground, on which the tenant has lately built a new house.

The improved yearly value of this tenement may amount to £30*[sic]* – –

Isaac Morgan holds by a Lease dated 7th of October in the sixth year of the Reign of her late Majesty Queen Anne *[1707]*: All that piece or parcel of coarse land known by the name of **Henclawdd**, containing by estimation two acres, situate and being in the Parish of Langevelach in the said County. To hold to the said Isaac Morgan for the term of four score and nineteen years if the said Isaac Morgan, Elizabeth his wife, and Roger Morgan their son or either of them shall so long live, at and under the yearly rent of five shillings payable half yearly at Lady Day and Michaelmas. The sum of five shillings *[Folio 56/57]* in lieu of a Heriot on the decease of every tenant dying in possession, and doing Suit of Court and Suit of Mill, and doing Services with oxen and horses when required.

It consists of two closes of pasture and rough ground, having the Commons called Mynnydd Puscodlyn on the north, the Common called Cwmdylais on the west, the lands of the late Owen Bevan called Skiach on the south, and the lands of the said Owen Bevan and Isaac Morgan on the east

The improved yearly value may amount to £1 – –

Thomas Lewis and John Morse, gentlemen, have by Lease dated the *[blank]* day of *[blank]* 1755, full power, liberty and authority for them, their Executors, Administrators and Assigns, to erect and make in upon and across all that brook, stream and current of water situate lying and being in the Parish of Langefelach commonly called and known by the name of **Clydach Yssha**, a certain **wear** of the height of one foot, and no more, for diverting and conveying of the same to and for the use of and working of a certain **iron battery** of the said Thomas Lewis and John Morse, erected on a certain tenement of lands of Herbert Mackworth esq., called Ithrim Yssha, situate in the Parish of Langevelach. In the doing whereof no prejudice, hinderance, or obstruction, is to be done to the Lord's water grist mill called Clydach Mill, [and] saving to the Lord, his Heirs and Assigns, the fishery thereof.

To hold to the said Thomas Lewis and John Morse for the term of twenty-one years at and under the yearly rent of two pounds, payable half yearly at Lady Day and Michaelmas, clear of all deductions.   £2   –   –

William David Eynon holds a cottage near **Clydach Bridge** in the Parish of
Langevelach, at the yearly rent of   £1 *[sic]* –   –

David Hopkin holds a cottage near **Clydach Bridge** in the Parish of
Langevelach, at the yearly rent of   £–   2   –

Geo. Venables Vernon esq. holds a cot garden and croft at **Keven y Park**
in the Parish of Langevelach, at the yearly rent of   £–   2   –

Mary, the wife of Mathew Price esq., and Thomas Price esq, her son, Executors of Thomas Popkin esq., deceased, have, by Lease dated the first day of August 1732 granted to the said Thomas Popkin, liberty for the erecting **a bridge over the River Tawy near Forrest House**. And to fish and erect wears for fishing in the said river, to burn lime in a limekiln encroached by the said Thomas Popkin on his Grace's wastes called Trewyddva Forrest, and to cut furze on Trewyddva Forrest, otherwise Graig Trewyddva. [And] for carrying of coals or other carriages over the said Common or waste called Trewyddva, or any other the Duke's Commons or wastes within the Lordship Royal of Gower, *[Folio 57/58]* and for diverting the water to the use of the **copperworks**. To hold to the said Thomas Popkin, his Executors, Administrators and Assigns, for the term of ninety-nine years if the said Thomas Popkin, Robert Popkin his son and Thomas Popkin<u>s</u>, son of the said Robert, or any of them, shall so long live. At and under the yearly rent of ten shillings payable on Michaelmas Day yearly.   £–   10   –

George Venables Vernon esq. holds a cot garden and three crofts at **Gellywast<u>o</u>d**
in the Parish of Llangevelach at the yearly rent of   £–   2   6

Phillip John Jones holds two gardens at **Gellywast<u>e</u>d** at the yearly rent of   £–   1   –

The same holds part of a garden at **Pen y Vedow** at the yearly rent of   £–   –   6

Leyson Morgan holds a potato garden on **Mynnydd Cadle** at the yearly rent of   £–   1   –

The same holds a piece of ground there containing *[blank]* at the yearly rent of £– 5 –

David Richard holds a cott garden and croft at **Gellygwm** in the Parish of Langevelach at the yearly rent of £– 4 –

Evan Llewelyn holds a garden and croft on **Graig Vawr** at the yearly rent of £– – 6

Thomas Price esq. holds a cot and croft on **Graig Vawr** at the yearly rent of £– 3 6

Rytherch Jenkin holds a cot garden and croft at **Gellygwm** in theParish of Langevelach at the yearly rent of £– – 6

David John holds a cot and garden and two crofts at **Gellygwm** in the Parish of Llangevelach at the yearly rent of £– 1 –

David Morgan Lewis and Thomas Jones have liberty of making a pond and a watercourse to a **furze mill at Skiach**, at the yearly rent of £– – 6

John William holds a cott and garden at **Gorse Eynon** in the Parish of Langevelach at the yearly rent of £– 2 –

Jane George lately held a cott and garden there (now vacant) £– – –

Thomas Price esq. holds a **pond on Mynnydd Carn Goch** at the yearly rent of £– – 6

Rees David holds a cott and garden at **Gorse Eynon** at [the] yearly rent of £– 4 –

Sarah Prichard, infant, holds a small garden on **Mynnydd Carn Goch** at the yearly rent of £– – 1
[Folio 58/59]

John George holds a cott and garden at **Gorse Eynon** in the Parish of Langevelach at the yearly rent of £– 2 –

William Powell esq. holds three pieces of waste land near **Pen y vilia** at the yearly rent of £– 5 –

Thomas Price lately held a small garden on **Mynnydd Carn Goch** (now laid open) £– – –

Thomas Richards holds a cot garden and croft at **Godre Garth** at the yearly rent of £– – 6

Richard John and William Roger lately held a piece of waste ground in **Cwm Egel** in the Parish of Languick (since laid open) *[blank]*

[Folio 59/60]

Borough and Manor of Swansea

This Borough is a Corporation by Prescription, consisting of a Portreeve, Aldermen and Burgesses, and is supposed to be very ancient; there being no Charter of Creation extant; but they have Charters of Privileges and confirmation as far back as Henry the 3rd. It is within and held of the Seigniory, and His Grace the Duke of Beaufort is the immediate Lord of it, and intituled to all Rights and Royal Jurisdictions in and over it.

The general boundaries are: the River Tawy, from the mouth of the Brook called Nant Bwrla near the old copperworks to the sea, on the east; the sea from the mouth of the River Tawy to Brinmill Water (anciently called St David's Ditch) on the south; the brook running by Brinmill quite from the sea to the spring head near the Cocket on the west. And thence to the house of John Thomas situate on the boundary. You enter the house door and turn through the stall or beast house[21] to the inclosure adjoining the Common called the Town Hill, and along the ditch of the inclosures to the road or lane leading to Weeg. And thence, still keeping along the inclosures till you come to a meadow lying south-west of Weig Vawr house. You there cross the meadow to the house, which lying on the boundary, go in at the door and out through a window of the house into the garden. And then turning eastward, keep on a slant through another meadow lying on the south-east of the house to the Hill, then along the brook of water called Nant Bwrla to the River Tawy on the north.

The Portreeve is an Annual Officer elected every Michaelmas Day. The method, according to ancient usage, of electing the new Portreeve is: the old Portreeve convenes the Aldermen on Michaelmas Eve at such house as he appoints, when four Aldermen are by ballot to be put in nomination, who are the next day returned to the Burgesses met for that purpose in the Guild Hall of the said Borough. Who elect two out of the said four, which two are to be returned and presented to the Lord's Steward, who is to swear in one of them. If any Portreeve should be sick, or absent so that he is not able to attend the business and the Courts of the Borough, he may by Custom appoint a Deputy who is to act for him. Or if the Portreeve die, a new one is to be immediately chosen. The senior Alderman residing within the Borough is to convene his brethren and the Burgesses, and then proceed as above.

The Aldermen are elected out of the Burgesses, the manner of which is for the Aldermen, at a meeting appointed by the Portreeve, to choose two of the Burgesses who are to be returned to the Steward, one of which he swears.

The Burgesses are elected in the following manner: At a Hall Day or Public Meeting of the Burgesses appointed by the Portreeve at the Guild Hall, the names of the persons desiring to be Burgesses are brought in and presented to the Portreeve by one of the Common Attorneys or one of the Burgesses, at the same time setting forth his claim or right. If [he is] a Burgess's son or

---

21. This description suggests that the building was a longhouse.

having served an apprenticeship to a Burgess, he is allowed by the Burgesses, paying five shillings to the use of the Corporation. If having married a Burgess's daughter, then paying thirty shillings, and if not intituled by either of these rights, then such sum as the Burgesses think proper (usually £3). And after being thus allowed, their names are entered in the Corporation Book as fit persons to be admitted. Their names are then given in by the Common Attorneys to the Jury at the Leet Court, who present them to the Steward and Portreeve who are to swear them.

The **Common Attorneys** are Officers of the Corporation. They are elected yearly on Michaelmas Day, the Burgesses returning four of their own body to the Steward and Portreeve, who appoint and swear in two of them. Their business is to attend the Portreeve on all public occasions, to collect all the Corporation rents and dues, and to disburse what sums are necessary for the uses of the Corporation, by the Orders of the Burgesses assembled, or of the Portreeve.

The **Serjeants at Mace** are also Officers of the Corporation, who are in like manner elected annually on Michaelmas Day, the Burgesses returning four of their own body to the Steward and Portreeve, who appoint and swear in two of them. Their Duty is to be attendant on the Portreeve *[Folio 60/61]* and constantly to attend the Borough Courts, and to execute all the Warrants and Processes issued out of the Courts, and make due return of them, and to take care of the common pound.

The **Haywards** are also annual Officers. The Jury at Easter Leet present four Burgesses for the Burroughs and four for the Hill, of which the Steward and Portreeve choose and swear in two for each. Their business is to take care that no trespass be done on the Burroughs and Hill, and to see that no persons turn any cattle to graze there except the Burgesses. But an Act having ['lately' in Bn] passed the last Sessions of Parliament for dividing and inclosing them, when that is done these Officers will become useless.

The **Learkeeper** is an annual Officer. The Jury at Easter Leets present two Burgesses to the Steward and Portreeve who appoint and swear in one. His duty is to take care of the navigation of the bar and river, to see that no ballast or other offensive matter be thrown into the river, and that all nuisances or whatsoever might be prejudicial or inconvenient to the ships should be removed.

The **Crier** is appointed by the Steward. He attends all the Courts which are held within the Borough, and proclaims everything within the Town.

The **Constables** are six within the Town, and two within the Franchise – one for each Division. They are appointed and sworn at Michaelmas Leet yearly.

These are held yearly within the Borough two general **Leet and Baron Courts**, before the Steward and Portreeve within a month of Michaelmas and Easter. These are appointed by Warrant under the hand and seal of the Steward, directed to the Serjeants at Mace who are to give notice of the Courts and return the Juries. There are also Courts of Pleas and Baron Courts held every three weeks on Monday by Adjournments, before the Steward and Portreeve, in which

The old Carmarthen Arms, at the corner of Castle Bailey Street and College Street, Swansea (see opposite page).
Photograph by Calvert Richard Jones, c.1845.

Swansea from the west in 1783, by Lieut. William Booth. Note the towers of the castle and the church.
The foreground house is St Helen's, near modern Brynymor Road. The fields were built over from 1830 onwards.

all manner of actions are brought and tried, arising within the Borough and Franchise. The time of holding the Leet and Baron Courts of the Borough as well as the Leet and Baron Courts for the Seigniory and the other Manors belonging to the Duke of Beaufort are usually proclaimed in the Town of Swansea on a Market Day, at least eight days before the holding of them.

Swansea is one of the Contributory Boroughs and joins with the Burgesses of Cardiff, Cowbridge, Lantrissent, Kenfig, Aberavon, Neath, and Loughor in electing a Burgess or **Representative in Parliament** for Cardiff. The method is: as soon as the Bailiffs of Cardiff have received a Precept from the Sheriff, they send their Precept directed to the Portreeve and Burgesses of each of the said Boroughs, requiring their attendance at a particular time specified, to join with them in the election: and the indenture has eight columns under it, one for the Burgesses of each Borough to sign in.

The Lord is intitutled to several rents within the Borough and Franchise

The Portreeve pays a Fee Farm or Quit Rent of £18 1 6 for the **Burgage Rents, Assise of Ale, the Toll, Pitching of Fairs and Markets,** and **Keelage of Ships and Vessels.**

David Jones holds the **Ferry Boat and House** from year to year, at the yearly rent of fourteen pounds a year.

[Folio 61/62]

Mary Phillips holds a messuage, stable and garden, situate in Castle Baily Street in the Town of Swansea, called the **Carmarthen Arms**, together with one close or parcel of land called Harbinger's Acre, containing about two acres, situate in the Franchise of Swansea. Which field is bounded or meared by the highway leading to Pantgwidire on the north and the lands of Messrs Hurst and Jones on all other sides thereof, at the yearly rent of £13 – –

William Walter holds a house and garden, situate in **Castle Baily Street**, from year to year at the yearly rent of £2 2 –

John Thomas holds a house in **higher Town Street**, from year to year at the yearly rent of £1 15 –

Thomas Hopkin holds a house in the same street, at the yearly rent of £1 15 –

John Jones holds a house in the same street, from year to year at the yearly rent of £3 5 –

David Lewis holds a house in the same street, from year to year at the yearly rent of £2 5 –

Jane Harry holds a house in the same street, from year to year
at the yearly rent of   £1   15   —

William Jones holds a smith's forge under **the Postern**, from
year to year at the yearly rent of   £–   10   —

Robert Morris esq. holds by Lease dated the 14th of February 1735, all that water corn grist
mill, commonly called **Green Hill Mill**, situate in the Franchise of the Town of Swansea, together
with all waters, watercourses, dams, ponds, floodgates, ways, privileges, and advantages thereunto
belonging. To hold to the said Robert Morris and his heirs for and during the lives of Bridget,
Margaret, and Mary, three of the daughters of the said Robert Morris, and the life of the survivor
of them. At and under the yearly rent of forty shillings, payable half yearly by even and equal
portions at Lady Day and Michaelmas, clear of all deductions. Two fat pullets or one shilling on
St Thomas's Day[22]. The sum of five shillings in lieu of a Heriot on the decease of every tenant
dying in possession. The sum of five shillings upon every Assignment or Alienation, and doing
Suit of Court on pain of 3s 4d for every default.

The improved yearly value of this mill may amount to   £20   —   —

[Folio 61/62]

Rachael Cooper holds by Lease dated 20th of December 1734, all that messuage or mansion
house situate, lying and being in a certain street called **High Street below the Gate**, together
with all outhouses, stables, stalls, courts, curtilages, gardens, passages, ways, waters, watercourses,
lights, commodities, privileges, easements and appurtenances to the said messuage belonging, or
in any wise appertaining. To hold to the said Rachael Cooper for and during the term of the
natural lives of the said Rachael Cooper, Rachael her daughter, and Simon Price, son of Aaron
Price of the Town of Swansea, joiner, and the life of the survivor of them. At and under the yearly
rent of two shillings, payable half yearly at Lady Day and Michaelmas by equal portions clear of
all deductions, together with two fat pullets, or one shilling, on St Thomas's Day yearly. And the
sum of five shillings for and in the name of a Heriot on the decease of every tenant dying in possession. And the sum of five shillings upon every Assignment or Alienation, [and] doing Suit of
Mill and Suit of Court upon pain of three shillings and four pence for every default.

The improved value of the messuage and garden may amount to   £10   —   —

Simon Llewelyn and Susanna his wife, the daughter of David Davies deceased, holds by Lease
dated the 20th day of July 1736 and granted to the said David Davies, all that water corn grist
mill and dwelling house thereto adjoining, called and known by the name of the **higher Brinmill**
And also all that water corn grist mill and dwelling house thereto adjoining, called by the name

---

22. 21st December.

of the **lower Brinmill**. All which said premises are situate and being within the Franchise of the said Town of Swansea, together with all ways, waters, watercourses, mill streams, ponds, dams, floodgates and appurtenances to the said mills belonging, or in any wise appertaining. To hold to the said David Davies for and during the natural lives of the said David Davies, Susannah Davies his daughter, and the said Simon Llewelyn, and the life of the survivor of them. At and under the yearly rent of £10 11 8, payable half-yearly, to wit: at Lady Day and Michaelmas by even and equal portions clear of all deductions whatever, together with two fat pullets, or one shilling in lieu thereof, on St Thomas's Day yearly. The sum of five shillings in the name of a Heriot on the decease of every tenant dying in possession, and the sum of five shillings for every Assignment or Alienation. And doing Suit of Court, upon pain of three shillings and four pence for every default.

The improved yearly value of these mills may amount to   £20   —   —

Elizabeth Evans, spinster, holds by Lease dated the 20th December 1734 and granted to Anne Dawkins, widow, her sister since deceased, all that messuage or mansion house, situate and being in a certain street called **Cross Street**, adjoining to the east side of the Church Yard in the Town of Swansea, together with all passages, ways, easements and appurtenances to the said messuage belonging or in any wise appertaining. To hold unto the said Anne Dawkins and her heirs for the lives of the said Anne Dawkin, Catherine Evans her mother and the said Elizabeth Evans, and the life of the survivor of them (of which lives the said Elizabeth is the only surviving one). *[Folio 62/63]* At and under the yearly rent of one shilling, payable upon the Feasts of the Annunciation of the Blessed Virgin Mary, and Saint Michael the Archangel, by even and equal portions clear of all deductions, together with two fat pullets, or one shilling in lieu thereof on St Thomas's Day yearly. The sum of five shillings in the name of a Heriot on the decease of every tenant dying in possession, and the sum of five shillings upon every Assignment or Alienation. And doing Suit of Mill and Suit of Court, upon pain of three shillings and four pence for every default.

The improved yearly value of this messuage amounts to   £5   —   —

James Griffiths of the Town of Swansea gent. holds ['lately deceased held' in Bn] by Lease dated the 20th of December 1734, all that messuage or mansion house situate and being upon the **Strand** adjoining to the east side of the Castle[23] in the said Town of Swansea, together with all and singular outhouses, stables, stalls, courts, curtilages, gardens, passages, ways, easements and appurtenances to the said messuage or mansion house belonging, or in any wise appertaining. To hold to the said James Griffith and his heirs from the Feast of Saint Michael then last past for the term of the natural lives of Hester, the wife, and James and William, the sons, of the said James Griffiths, and the life natural of the survivor of them. At and under the yearly rent of one shilling payable at Lady Day and Michaelmas yearly, by even and equal portions clear of all deductions, together with two fat pullets, or one shilling in lieu thereof, upon St Thomas's Day yearly. And also the

---

23. This house is well-shown in the Buck brothers' 'East View of Swansea', 1748.

Detail from the Buck brothers' 'East View of Swansea', 1748. The large house touching the castle is James Griffiths'. The small tower with its pyramid roof is the summer house in the Castle Gardens. See opposite page.

Swansea Castle. In 1750 it was leased for use as the town's poor-house. See opposite page.

sum of five shillings in lieu of a Heriot upon the decease of every tenant dying in possession. And also the sum of five shillings upon every Assignment or Alienation, and doing Suit of Mill and Suit of Court, upon pain of three shillings and four pence for every default.

> *[Added note, in Sa only:]* This lease is lately expired and is now let out at the clear
> yearly rent of   £6   –   –

The Churchwardens and Overseers of the Poor of the Town of Swansea for the time being, hold by Lease dated 22nd of October 1750, and granted to Gabriel Powell and John France, gen[tlemen], then Churchwardens, and Edward Westley and John Gwyther, Overseers of the Poor: all that **the Castle of Swansey**, together with all and singular the rights, members and appurtenances thereof. To hold unto the said Gabriel Powell and John France, Edward Westley and John Gwyther, their Executors, Administrators and Assigns, for the use of the inhabitants of the Town of Swansea, from the 29th of September then last past, for the term of forty-two years thence next ensuing. At and under the yearly rent of five pounds and nine shillings, payable at Lady Day and Michaelmas yearly, by even and equal portions without any deduction whatsoever, together with two fat pullets, or one shilling in lieu thereof, on the Feast of St Thomas the Apostle yearly.   £5   9   –

[Folio 63/64]

George Venables Vernon esq. held by lease which expired at Lady Day 1762, and now holds from year to year, all those two gardens called the **Castle Gardens**, and the summer house thereto belonging, having the back court belonging to the dwelling house in the possession of Sir Edward Mansel and the garden of William Hurst and Calvert Richard Jones esqs. on the west, the new Postern on the south, the Strand towards the east and the old Postern on the north.
£2   2   –

Henry Mackordy holds from year to year a house and garden under the new Postern, at the yearly rent of   £3   –   –

Robert Morris esq. holds from year to year a ballast bank, having the river on the east, the building bank in possession of Henry Squire on the south, the Strand on the west and the building bank in the possession of Thomas Maddocks, shipwright, on the north.   £–   10   –

Hopkin Walters of the Town of Swansea holds by lease granted to Hopkin Walters, his father, [dated] 19th October 1754, all that messuage or dwelling house situate in the Town of Swansea in a certain street there called **Castle Baily Street**. To hold to the said Hopkin Walters, deceased, for the term of the natural lives of him, the said Hopkin Walters, Sarah his wife (both since deceased) and the said Hopkin Walters, their son, and the survivor of them. At and under the yearly rent of one shilling, payable at Lady Day and Michaelmas by even and equal portions without any deduction whatsoever, together with two pullets, or six pence in lieu thereof, on the Feast of St Thomas the Apostle yearly. And the sum of five shillings in the name of a Heriot upon the decease of every tenant dying in possession. And also the sum of five shillings upon every Assignment or Alienation. Doing Suit of Mill and Suit of Court, upon pain of three shillings and four pence for every default.

The same Hopkin Walters, deceased, had for the building of the said house ten ton of timber and a few feet more at 32s per ton, and was by agreement to pay interest for the same during the continuance of the lease, at the rate of five per cent, and therefore pays for the same the yearly rent or sum of 16s 3d.

The improved yearly value of the above premises may be about   £6   —   —

Mr John Flemming of Swansea, mariner, holds by virtue of a lease or grant bearing date the first day of July 1735, granted to William Watkins of the Town of Swansea, gentleman, a ground plot or parcel of waste ground lying on the east side of the curtilage belonging to the then freehold dwelling house of the said William Watkins in **Castle Baily Street** in Swansea aforesaid (which house is since purchased by the said John Flemming). In measure from the court wall there of the said house, to the corner of the stable there, being five feet and four inches, and thirteen feet the other way, and leading from the said curtilage down to the Strand in Swansea aforesaid. With liberty for conveying all waters and watercourses, under ground or otherwise, from the said curtilage down to the Strand in Swansea aforesaid. To hold unto the said William Watkins for the term of 99 years, at and under the yearly rent of one penny, payable on the First day of July yearly.

[The following paragraph appears only in Bn.]

Gabriel Powell gent. holds by Lease dated the 26th of March 1753, all that parcel of land called the **Orchard Close**, for 21 years at the yearly rent of £5 payable at Lady Day and Michaelmas, [with] Suit of Court and Suit of Mill. This field contains 6 acres, of which Messrs. Hurst and Calvert Richard Jones claim one, and are paid a yearly rent of 16s 8d for it, but in what part of the field this acre lies is not known.

The improved value may be about   £7   10   —

[Folio 64/65]

Borough and Manor of Loughor

This is also a Corporation by Prescription, having no Grant, Charter or any other proof in writing of their creation or privileges. It is constituted of a Portreeve, Aldermen, and Burgesses, and is one of the Contributory Boroughs joining with the others in electing a **Representative to serve in Parliament** for Cardiff.

This Borough is thought to be very ancient and to be the Leucarum mentioned in Caesar's Commentaries. It lies within and is held of the Seigniory of Gower, and the Duke of Beaufort is immediate Lord of it, and has the same Royal Jurisdiction over this Borough as over the rest of the Seigniory.

The general boundaries are: Beginning at the ferry opposite the church, up along the middle of the river where ever it runs, to the mouth of the Island Pill Then turning east up the middle of the pill to Pentre Bach, and then along the brook to the road or way that leads to Pentre Bach House, keeping the garden on the south or right hand, till just at the upper end cross-slanting to an oak growing by the brook side. Then along the brook to the Common or moor called Loughor Moor, and along the gripe or ditch of the inclosures to the corner at Tavern y Piod, and thence to a large grey stone on the Common. And then [in] near a direct line east to another grey stone on the Common, and thence keeping east to another grey stone on the Common, near Wain y Gorse Ditch. Thence along the ditch between Wain y Gorse and Gorse Velin, leaving Rheed y Pollon on the south, and so along the ditch at the bottom of Gorse Velin to Llyw River. Then across the river to Wain y Trap, and round the upper part of Wain y Trap, then cross over to the road and crossing the road to Caer Bont, and round the east and south sides of Caer Bont to the River Llyw. And along the river down to the marsh, there crossing Morva Glasse to Wain Trebinog, and round Wain Trebinog to Morva Shewy. And thence to Morva Arllwydd, and thence to Cobbs Bridge, and along the river called Llyw Itha till you cross it to Morva Llyw. And then along a pill or ditch just under the inclosures to a little stone bridge at the mouth of Berthllwyd Lane. Then turning west along Sluice Pill to Loughor River, leaving the coal bank to the north on the right hand. And so up along the middle of Loughor River to the ferry, where the boundary was begun.

The Portreeve is an Annual Officer appointed at the Michaelmas Leet Court, the Jury presenting two of the Aldermen to the Steward who swears in one of them.

The Aldermen are chosen out of the Burgesses, the Jury at either of the Leet Courts, upon a vacancy, presenting the names of two Burgesses to the Steward. He appoints and swears in one.

The Burgesses are chosen in the following manner: the Jury at either of the Leet Courts present the names of such persons as they think proper to the Steward, who is to admit and swear them. They are generally persons who have Estates within the Borough, Burgesses' sons, [those] who have married Burgesses' daughters, or [those who] have served apprenticeships within the Borough.

There are two **Serjeants at Mace** chosen yearly at Michaelmas Leet, the Jury presenting the names of four of the Burgesses, of whom the Steward appoints and swears in two.

There are also two **Constables** appointed at every Michaelmas Leet Court for the Borough.

[Folio 65/66]

There are **Heywards** appointed and sworn every May Leet for the Moor and Marsh, the Jury presenting the names of two of the Burgesses for each, of whom the Steward appoints and swears in one for the Moor and another for the Marsh.

There is at Michaelmas Leet yearly a **Learkeeper** appointed and sworn, the Jury presenting two of the Burgesses to the Steward who is to swear in one.

There is also appointed at Michaelmas Leet yearly an Officer called an **Aletaster**, who is appointed and sworn in the same manner. He is in the nature of a Clerk of the Market. His business is to see that no unwholesome meat or drink be sold within the Borough and to examine the weights and measures.

There are held within the Borough yearly, within a month of Easter and a month of Michaelmas, **Leet Courts, Courts of Pleas and Baron Courts**, before the Steward and Portreeve. And great care should be taken to keep the Leet Courts regular, especially that at Michaelmas, for as all the Officers are by the custom to be appointed yearly at that Court, if it should be neglected but one year, the Borough will be lost.

At the Court of Pleas all manner of Actions may be brought, and for any sum, and though it is generally held but twice a year at the time of the Leet Courts, yet it may, as well as the Baron Court, be held oftener. But as there are but few inhabitants and no trade, the holding of Courts twice a year is sufficient for the business.

There is one Fair held annually within this Borough on old Michaelmas Day[24]. And they have lately proclaimed another to be held yearly on the first Monday in June, but there are no Markets. The Toll and Pitching at the Fairs as well the Keelage and Moorage of ships are received by the Portreeve, for which he pays the Lord yearly at Michaelmas ten shillings.

The Portreeve receives the Burgage Rents, [and] the Rent for the Castle and Marsh, for which he pays the Lord at Michaelmas yearly the rent of two pounds sixteen shillings and sixpence.

There is within the Borough a large Common called Loughor Moor, situate on the north and east sides of the Borough, on which the Burgesses and inhabitants claim a right of Common without number, but the soil and all mines, minerals and quarries of stone and slate belong to the Lord. There are under it some mines of coal, which are held by Miss Anne Mackworth. There is also another large Common called Loughor Marsh, which lies on the south side of the Borough. It is, on spring tides, overflown. The Burgesses and inhabitants intercommon on this, but pay the Lord an annual rent of 5s 4½ for [it], which is collected by the Portreeve and included in the above rent of £2. 16. 6.

[Folio 66/67]

---

24. i.e. the day on which 29th September would have fallen, prior to the 'loss' of eleven days in the calendar adjustment made on 3rd September 1752. So 'old Michaelmas' was 10th October 'new style'.

A Rent Roll of the Burgage & Marsh & Moor Rent
within the Borough of Loughor

No.	Freeholders Names	Tenements	Tenants	Rents per Annum		
				£	s	d
1	Thos Popkin esq. & Mr Robt Whitta	Pen y Bayley		–	4	9
2	Thos Popkin esq.	Vernel Yssha		–	5	–
3	Miss Anne Mackworth	Sanctuary		–	7	2
4	Mr John Dawkins	Coedbridwen		–	5	–
5	Richard David			–	2	–
6	Hugh Morgan Rees	Tyr Chas. Bowen		–	4	2
7	Owen William, Rees Thomas, & Lemuel Allen	Penseallan		–	1	7
8	Elizabeth Richards, infant	Tyr Wrie & other land		–	4	2
9	John Thomas	Lands in the upper Town, late David Leyson's		–	1	–
10	Phillip Bevan	Vernhill ycha		–	1	–
11	Mr Gamaliel Hughes			–	–	6
12	Thos Bonnor, late Mrs. Watkins	Pen Suallan [?] ycha & Catherine Jacobs Cott		–	2	7
13	Mr John Dawkins	Vernel Land		–	–	7
14	William David, Alice Llewelyn and John Evan	Tyr John David		–	–	7
15	John Thomas	Vernel Land		–	–	8
16	Wm Harry & Edwd Bowen	House & lands at Vernel		–	–	6
17	Catherine Bowen, widow	Tyr David Bowen		–	–	7
18	Timothy Matthews	A house & lands		–	1	–
19	Willm Dawkin esq., infant	House & lands	Thomas Bear	–	–	11
20	Enoch Bowen	A house and garden		–	–	4

No.	Freeholders Names	Tenements	Tenants	Rents per Annum		
				£	s	d
21	Jos. Matthew & Rowd Bevan	Part of Tuy yn *[—?]*		–	–	2
22	Thomas Bear & his wife, Howell Howell & his wife, & Catherine Minors, widow	Late Wm Johns		–	–	6
23	William Dawkin esq.	Lands at [G]w[y]nvain	Richard David	–	2	–
24	William Phillip	Lands in the Upper Town	William John	–	–	4
25	*[blank]*	Whiteley Vach	John Parry ['John Morris' in Bn]	–	–	4
26	Thomas Bonnor	Whiteley Vawr	John Morris	–	–	7
27	Catherine Vaughan, widow	Wain Vach		–	–	4
28	Hugh Morgan Rees	Part of Tyr Chas Bowen		–	–	3
29	William Dawkin esq.	Lands at Wun Wen	Thomas Morgan	–	–	7
30	Thomas Jones	Red House		–	–	6
31	William John	A house & croft	John Prothero	–	–	2
32	Thomas Price esq.	The Great House	Eliz. Morris	–	–	6
33	Deborah Davies	Stoutwell		–	1	–
34	*[blank]*	Cottage garden & lands near the Common		–	–	2
35	Mr John Dawkins	Pont y Brennin		–	–	8
				£2	12	2

[Total is blank in Bn]

A Rent Roll of the Marsh Rent within the Borough of Loughor

	Rent per Annum		
	£	s	d
Catherine Minors	–	–	2
Elizabeth John	–	–	1
Catherine Allen	–	–	1½

Timothy Mathews	–	–	3½
Moses David	–	–	2
Thomas Bear	–	–	4
Ann Harry and John Prother[o]	–	–	2½
John Fray	–	–	3½
William Jones	–	–	2
John Prothero the younger	–	–	2½
Marmaduke Jenkin	–	–	1½
William Hugh	–	–	2
David Bedow	–	–	3½
William John Griffith	–	–	3
John Jeffrey	–	–	3½
William Harry Hugh	–	–	3
Edward Bowen	–	–	3½
William David	–	–	1½
Thomas Evan	–	–	3½
Thomas Evan, mason	–	–	2
John Morgan	–	–	4
William Harry, labourer	–	–	1
Samuel David	–	–	2
Enoch Bowen	–	–	2
William John	–	–	2
John Morris	–	–	1
	0	5	4½

[Folio 68/69]   [Total is blank in Bn]

The Lord is intitutled to the several Demesne Lands hereinafter mentioned within the Borough and Manor of Loughor

Miss Anne Mackworth holds from year to year at the yearly rent of eight pounds: All those several fields or parcels of lands commonly called or known by the several names following: Cae Pen y Coyd, containing 1½ acres; Cae Mawr, 4 acres; Cae Dryssyog Mawr, 2 acres; Cae Dyssyog Vach, ½ acre; Croft Coed, ½ acres; Wain Dan y Coed, 10 acres; Cae Wern, 4 acres; Cae Gloe, 1½ acres; Wain Arllwydd, 8 acres; and Wain Fa, 3 acres.

All which said closes and parcels of land are situate and being in the Borough and Parish of Loughor aforesaid, and are bounded as follows[25]:

Cae Pen y Coed (in possession of Edward Bowen): by the Common on the west, the highway on the north, the lands of Elizabeth Richards and Miss Mackworth on the south and Cae Mawr on the east. There are quarries in the middle of it;

Cae Mawr alias Cae Kenol (in the possession of Mrs Minors): by the highway on the north, Cae Pen y Coed and Miss Mackworth's lands on the west, Wain Dan y Coed on the south, and by a field of Mr Dawkin, Cae Dryssyog mawr and Cae Dryssyog vach on the east;

---

25. The following list of boundaries is in Bn but not in the body of Sa. However it survives in Sa in the Miscellanea volume, in the form of a final draft in Gabriel Powell's hand, from which his clerk would have made a fair copy.

Cae Dryssyog mawr (in the possession of Mrs Minors): by Mr Dawkin's land on the north, Cae mawr on the west, Croft y Coed on the east, and Cae Dryssyog vach on the south;

Cae Dryssyog vach alias Croft Pen y Twyne (in the possession of Mrs Minors): by Cae Dryssyog mawr on the north, Cae mawr on the west, Cae Gloe on the south, and Wain Arllwydd on the east;

Croft Coed alias Croft yr Odin (in the possession of Mrs Minors): by Cae Dryssyog vawr on the west, and the lands of Mr John Dawkin on all other sides thereof;

Wain Dan y Coed (in possession of Mrs Minors): by Cae Mawr on the north, the land of Miss Mackworth on the west, the land of Mr Wm Dawkin on the east, and the land of Mr Gamaliel Hughes on the south. A great part of this field is full of thorns;

Cae Wern alias Coed tyr y Portreeve (in possession of Mrs Minors): has the same boundaries as Wain Dan y Coed;

Cae Gloe, otherwise Cae Gwaith (in possession of Mrs. Minors): by Wain Dan y Coed on the south, Mr John Dawkin's lands on the east, Cae Wern on the west, and the lands of Mr John Dawkin on the north.

Gwain Arllwydd (in possession of Maud Morgan): by Wain y Fa and Loughor Moor on the north, and the lands of Elizabeth Richards, and Mr John Dawkin's on all other parts;

Gwain y Fa (in the possession of Maud Morgan): by the lands of Mr Popkin and Mr John Dawkin on the west, the Moor on the north, and Wain Vawr on the south and east.

The same **Miss Anne Mackworth** has by Lease granted her the seventh day of October 1754, all the veins mines and seams of coal and culm, and **coal and coal works** then had, opened or found then, [or] after to be had, opened, or found, in, upon or under all that tenement and land commonly called or known by the name of **Gurnos**. And also in, upon and under, all the parcels of lands mentioned in the next preceding tenement. And also in upon and under all those several Commons or wastes commonly called or known by the several names of Loughor Moor, Loughor Marsh, Mynnydd Rhose Bishwell and Mynnydd Stafford. All which tenement, fields, parcels of lands and Commons are situate lying and being in the Borough and Parish of Loughor aforesaid. With full and free liberty, power and authority to and for the said Anne Mackworth, her Executors and Administrators, to pursue and work the said veins and mines in upon through and under as well the inclosed lands as any other Commons or wastes, highways, open and uninclosed lands of the said Duke's which the said veins and mines of coal and culm may extend themselves into, or run through or under, within the Borough and Parish of Loughor aforesaid. With full and free liberty and authority to and for the said Anne Mackworth, her Executors, Administrators and Assigns, factors, servants, agents, colliers, workmen and labourers at all times during the term thereby granted to bore, try, search, dig, mine, work, raise, and land, all coal and culm that should or might be found in or under the premises hereinbefore for that purpose mentioned. And to make dig and sink any pit or pits, shaft or shafts, gutter or gutters, trench or trenches, engine or engines, or any other acts or devices whatsoever needful or convenient in or about the same, [but] so that in doing thereof no hurt or prejudice whatever be done to any mills which the said Duke had a power to grant. To hold all and singular the said veins, mines, and seams of coal and culm thereby granted, with the several liberties and authorities aforesaid, unto the said Anne Mackworth, her Executors, Administrators and Assigns, from the Feast of Saint Michael the Archangel then last past for and during the term of twenty-five years. Yielding and paying unto the said Duke, his Heirs and Assigns, the sum of three shillings per weigh for every weigh of coal or culm that shall be wrought, raised, or landed from or under the said lands and premises, and so in proportion for any greater or lesser quantity than a wey *[sic],* each wey to contain fifty bags or sacks, and each sack to contain twenty-four Winchester gallons and no more[26]. The said rent or land money [is] to be accounted for and paid quarterly, on the Feast of the Nativity of St John Baptist, St Michael the Archangel, the Birth of our Lord Christ, and the Annunciation of the Virgin Mary. Such payments to be made respectively on such of the said four days of payment as shall happen next after the landing [of] the said coal or culm, for which the same is to be paid within fifteen days after. And also four horse-loads of coal weekly to *[Folio 69/70]* be delivered at the pit's side.

And also yeilding and paying to the said Duke, his Heirs or Assigns, the sum of six pence for every weigh of coal as shall be wrought by the said Anne Mackworth, her Executors or Administrators, from or under the lands of any other person, which shall be landed or laid on the lands and premises before mentioned, or for the working or raising whereof any pit or pits, gutter or gutters, level or levels, engine or engines, made or to be made on the lands before mentioned [which] shall be in any respect useful and serviceable, to be accounted for and paid in manner aforesaid.

William John holds by Lease dated the 16th day of November 1762, all that water corn grist mill called and known by the name of **Loughor Mill**, together with the house and garden thereunto belonging, situate and being in the Borough of Loughor. To hold the said water corn grist mill, house and garden, unto the said William John, his Executors, Administrators and Assigns, from Michaelmas 1761 for the term of 21 years, at and under the yearly rent of £5, payable half-yearly at Lady Day and Michaelmas. And doing Suit of Court to the Court of the Manor of Loughor.

£5   –   –

Edward Griffith holds by Lease dated the 10th of July 1741, all that messuage and tenement of lands called and known by the name of **Gorse y Velin**, situate in the Borough and Parish of Loughor. To hold to the said Edward Griffith [also 'Mary Gamage, and Martha Gamage' included in Bn], his Executors and Administrators, for the term of 99 years if the said Edward Griffith, Mary Gamage, and Martha Gamage, or either of them should so long live. At and under the yearly rent of two pounds, payable half-yearly on every the Feast of the Annunciation of our Blessed Lady the Virgin Mary, and St Michael the Archangel. Together with two fat pullets, or one shilling in lieu thereof, on St Thomas's Day yearly, [and] the sum of five shillings on the decease of every tenant dying in possession. And also the sum of five shillings upon every Assignment or Alienation, and doing Suit of Mill and Suit of Court, on pain of two shillings for every default.

It consists of a house, garden and stall and the four closes or crofts following: Wain Tew, Wain Tynny, Caer Velin and Cae wrth y Tuy. The whole containing about three acres, and are bounded

---

26. In the Swansea area the weigh, or wey, was reckoned at five tons.

by the lands of Mathew ['Thomas' *struck through and replaced by* 'Mathew' *in Sa*] Pryce esq. on the north and east sides, the Lords Common on the west, and the mill on the south.

The improved yearly value whereof amounts to	£3	–	–

David Beynon ['Henry Squire' in Bn] has **liberty to build ships** on the beach within the Borough, paying to His Grace yearly during His Grace's pleasure the rent of

	£	s	d
	–	1	–

Charles Llewelyn has the like liberty paying the yearly rent of

–	2	–

Mr Thomas Morgan of Penddery has the use of a **limekiln** and liberty to lay down stones at Bwlch y Mynnydd, paying to the Lord the rent of 6d yearly
[Folio 70/71]

–	–	6

Thomas Bedow holds a cottage and garden at **Bwlch y Mynnydd** within this Borough at the yearly rent of

–	1	–

Richard Richards holds a cottage and garden there at the yearly rent of

–	8	–

Miss Mackworth holds a cottage and garden there at the yearly rent of

–	1	–

Rees Bevan holds a limekiln there at the yearly rent of

–	1	–

Richard Richards holds two limekilns there at the yearly rent of

–	2	–

Mr John Dawkin holds a limekiln there at the yearly rent of

–	–	6

John Walter holds a small garden there at the yearly rent of

–	1	–

Thomas Bedow and others have liberty to lay down coal on the beach, paying yearly the sum of

–	1	–

The Portreeve for the time being pays to the Lord at Michaelmas Day yearly for **Burgage Rents, Marsh and Castle**, the rent or sum of £2. 16. 5.   See the Rent Roll on Folios 67 & 68 *[p.133-135.]*

2	16	5

The Portreeve also pays the Lord the yearly rent of ten shillings on Michaelmas Day for the **Toll, Pitching, Keelage and Moorage of ships** within this Borough

–	10	–

[Folio 71/72]

The Manor of Pennard, with the Fiefs or Fees of Kittle, Lunnon and Trewyddfa which are Members of the said Manor; and the said Manor and Fees are Members and held of the Seigniory

Pennard is a mere Copyhold Manor. All the tenants within the same hold their lands of the Lord by Copy of Court Roll at the Will of the Lord, according to the Custom of the Manor: and there are no Freehold lands within the Manor of Pennard, or either of the Fees, except in the Fee of Kittle as hereinafter mentioned.

The Manor of Pennard is bounded by the sea on the south, by Pennard's Pill on the west, by Fairwood's Moor and a brook called Dyfnant on the north, and the brook which runs from Bishopston to Pwll Duy on the east.

There are within this Manor three large Commons, to wit: Pennard's Moor, lying on the north side of the said Manor, for which the tenants of the said Manor and the tenants of the Fee of Kittle pay the Lord yearly for liberty to graze it, the sum of 13s 4d. Some of the inhabitants of the Manor of Bishopston have also liberty to turn their cattle there, paying the Lord yearly 13s 4d; Pennard's Cliffes, which lie on the south side of the said Manor and extend from the three Cleeves on the west, to Pwll duy on the east, this Common or waste belongs to the Lord but the tenants have liberty to graze it, paying yearly 13s 4d. There are on these Cliffes, particularly at Pwll Duy, quarries of limestone which are worked and sold by the Lord's tenant (now Mrs. Mary Watkins); Pennard's Burroughs lies on the west end of the Manor between the inclosures and Pennard's Pill On this waste stands an old ruinous castle belonging to the Lord, and the ruins of an old church, reputed to have been formerly the Parish church, though more probably a chapel belonging to the castle. But it is now entirely overwhelmed with sand, and the tenants now turn their cattle there claiming it as a Common.

Many of the inhabitants within this Manor fish in the sea by drawing nets, and sometimes by fixing them with poles drove into the sands, and also take lobsters and crabs in the rocks, for which they pay the Lord an annual acknowledgment of six pence each. The names of those persons that paid last year are: John Jenkin; Daniel Taylor; Benjamin Bynon; John Gamon; Thomas Gamon; John Thomas; Jno. Smith and John Jenkin.

The Copyhold Rents within this Manor, with the rents for the moor and cliffes [are] collected by the Reeve. Part of the Copyhold rent is collected at Michaelmas and the other part at May, yearly.

[Folio 72/73]

A Rent Roll of the Customary or Copyhold Rents within the Manor of Pennard, together with Cliff and Moor Rent collected at Michaelmas yearly

	Customary Rent			Cliff Rent			Moor Rent		
	£	s	d	£	s	d	£	s	d
Rowland Dawkins esq.	–	2	2	–	–	–	–	1	–
Representatives of Mrs Dawkins for Hunts	–	16	–	–	1	6	–	3	–

Sheep still graze the cliffs at Pennard.

Looking south-east over Southgate, Pennard. Dobbins Plud (opposite page) is the dark strip half-way up the photograph, to the right of the curved field boundary. Pwlldu Head and the sea are in the distance.

	Customary Rent			Cliff Rent			Moor Rent		
	£	s	d	£	s	d	£	s	d
Owen Brigstock esq.	–	9	4	–	–	6	–	–	6
Mrs Anne Watkins for Highway	1	8	8	–	1	6	–	1	6
Thomas David of Green Lane	–	12	10	–	–	9	–	1	–
John Griffith for Highway	1	–	–	–	1	4	–	1	–
John David for James Grove	–	12	4	–	1	–	–	–	10
John Griffith for Broadway	–	10	4	–	–	10	–	–	6
Benjamin Bynon for Southgate	–	7	2	–	–	4	–	–	6
John Gamon for Southgate	–	9	–	–	1	2	–	–	2
Thomas Parry of High Pennard	–	5	–	–	–	4	–	–	4
Mary Gamon, widow, for Heal	–	4	–	–	1	–	–	–	8
Daniel Taylor for an acre of land at Hael	–	–	4	–	–	–	–	–	–
Robert Jone for Buddy Acre	–	3	8	–	–	6	–	–	3
Daniel Taylor for land at Southgate	–	6	3	–	–	3	–	–	4
Daniel Taylor of Heal	–	2	4	–	–	6	–	–	2
Daniel Taylor of High Pennard	–	1	8	–	–	3	–	–	2
The Representatives of Mrs Dawkin for Limpit	–	2	4	–	–	3	–	–	2
John Lucas esq. for Dobbins Plud & the Drangs	–	1	7	–	–	3	–	–	–
Henry Jone for Southgate	–	2	10	–	–	2	–	–	3
Henry Eaton for Norton	–	2	–	–	–	5	–	–	2½
Thomas David for Norton	–	–	8	–	–	1	–	–	–
Thomas David for lands late David Hopkins	–	2	–	–	–	3	–	–	1
Daniel Taylor for the land of John Dawkin	–	2	–	–	–	4	–	–	3
Mrs Watkins for land late Rees Mathews	–	1	10	–	–	2	–	–	2
The Representatives of Mrs Dawkin for a meadow by Wimblewood called Wain Belaph	–	–	4	–	–	–	–	–	–
Samuel Grove for the Lord's lands at High Pennard	–	1	8	–	–	2	–	–	–
Samuel Grove	–	–	3	–	–	–	–	–	–
Thomas Parry	–	–	1	–	–	–	–	–	–
Thomas Gamon for a house & land at High Pennard	–	–	8	–	–	–	–	–	–
Meredith David	–	–	2	–	–	1	–	–	1

The persons hereunder-named live out of the Manor and are permitted to turn their Cattle to the Moor

	£	s	d
John Parry of Kittle	–	–	3
William Atkins & William Collins	–	–	3
Mr Elias Jenkins for Brinmoyl	–	–	3
William Cornelius for Wirgin Rews	–	–	3
William Lewis for Killay	–	–	3
Charles Robert of Kittle	–	–	3

[Folio 73/74]

A Rent Roll of the Customary or Copyhold Rent within the Manor of Pennard collected at May yearly

	£	s	d
The Representatives of Mrs Dawkin for Hunts	–	10	–
The Representatives of Mrs Jennings	–	3	4
Thomas David	–	11	3
Mrs Watkins	1	2	6
John Griffith	–	14	–
John David	–	12	4
John Griffith for Broadway	–	4	–
Benjamin Bynon	–	5	–
John Gamon	–	4	10
Thomas Parry	–	3	–
Mary Gamon, widow, for Heal	–	4	–
Daniel Taylor	–	–	4
Robert Jone	–	1	6
Daniel Taylor for lands at South Gate	–	2	3
The same for Heal	–	1	–
Samuel Grove	–	1	–
The Representatives of Mrs Dawkins for ['of' in Bn] Limpit	–	2	1
John Lucas esq. for Dobbins Plud & Drangs	–	1	–
Thomas David for the lands late David Hopkins	–	1	–
Mrs Watkins for lands late Rees Matthews	–	–	6
Henry Jones	–	1	4
Henry Eaton	–	2	–
Benjamin Bynon	–	–	4
Joseph Webb	–	–	4
Mrs. Watkins for a house at High Pennard	–	–	2
	£5	9	1

[No total in Bn]

The Lord is intitutled to the several Demesne tenements hereafter mentioned within the said Manor of Pennard

Edward William holds from year to year those two water corn grist mills called **Park and Stone Mills**, situate in the Parishes of Penmain and Ilston. Within this Manor there is a small piece of ground containing about ¼ acre called the Pound, at the end adjoining to the Pound of Stone Mill, between it and the Horse Way. There is also belonging to Park Mill a small house and garden adjoining to it, and a kiln for drying oats under the cliff opposite to it. There is also a piece of rough furzy ground called the Tucker's Grove, lying on the side of the hill, containing about ten acres, having a foot-way on the south, the mill leat on the west, John Austin's Customary lands in possession of Phillip Bevan and the land of Nathaniel Bowen on the east, and part of Willoxton on the north. There is also another small piece near the mill, called the Orchard, and another small piece of moist ground adjoining called the Paddock alias the Werne. There is also another meadow *[Folio 74/75]* called the Splotts, containing about ½ an acre, having the brook on the west, the highway on the north, the mill meadow on the south, and the meadows of David Harry and the late Mrs Dawkin on the east The mill meadow contains about 2½ acres, having the brook on the east, Nothills Meadows on the south, and the highway on the north.

For which mills and closes the tenant pays the yearly rent of £19 17 0

[Added note in Sa, also in Bn.]   This is let out since by lease.

Mrs Mary Watkins holds from year to year a farm called **Nothills** within this Manor, situate part thereof in the Parish of Ilston, and part in Penmaen Parish.

   It consists of the following closes:

	Acres	Qrs
The Nine Acres containing	9	–
The Four Acres containing	4	–
The Three Acres by Nothills containing	3	–
The Three Acres by the lane containing	3	–
The Five Acres Close containing	5	–
The New Close containing	2	2
A rough piece of woody ground in which there is about half an acre of arable land containing in the whole about five acres	5	–
A meadow lying in the bottom between Park Mill and Park Farm, called New Meadow, containing about 5 acres, three of which are in Penmaen Parish & two in Ilston	5	–
One other close, called the Nine Acres, containing	9	–
The Acre containing	1	–
The long Three Acres containing	3	–
The Stanterns containing	2	2
The Higher Four Acres containing	2	2
	54	2

For which the tenant pays the yearly rent of £18 2 –

The outward bounds of this tenement are: on the south, the road leading from Park Mill to Penmaen Church; two small fields of Mrs. Mansels called Nothills on the west between it and Keven Bryn; Park Farm and Redden Hill on the north and east.

The same **Mrs Mary Watkins** holds from year to year a messuage and tenement called **Furzeland**, situate in the Parish of Ilston within this Manor. It consists of an old ruinous house, now converted into a barn and beast house.

   It consists also of:

	Acres	Qrs
A close called White Wells, situate in the western side of Lunnon containing	6	–
A rough close called Coed Kae, situate on the west of Willoxton Lane & adjoining to Luke Austin's house	6	–
Barrions Close containing	3	–

	Acres	Qrs
Hoarston containing six acres of meadow	6	–
One other arable close containing	1	–
One meadow called the eastern Meadow, alias the Three acres by the House, containing	3	–
One other meadow called the Middle Meadow containing	3	–
The Field by the House containing	2	–
Little Hoarstone by the Barrions Close containing	2	–
A field on the western side of Lunnon Lane containing	2	–
One other field on the western side of Lunnon Lane	2	–
A furzy field by Pengwern Moor containing	1	–
The little Acre containing	1	–
A quarter of an acre in a meadow of Luke Austin's, by the house, having the lane leading from the moor to the east, & an old ditch on the west the whole length	1	–
[Folio 75/76]		
On the eastern side of Lunnon Lane, a furzy field by the moor	2	–
One other field there containing	2	–
Pitclose lying below Furze Hill lane containing	1	–
Acres	50	1

For which the tenant pays the yearly rent of   £17   5   –

This tenement is bounded on the east by the Copyhold lands of John Gorton and William Jone; on the west by Lunnon Lane; the moor on the north; and Furze Hill Lane on the south.

John Rowland holds by virtue of a Lease granted him on the 15th of December 1752, all that messuage, tenement and lands called by the name of **Lletherid**, situate in the several Parishes of Lanridian and Ilston in the County of Glamorgan. To hold unto the said John Rowland, his Executors, Administrators and Assigns, from thenceforth for and during the natural lives of Mary, the wife of the said John Rowland, John Rowland the younger their son, and Elizabeth Rowland, spinster, sister of the said John Rowland (the lessee), and the life of the survivor of them. At and under the yearly rent of ten pounds, payable half yearly at Lady Day and Michaelmas, by equal portions clear of all deductions whatsoever, together with two fat pullets on the Feast of St Thomas the Apostle yearly, or one shilling in lieu thereof. And also the sum of five shillings on the decease of every tenant dying in possession, and the like sum of five shillings upon every Assignment or Alienation. And doing Suit of Mill to the Lord's Mill called Park Mill, and Suit of Court to the Court of the Manor of Pennard and Fee of Lunnon, on pain of three shillings and four pence for every default in either of the said Suits.

It consists of a dwelling house, stable, two beast houses, one barn, two gardens, one orchard, and the following closes of land:

	Acres	Qrs
Cae Hendy containing	3	–
Cae Mawr containing	6	–
The western Cae Mawr containing	6	–
The Higher Cae Bach containing	3	–

	Acres	Qrs
The lower Cae Bach containing	4	–
Cae Garw containing	7	–
The lower Roach containing	7	–
The middle Roach containing	7	–
The higher Roach containing	7	–
Cae John Owen containing	10	–

The above closes are in Lanridian Parish

	Acres	Qrs
Higher Meadow by the Moor containing	3	–
Lower Meadow by the Moor containing	3	–
The Little Meadow by the House containing	2	–
The Great Meadow by the House containing	6	–
The Higher Coombs containing two acres, one in Lanridian & one in Ilston	2	–
Cae Funnon, containing	4	–
Balls Close containing	4	–
Cross Ways containing five acres, two parts in Lanridian and one part in Ilston	5	–
	89	–

[Folio 76/77]

The last mentioned closes are situate in the Parish of Ilston.

There is a large parcel of woody ground, about ten acres, on which are several oak and ash timber trees. There is also situated on the said farm a small cottage now let by the tenant to one Robert Lloyd. There are two limekilns on the premises, in which lime is burnt by the neighbouring tenants, and the tenant is paid by them 3d for every score of horse-loads.

This tenement is bounded on the west by the lane leading to Lodge, on the south by the lands part of Lodge and a small part of Park, on the east, by the Green [way?] leading from Park to Willoxton and a part of the Copyhold tenement of Mrs. Dawkin's called Pengwern, and on the north by the said tenement called Pengwern and part of Pengwern Moor.

The improved yearly value of this tenement amounts to	£40	–	–

John Jones holds by virtue of a Lease granted to Elizabeth Jones, widow, dated 28th of October 1735, all that messuage or mansion house called or known by the name of **Lodge**, together with the several fields or parcels of land called:

	Acres	Qrs
The western Park containing	5	–
The Deer Park containing	4	–
The Barn Park containing 3–		
The Coombe Close containing	3	–
The Five Acres in the Wood, adjoining to Cae Draw belonging to Park & the Coombs containing	5	–
The Great Rye Cats [sic] Close containing	6	–
The little Cae yetts, alias the Close about the Garden containing	3	–

	Acres	Qrs
The meadow called Grass *[sic]* – [?'Great'] – Kae Yetts containing	3	–
The little meadow containing	1	–
The little acre joining to Coomb Close containing	1	–
Lodge Crofts in the Wood adjoining the three acres	2	–
The three acres adjoining to the Five Acres	3	–
The Coombe containing	1	–
There is also a parcel of wood on each side Combe *[sic]* containing about	5	–
	45	–

To hold to the said Elizabeth Jones for the term of the natural lives of Rowland Jones, Elinor Jones, and Margaret Jones, the son and daughters of the said Elizabeth Jones, and the life of the survivor of them, who are all in being. At and under the yearly rent of six pounds, payable half yearly at Lady Day and Michaelmas, together with two pullets, or one shilling, on St Thomas's Day yearly. And also the sum of 5s on the decease of every tenant dying in possession. And also the sum of 5s upon every alienation, and doing Suit of Mill and Suit of Court to the Court of Gower Anglicana, on pain of three shillings and four pence for every default.

This tenement is bounded on the west by Kellibion lands and the lane leading to Letherid, on the north [by] Lletherid, on the east [by] part of Lletherid and Park, and on the south by Long Oaks.

The improved yearly value of the tenement amounts to	£16	–	–

[Folio 77/78]

Abraham Morgan holds by virtue of a Lease granted to David Morgan, his father (deceased), dated 23rd day of July 1736, all that messuage called **Park le Bruce** consisting of a dwelling house, stable, beasthouse, barns, and other outhouses, gardens and orchard, and the several closes following:

	Acres	Qrs
Brockhills containing	10	–
Hen gae or the old Close by Lunnon containing	1	2
Brockhills Close containing	8	–
The Great Close containing	7	–
The Close below the Barn containing	7	–
Hams Close containing	2	2
Small Close containing	1	2
A Furzy Piece called Pennard's Close adjoining to Kevenbrin containing	15	–
Pitt Close containing	2	2
Kitchen Well containing	10	–
Swinging Close now divided into two pieces containing	10	–
Redden Hill containing	8	–
Round Lays containing	7	–
Calves Close containing	7	–
Church Hill containing	3	–

	Acres	Qrs
Green Coombs containing	8	–
Carn Hills containing	4	–
Mill Pond Green containing	–	2
Comb Grove near the Mill adjoins the road going to		
Lunnon & Jno. Austin's lands	1	2
Cae Draw adjoins to Brockhills in the		
Parish of Lanridian containing	7	–
The meadow under the house containing	6	–
The meadow called the Quobs containing	9	–
The meadow called the Orchard Close containing	1	–
An acre of wood in Ilston Combe adjoining to Joseph Webbs	1	–
A cottage and garden called the Higher House,		
with two Crofts containing	2	–
This adjoins to Kevenbryn and Furzey Close, alias		
Pennard's Close, now in the possession of John		
William and Mary Lewis, as undertenants to Abraham Morgan	2	–
The little cottage and garden and two fields belonging,		
now in possession of Richard Watkins, as undertenant to		
Abraham Morgan, containing	2	–
A cottage, garden and three crofts, containing about		
three acres & a half, called Matthew Rees's cott, now		
in the possession of Edward Williams, adjoining		
to Kevenbrin & the Furze alias Pennards Close	3	2
A cottage, garden and two crofts, containing about		
one acre, adjoining to Quabs and Pennards		
alias Furze Close, and Kevenbryn	1	–
	136	–

['147' in Bn]

There are on this tenement several very large coppice woods, containing about fifty acres, on which there are several timber trees of oak and ash interspersed. And [it] is bounded by Kevenbrin and Nothills on the south; Long Oaks and Lodge on the west; Lletherid, a Copyhold tenement of the late Mrs Dawkin of Kittlehill called Pengwern, and part of Willoxton on the north; [and] part of Willoxton, Nothills Meadow and Reddenhill on the east.

The improved yearly value of this tenement may amount to	£60	–	–

[Folio 78/79]

John Rowland holds by virtue of a Lease granted to Leyson Bowen of Oystermouth, shipwright, dated 18th of March 1750, which Lease was mortgaged by the said Leyson Bowen to Sir Robert Long, Bart., Norborne Berkley, and John Talbot esqs., Executors of the Most Noble Charles, late Duke of Beaufort, for the sum of £404 due to the said Duke in his lifetime. And by them afterwards assigned to the said John Rowland, by the direction and consent of the said Leyson Bowen, who at the same time conveyed the equity of the said Lease to the said John Rowland for the sum of *[blank]*: All those two several messuages and tenements of land called **upper and**

lower Willoxtones, situate in the Parish of Ilston in the said County of Glamorgan. To hold to the said Leyson Bowen for and during the natural lives of Joannah, the wife of the said Leyson Bowen, Mary Bowen and Magdalen Bowen, two daughters of the said Leyson Bowen, and the life of the survivor of them. At and under the yearly rent of ten pounds, payable at Lady Day and Michaelmas yearly by even and equal portions, together with two fat pullets on the Feast Day of St Thomas yearly, or two shillings in lieu thereof. And the sum of five shillings upon the decease of every tenant dying in possession, and the like sum of five shillings upon every Assignment or Alienation. And also doing Suit of Mill to the Lord's Mill called Park Mill, and Suit of Court to the Court of the Manor of Pennard, on pain of three shillings and four pence for every default.

It consists of two dwelling houses, two stables, 2 beasthouses, 2 barns, two gardens, and four orchards, and the several pieces of ground following, to wit:

	Acres	Qrs
The Bakehouse Meadow containing	3	–
The Haggard Meadow containing	1	–
The Higher west Close containing	3	–
The Lower west Close containing	6	–
New Close containing	6	–
Carrion Close containing	8	–
Well Head Close containing	2	2
The Two Acres by the Well Head Close containing	2	–
Hitch Cocks containing	5	–
Coomb containing	1	–
Ashen Pitts containing	4	–
Fur[z]land containing	4	–
Huggrove containing	–	2
The Lower Brower containing	6	–
The Higher Brower containing	4	–
Quar Close containing	4	–
Old Close containing	6	–

All the above closes are the lower side of the lane leading to the House.

Above the road:		
Higher Cunnigaer, – containing	2	2
Lower Cunnigaer	3	–
Rough Close	6	–
Mayas Close	2	2
	80	–

This tenement is bounded on the east by the high road called Lunnon Way and the Copyhold lands of John Austin, Joseph Austin, Morgan Harry, Griffith Hopkin, and Henry Eaton; on the west by the Copyhold lands late Mrs Dawkin and Nathaniel Bowen and the Demesne lands called Park le Bruce; on the north to other Demesne of the said Duke called Furzeland.

[Folio 79/80]

	Acres	Qrs
There is also a cottage garden and little meadow containing about one acre of ground situate at Cardus Ford. Part of this tenement now let by the tenant to one Margaret Stephen	1	–
There is also a piece of meadow ground called theYnys, situate at Cardus Ford, which is bounded by Fairwood's Moor on the east, by Cardus Ford little Meadow on the south, by the encroached fields in possession of William David on the west, and part of lower Wimble Wood and Ilston Glebe on the north, containing	8	–
There is also a parcel of meadow ground lying in Lletherid's Meadows, containing by estimation ten acres, and is divided into landshares[27], nine whereof lie in great Lletherid's meadow, and one acre in higher Lletherid's Meadow, which meadows are situate between Pengwern Moor and Welsh Moor.	10	–
The improved yearly value of the whole (including the above reserved rents and Duties) amounts to	£50 – –	

There is one acre of woody land in **Ilston Coombe** on the north side thereof, having a meadow of Joseph Austin's on the south side; William Bynon's wood on the east side, without any fence, the path or footway being the boundary on that side; the landshare lands between John Harry and Joseph Austin, called the three Acres on the north side; and the three Acres Wood, which is between John Harry, David Atkins and William Jones, on the west side. Not let to any tenant but having a few young oaks and ashes and some hazel growing there.
[Folio. 80/81]

Cornelius William holds by Lease dated 28th October 1735, for the term of the natural lives of Anne Williams, wife of the said Cornelius, and Cornelius and Anne, their son and daughter, and the life of the survivor of them: A messuage and tenement called **Long Oaks**, situate in the several Parishes of Penmaen and Lanridian, at and under the yearly rent of eight pounds payable at Lady Day and Michaelmas, by equal portions, together with two fat capons on St Thomas's Day yearly, and doing service with horses and oxen when and as often as required. Paying the sum of twenty shillings in lieu of a Heriot on the decease of every tenant dying in possession, and the like sum upon every Assignment. and also doing Suit of Mill and Suit of Court, on pain of five shillings.

It consists of a dwelling house, stable, beasthouse, barn, two gardens and one orchard,and the following closes of land, to wit:

	Acres	Qrs
The Rush Park containing	7	–
The two little Rush Parks containing	3	–
The Meadow containing	3	–
Harry Griffiths Close containing	5	–

27. Intermingled strips in various ownerships.

	Acres	Qrs
Long Oaks Close containing	7	–
The Oat Land, otherwise the four acres, containing	4	–
Two Closes called the Trenches containing	2	–
Cae William containing	5	–
The Middle Park containing	9	–
The Seven acres otherwise Kae'r Odyn containing	7	–
Cae Tom Griffith, alias the five acres, containing	5	–
The Great Close, alias Caer Pwll, containing	8	–
The Acre, otherwise the little Meadow, containing	1	–
The Great Meadow containing	8	–
The Six Acres containing	6	–
There are about Five acres of Wood	5	–
Acres	85	–

This tenement is bounded on the south by Kevenbrin; by Park Farm on the east; Lodge on the north; and part of Walterston, in the possession of John Walter, on the west.

The improved yearly value of this tenement amounts to   £30   –   –

The same **Cornelius William** holds by Lease dated 28th October 1735 another part of **Long Oaks**, consisting of an old ruinous house, which with the outhouses are now fallen down, and:

	Acres	Qrs
Three ['Four' in Bn] little meadows containing	7	–
One small field adjoining to the meadows containing	2	–
Harry Griffith's Close containing	1	–
A croft by the house containing	–	2
Acres	10	2

To hold to the said Cornelius William for his own life, and the lives of Cornelius and Anne, his son and daughter, at and under the yearly rent of twenty shillings, payable at Lady Day and Michaelmas by even and equal portions, together with two capons, or one shilling in lieu thereof. The sum of five shillings in lieu of a Heriot, and the sum of five shillings upon every assignment. And doing Suit of Mill and Suit of Court, on pain of three shillings and four pence for every default. This little tenement is bounded by Kevenbrin on the south, Walterston Wood on the west, the Great Meadow belonging to Long Oaks on the north, and the field called Long Oaks ['on the east' in Bn].

The improved yearly value of this small tenement may amount to   £5   –   –
[Folio 81/82]

Edward William holds by Lease dated 20th October 1738, all that messuage, tenement, and lands called **Redden Hill**, situate and being in the Parish of Penmaen in the County of Glamorgan. To hold unto the said Edward William, his heirs and assigns for and during the natural lives of the said Edward William, John William, and Benjamin William, brothers of the said Edward William, and the life of the survivor of them. At and under the yearly rent of twenty shillings, payable at Lady Day and Michaelmas by equal portions, and two pullets, or one shilling in lieu thereof, on St Thomas's Day yearly, [and] the sum of five shillings in lieu of a Heriot.

It consists of a dwelling house, stable, beasthouse, barn, garden, potato garden, and the following pieces of ground, to wit:

	Acres	Qrs
The Close below the Garden containing	1	–
The Field below the Green	2	–
The little Field containing	1	–
The Middle Field containing	2	–
The Rock Field containing	3	–
The Croft containing	–	2
There is also a large piece of waste and rough woody ground, containing about ten acres, and lying on the south of the way leading from Park Mill to the house	10	–
Acres	19	[2]

This tenement is bounded on all sides by Park and Nothills Farms, belonging to the Lord, and the improved value will amount to £8 – –

Daniel Taylor holds a small piece of land at **High Pennard** for which he pays the Lord the annual sum of one shilling £– 1 –

*   *   *

The Fief or Fee of Kittle, a Member of the Manor of Pennard, consists of

Freehold and Copyhold lands, and lies altogether in the Parish of Pennard. And [it] is bounded on the east by the Parish and Manor of Bishopston; on the south by a place called the Sheep Wash and the Manor of Pennard; on the west by the Fee of Lunnon and Trinity Well; and on the north by Mounck lake and Pennard's Moor, and part of the Parish of Bishopston. The Free and Copyhold Tenants within this Fee pay to the Lord yearly the sum of *[blank]*.

A Rent Roll of the Copyhold lands within Kittle

	Acres	Qrs	£	s	d
The late Mrs Dawkin for part of Kittlehill	81	–	–	2	2
The same for a messuage and croft at Kittle	–	–	–	2	–
John Parry for a messuage and lands called Kittle	10	2	–	7	–
The late Mrs Dawkins [for] a messuage and lands at Kittle late Mr William Roberts	10	–	–	7	1
The same for lands there	2	–	–	1	4
Acres	103	2	£3	12	7

Looking north over Lunnon village, with vestiges of open-field strips, now enclosed.
Two parallel lanes lead north to Pengwern Common, alias Lunnon Moor. See pages 154 to 156.

Lunnon Moor (Pengwern Common) and the ancient rectangular enclosure of Newclose. See page 155, under 'Moor Rent'.

[Folio 82/83]

A Rent Roll of the Free Rents within the Fee of Kittle

	£	s	d
The late Mrs Dawkin for part of Kittlehill	–	–	6
The same for other parcels of lands	–	1	7
The same for lands called the Ynisland	–	–	11
William Dawkin esq. for Rytherchs	–	1	6
John Parry for part of his land at Kittle	–	–	4
The late Mrs Dawkin for Pen y Pwll, in possession of Phillip Bevan	–	1	1½
The same for Girland in possession of Phillip Knaeth	–	–	6½
Mr William Richards for Great Kittle in possession of John Gwyn	–	2	6
Catherine Walters, widow, for part of Pwll y Bloggy, in possession of *[blank]*	–	–	7
John Jennings esq. for part of Pwll y Bloggy in possession of John Gwyn	–	–	7
	£–	10	2

Rowland Rowland holds by virtue of a Lease granted him 23rd July 1736, a cottage, garden and small stable on **the Bank at Kittle**, which he now lets to one William Thomas.

	Acres	Qrs
A cottage, three gardens and stable on the Bank at Kittle	*[no entry made, final total suggests 2 Qrs.]*	
A croft lying over the Pit containing a quarter of an acre, called Pit Croft	–	1
One other croft called the Croft below the Garden, containing 3 Quarters, now let to David Rees	–	3
He also by the same Lease holds one other croft situate in the Parish of Bishopston, having a small croft of the Earl of Warwick's on the south and the Lord's waste on all other sides thereof, containing about half an acre	–	2
He also by the same Lease holds a parcel of rough ground in Bishop's Wood, having Thomas Edwards' land on the south, the boundaries of Oystermouth Parish on the east, the lands of George Bowen and David Webbern on the north, and the lands of Mrs Anne Watkins of Highway on the west It contains about two acres, though commonly called one acre	2	–
	4	–

He also holds a house and garden near Bishop's Cross called the Stone House. To hold to the said Rowland Rowland and his heirs for the lives of John Rowland, Elizabeth Rowland, son and daughter of the said Rowland Rowland, and Mary Thomas, step-daughter of the said Rowland Rowland, and the life of the survivor of them. At and under the yearly rent of three shillings, payable at Lady Day and Michaelmas by equal portions, together with two fat pullets on St Thomas's Day yearly, or one shilling in lieu thereof; the sum of five shillings on the decease of every tenant dying in possession, and the like sum of five shillings on every Assignment or Alienation, and doing Suit of Mill, and Suit of Court to the Court of the Manors of Pennard and Bishopston, on pain of 3s 4d for every default.

The improved value of the whole will now amount to	£5	–	–

[Folio 83/84]

[The] Fief or Fee of Lunnon – a Member of the Manor of Pennard, consists of Copyhold Lands, and is situate within the several Parishes of Ilston, Penmaen and Lanridian, and is bounded[28] on the south by the old Park Ditch; by the Marsh near Stone Mill on the west; by the old Park Pales at Walterstone Field on the north; by a parcel of land called Bryn y Gwase and the river of Lunnon and Trinity Well, Coombe Chappel and Cardus Ford on the east.

There is within this Fee a large Common called Lunnon, otherwise Pengwern, Moor which is held by the tenants and inhabitants of the said Fee at the yearly rent of five pounds, which is paid in the proportions following:

Moor Rent for Lunnon Moor[29]

	Per year		
	£	s	d
John Morris for Middle Pengwern	–	6	0½
David Austin for the western Pengwern	–	5	0¾
Ditto for Wreckland	–	–	4
Leyson Bowen for Willoxton	–	4	8
Joseph Webb for Lunnon	–	2	3
John Rowland for Lunnon	–	4	7¾
Ditto for Furze hill	–	2	3
Nathaniel Bowen for Lunnon	–	4	7¾
Joseph Austin and Morgan Harry for Lunnon	–	6	0½
John Austin for Lunnon	–	5	6
Griffith Hopkin for Lunnon	–	4	3
Morgan Harry, William Jones, & William Atkins for Furzehill	–	4	1¾
Henry Eaton for Lunnon	–	2	3¾
Rowland Rowland for George Evans's Land	–	1	6
John Smith for Lunnon	–	1	3½
William Austin for Lunnon	–	–	3½
William Austin and Joseph Webb for Lunnon	–	1	–
John Morris for lands late Mary Harris at Pengwern	–	1	6
Luke Austin for Pengwern	–	4	7¾
Griffith Jone for Llethrid	–	2	6
Griffith Jone for a meadow near Llethrid	–	0	6
John Austin for Furzeland	–	1	6
Avis Gorton for Furzehill	–	3	2½
John Webb's land sold to Mr Richd Gorton 5¾ ac. 1s..7¼d;			
[to] Jno. Dunn 4½ ac., 1s..3d; [and to]	–	4	5¾*
Wm Atkins 5¾ ac., 1s..7¼d:	[*sic for 4		5½]

---

28. In the originals the punctuation is as given here, but the description does not accord with the topography. A suggested correction is to delete the first reference to the Park Ditch, and then to read: "bounded on the south by the Marsh near Stone Mill; on the west by the old Park Pales at Walterston Field; on the north by a parcel of land called Bryn y Gwas; and the river of Lunnon and Trinity Well, Coombe Chappel and Cardus Ford on the east." This would make sense in the field and on the map.

29. This list of Moor Rent payments is bound into the Miscellanea volume of Sa. It is a contemporary copy of the one on Sa Folio 84, and is used here because it includes more of the names of the tenants' holdings.

	Per year		
	£	s	d
William Beynon Furzehill, now Francis Batcock in	–	4	4¾
the possession of Elizabeth Jone			
William David, Cardus ford	–	1	0
Thos Austin for Flemings Land	–	1	0
John Dunn for western Hills	–	3	0
John Awbrey eastern Hills	–	6	1
David Morgan for Kae Howell	–	5	1
Mathew Jone for Black Lane	–	1	6
	£5	0	8½

Henry Evan for new Close 1s.
Jno. Kneath for Gorses land 1s.
Jno. David for Cardus ford 1s.

[Folio 84/85]

Copyhold Rents in Lunnon

The Copyhold tenants within the Fee of Lunnon pay to the Lord yearly the sum of sixteen pounds seventeen shillings and four pence, which is collected by the Reeve from the persons hereunder named:

	£	s	d
Morgan Harry & Joseph Austin Lands at Lunnon	1	6	8
The same for the Coome	–	–	8
for Killy whilly	–	1	4
for Button's Pitt	–	–	6
for William Harry's land called Quadditch	–	1	–
for Broad Close	–	1	4
John Austin messuage & lands at Lunnon	1	2	8
John Austin for rough Close	–	3	–
Henry Eaton lands at Lunnon	–	9	4
Henry Eaton for William Harry's land	–	–	8
John Smith Lands at Lunnon	–	3	9
William Austin ditto	–	–	11
Rowland Rowland George Evans late lands	–	5	–
Richard Bowen lands at Iltstone *[sic]*	–	14	2
Leyson Bowen Willoxtone	2	15	2
John Rowland for Lunnon	–	12	6
John Rowland for Furzehill	–	4	8
Nathaniel Bowen messuage & lands at Lunnon	–	12	6
Joseph Webb Furzehill	–	4	8
William Austin for Lease Land	–	2	4
Thomas Simpson for Flemming Land	–	2	8
John Webb for the Lane }	–	–	2
John Webb Furzehill } Sold to Mr Richd Gorton 5¾a, 3s 10d.			
to John Dunn 4½a, 3s.	–	10	8
to Wm Atkins 5¾a, 3s 10d.			
The Heirs of George Harry } vizt. John Harry, Wm Jone	–	17	8
} & Wm Atkin			

	£	s	d
David Austin Pengwern: Thomas Popkins esq. landlord	1	10	4
David Austin for Wreckland do.	–	2	8
John Morris for Pengwern do.	1	15	4
Avis Gorton for Furzehill	–	11	8
Luke Austin for Pengwern do.	–	9	4
Griffith Hopkin Lunnon	–	19	4
Morgan Harry lands by Stone mill	–	7	–
Joseph Webb Ho. & lands by Park Mill	–	2	4
William Beynon Furzehill	1	1	6
Mary David, widow Lunnon	–	6	–
Joseph Price esq. for Carter's Meadow	–	1	–
Abraham Morgan	–	2	–
Maysod Dawkin, widow for the Meadows	–	2	–
David Jone for the house at Park Mill called Cold Comfort	–	–	4
	£18	4	10

[Folio 85/86]

John Awbrey's widow holds from year to year *[blank]* crofts situate on the north side of **Pengwern Moor** within the said Fee of Lunnon, at the yearly rent of

	£	s	d
	1	10	–

John Morris holds two meadows there, at the yearly rent of

| | 2 | 10 | – |

Mary Gorse, widow, holds from year to year a house and six small crofts situate on the north and east sides of the said Moor, at the yearly rent of

| | 3 | – | – |

William David holds a house and three small crofts from year to year, situate on the east side of the said Moor, at the yearly rent of

| | 2 | 10 | – |

Leyson Bowen holds from year to year a croft and garden there, at the rent of

| | – | 2 | – |

Robert Loyd holds from year to year a small croft there, at the yearly rent of

| | – | 1 | – |

David Stephen holds from year to year a smith's forge situate near **Cardus Ford** at the yearly rent of

| | – | 1 | – |

[Folio 86/87]

The Fief or Fee of Trewyddva, a Member of the Manor of Pennard[30]

Trewyddva Fee, a Member of the Manor of Pennard, consists of Customary or Copyhold lands and is situate in the Parish of Langevelach about six[31] miles distant from the Manor of Pennard. And the bounds thereof are: Beginning at the River Tawy where the brook Vilast discharges itself into the said river, up along the said brook on the south side of the said Fee to the highway leading from Swansea to Langevelach. Then crossing the said highway to the corner of a meadow

---

30. The heading is in the Bn version, but not in Sa.
31. Actually nine miles.

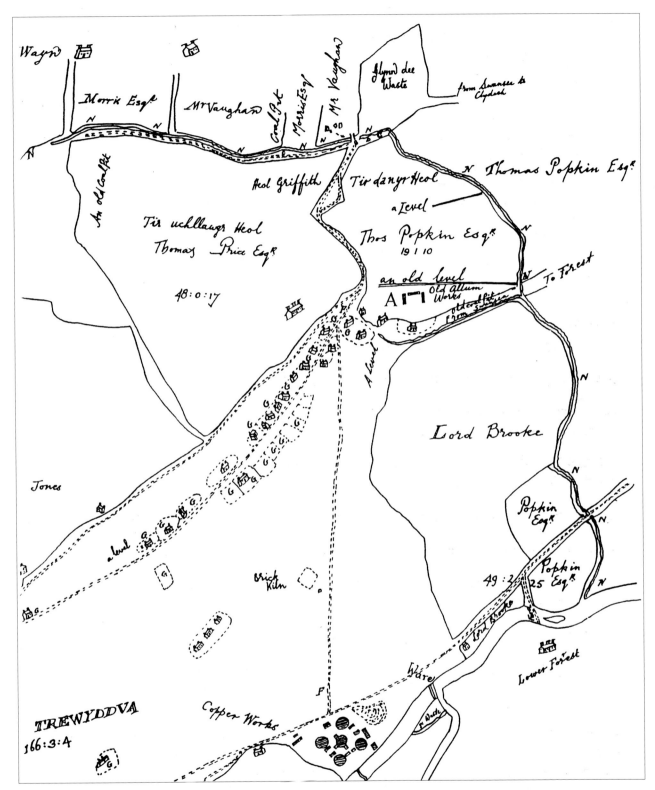

Part of a map of the Fee of Trewyddfa, 1761. Morriston was later built on the land shown here as belonging to Lord Brooke. Note the (Forrest) "Copper Works", and, at 'A', the "Old Allum Works" which related to the lease dated 1735 set out on pages 163 to 165. See also note 33, p.164.

belonging to the tenement called Pen y vilia and along the ditch of the said tenement, leaving the said tenement on the west, as far as the said tenement adjoins the Treboth Common. Then turning westward up along the ditch of Pen y lan vach to the new inclosure on Cadley Common, then turning to the north round the Copyhold tenement of Thomas Popkin esq. called Tyr Doynau to Heol Ddee. And along the ditch (on the north side of the said highway) of a tenement of lands of Thomas Price esq., lately purchased of Mathew Franklen, as far as the highway leading from Swansea to Langevelach. And crossing the highway along the brook to Mynnydd Carn Llwyd, and from the mouth of the lane to a stone on the bank which lies eastward of the lane. And thence to a heap of stones which lies on the Common, south of Mr Walter Vaughan's field called Kae Newydd, and thence along the mear stones to a May tree growing in the hedge of a meadow of Mr Walter Vaughan's called Wain y Maen. And thence along the ditch as far as the gate which leads to the house of Robert Morris esq., in the possession of *[blank]*, and thence along the water course which runs in the ditch on the north side of Heol Griffith to the highway leading from Swansea to Clydach. And thence along the brook between the lands of Thomas Popkin esq. called Pentrepoth and Bryth Tyr, otherwise Tyr Dan yr Heol, to a by way of the Lord's called Heol Hen Sage. And thence along the brook to the highway leading from Swansea towards Forrest, and thence crossing the said highway along the brook to the River Tawy, and down the said river to the mouth of the brook Vilast.

There are within the said Fee, four wastes or Commons, called Treboth; Mynnydd Carn Llwyd; Knapllwyd; and Graig, otherwise Forrest Trewyddva; for which particular rents were formerly paid the Lord. But these rents have been for many years consolidated with the Customary or Copyhold rents, which amount to the sum of two pounds ten shillings and nine pence per annum, and are collected by the Reeve in the proportions following:

A Rent Roll of the Copyhold Rent within the Fee of Trewyddva

Copyholders Names	Tenements	Tenants	Rent per Annum		
			£	s	d
Robert Popkin esq. ['Thomas P.' in Bn]	Ynishowell	*[blank]*	–	3	9
The Earl of Warwick	Tyr Hopkin Edmund [blank in Bn]	Robert Morris esq.	–	2	8
Robert Morris esq.	A meadow called Mynnydd Carn Llwyd	James Grey & Thos David Rees	–	1	–
Robert Popkin esq. ['Thomas P.' in Bn]	Tyr Dan yr Heol alias Bryth Tyr	George Zachariah	–	2	–
Thomas Price esq.	Tyr Ych lawr yr Heol alias Tyr Llan	Jennet Thomas	–	6	2
Thomas Jones gent.	Trewyddva Ycha	Margaret Jones	–	10	–

Copyholders Names	Tenements	Tenants	Rent per Annum		
			£	s	d
Mary Franklen infant	Cwm Gelly	John Franklen	–	5	3
Thomas Popkin esq.	Tyr Doynaw	Evan Griffith	–	–	9
Anne Franklen	Tyr Doynaw	Her own possession	–	–	9
Mrs. Mary Vaughan	Wain Gron	John Thomas	–	–	5
John Landeg	Trewyddva Yssha	His own possession	–	4	9
Robert Popkin esq. ['Thomas P.' in Bn]	Coedkae Dee	John Landeg	–	–	6
The same	Griffith Rees's land, old Copperworks	John Landeg	–	7	3
The same	David Williams lands alias Tyr Skybor Degwm	John Landeg	–	5	9
			–	–	–
			£2	11	–

Demesne Tenements within the Fee of Trewyddva

George Venables Vernon esq. holds from year to year a piece of meadow ground called **Morva Bach**, situate in the Parish of Langevelach and within the said Fee of Trewyddva, at the yearly rent of two shillings and six pence. *[Folio 87/88]* It abuts or joins with the lands of Thos Popkin esq., called Ynishowell and Trewyddva Common, on the north and west sides, Place y Marle on the south, and the River Tawy on the east.

Richard Lockwood of Deweshall in the County of Essex esq., John Lockwood of the City of London esq. and Robert Morris of Swansea in the County of Glamorgan esq., hold by virtue of a Lease granted to them the 24th Day of June 1754 by the Most Noble Charles Duke of Beaufort, deceased: All that piece or parcel of marsh land commonly called or known by the name of **Morva'r Arllwydd** or the Lord's Marsh, containing four acres or thereabout, having the River Tawy on the east, the great road, or common highway leading from Swansea to Neath by Forrest Ycha on the west, the said Lord Duke's waste lands under the little mill [on the] south, and a certain piece of open and uninclosed lands of the said Lord Duke's called Place y Marle on the north, and situate in the Parish of Langevelach within the said Fee of Trewyddva. To hold unto the said Richard Lockwood, John Lockwood and Robert Morris, their Executors, Administrators and Assigns, from the Feast Day of the Annunciation of the Blessed Virgin Mary which was in the year of our Lord 1746, for during and unto the full end and term of ninety-nine years thence next ensuing and fully to be complete and ended. At and under the yearly rent of four pounds and ten shillings payable at Lady Day and Michaelmas by equal Portions   £4   10   –

They also by the same lease hold forty cottages[32] at the yearly rent of two shillings each cottage, and have liberty of erecting new ones, paying two shillings for each new erected one, on Michaelmas Day yearly, which cottages are now held by the several persons hereafter named

	£	s	d
John Borlace holds a cottage & gardens situate at **Brimmellin** in the Parish of Swansea	–	2	–
John Richard, collier, holds a cottage & gardens situate at **Treboeth** in the Parish of Langevelach	–	2	–
Mathew William, collier, holds a cottage & gardens situate at **Treboeth** in the Parish of Langevelach	–	2	–
John Thomas, smith, holds a cottage & gardens situate at **Treboeth** in the Parish of Langevelach	–	2	–
John Prees, collier, holds a cottage & gardens situate at **Treboeth** in the Parish of Langevelach	–	2	–
John Thomas, smith, holds **Croft Lewelyn**, now divided into 2 parcels at ditto [Not in Bn]	–	2	–
Thomas Lewis, collier, holds a cottage & garden situate at **Treboeth** in the Parish of Langevelach	–	2	–
[blank] held a cottage at **Mynnydd Carn Llwyd** which is since fallen down	–	–	–
John Grey, collier, holds a cottage & gardens at **Knapllwyd** in the Parish of Langevelach	–	2	–
John David, copperman, holds a cottage & gardens at **Knapllwyd** in the Parish of Langevelach	–	2	–
Roger landeg, smith, holds a cottage & gardens at **Knapllwyd** in the Parish of Langevelach	–	2	–
John Mordecai, copperman, holds a cottage & gardens at **Knapllwyd** in the Parish of Langevelach	–	2	–
Griffith Jenkin, copperman, holds a cottage & gardens at **Knapllwyd** in the Parish of Langevelach	–	2	–
John Franklen, copperman, holds a cottage & gardens at **Trewyddva** in the Parish of Langevelach	–	2	–
David Phillip, copperman, holds a cottage & gardens at **Trewyddva** in the Parish of Langevelach	–	2	–
Evan Grey, collier, holds a cottage & gardens at **Trewyddva** in the Parish of Langevelach	–	2	–

32. Compare this list with that dated 1775-76 in Appendix III, p.228-230.

David Lot, copperman, holds a cottage & gardens at **Trewyddva** in the Parish of Langevelach	–	2	–
Hopkin Perkin, mason, holds a cottage & gardens at **Trewyddva** in the Parish of Langevelach	–	2	–
Edward Lewis, *[blank]*, holds a cottage & gardens at **Trewyddva** in the Parish of Langevelach	–	2	–
Catherine Grey, widow, holds a cottage & gardens at **Trewyddva** in the same Parish	–	2	–
Elizth Thomas, widow, holds a cottage & gardens at **Trewyddva** in the same Parish	–	2	–
Thos John Hugh, collier, holds a cottage & gardens at **Trewyddva** in the same Parish	–	2	–
William Hugh, collier, holds a cottage & gardens at **Trewyddva** in the same Parish	–	2	–
Honour Hugh, widow, holds a cottage & gardens at **Trewyddva** in the same Parish *[Folio 89/90]*	–	2	–
Thos William Hugh, collier, holds a cottage & gardens at **Trewyddva** in the Parish of Langevelach	–	2	–
John Thomas Hugh, collier, holds a cottage & gardens at **Trewyddva** in the Parish of Langevelach	–	2	–
Thomas Jenkin, copperman, holds a cottage & gardens at **Trewyddva** in the same Parish	–	2	–
Hopkin Terry, collier, holds a cottage & gardens at **Trewyddva** in the same Parish	–	2	–
William Lewis, collier, holds a cottage & gardens at **Trewyddva** in the same Parish	–	2	–
James Grey, collier, holds a cottage & gardens at **Trewyddva** in the same Parish	–	2	–
Henry David, collier, holds a cottage & gardens at **Trewyddva** in the same Parish	–	2	–
Morgan Thomas, collier, holds a cottage & gardens at **Trewyddva** in the same Parish	–	2	–
Isaac Bromfield, copperman, holds a cottage & gardens at **Trewyddva** in the same Parish	–	2	–
Maud Evan, widow, holds a cottage & gardens at **Trewyddva** in the same Parish	–	2	–
John Hugh, collier, holds a cottage & gardens at **Trewyddva** in the same Parish	–	2	–
Samuel Jones, schoolmaster, holds a cot. or schoolhouse at ditto. [In Sa., not in Bn]	–	2	–
Rees Wilcox, copperman, holds a cottage & gardens at **Heol Hene Sage** in the same Parish	–	2	–
David Perkin, mason, holds a cottage & gardens at **Place y Marle** in the same Parish	–	2	–

	£	s	d
John Abraham, collier, holds a cottage & gardens at **Place y Marle** in the same Parish	–	2	–
John Thomas, mason holds a cot. & garden at ditto. [In Sa., not in Bn]	–	2	–
Elizabeth Matthew, widow, holds a cottage & gardens at **Place y Marle** in the same Parish	–	2	–
David David, collier, holds a cottage & gardens near the **Marsh Side** in the same Parish	–	2	–
David Rees, collier, holds a cottage & gardens near the **Marsh Side** in the same Parish	–	2	–
William Powell, engineer, holds a cottage & gardens near the **Fire Engine** in the same Parish	–	2	–
Thomas Morris, collier, holds a cottage & garden near the **Fire Engine** in the same Parish	–	2	–
David Jenkin, copperman, holds a cottage & garden near the **Copperworks** in the same Parish	–	2	–
William Hopkin, copperman, holds a cottage & gardens near the **Copperworks** in the same Parish	–	–	2
Methusalem David, copperman, holds a cottage & gardens near the **Copperworks** in the same Parish	–	2	–
Thomas Howell, bargeman, holds a cottage & gardens near the **Copperworks** in the same Parish	–	2	–
William John, copperman, holds a cottage & gardens near the **Copperworks** in the same Parish	–	2	–
John Robert, copperman, holds a cottage & gardens near the **Copperworks** in the same Parish	–	2	–
Benj. John David, *[blank]*, holds a cottage & gardens near the **Copperworks** in the same Parish	–	2	–
Christmas Miles, *[blank]*, holds a cottage & gardens near the **Copperworks**	–	2	–

[Added marginal note: 'for further particulars of cottages see the latter end of this book', i.e. Appendix III.]

The said Richard Lockwood, John Lockwood, and Robert Morris esqs.
also hold by the same Lease all that piece or parcel of waste ground whereon their
Copperworks or **Smelting Houses** are now built, paying to the Lord yearly
the sum of five shillings on Michaelmas Day   – 5 –

Margaret Jones, widow, holds from year to year **two lime kilns at
Place y Marl** in the Fee of Trewyddva, paying to the Lord yearly   – 1 –

Robert Morris esq. holds from year to year **a limekiln** there, at the yearly rent of	–	1	–
Mr Thomas Lewis holds from year to year **a limekiln** there, at the yearly rent of	–	1	–

[Folio 90/91]

Mr Rowland Bevan holds from year to year **a limekiln** there, at the yearly rent of one shilling payable at Michaelmas yearly	–	1	–
Mr Thomas Jones holds from year to year a potato garden and court before a cott of his on **Mynnydd Carn Llwyd** within the Fee of Trewyddva, paying the Lord at Michaelmas yearly the sum of	–	2	–
Ann Franklen holds from year to year a small piece of waste land opposite her house at **Treboeth** in the Fee of Trewyddva, paying to the Lord at Michaelmas yearly the sum of	–	–	6

The Lord claims within the said Manor and Fees all manner of Royalties in as large and ample manner as he is intituled to enjoy them within the Seigniory.

He is also intituled to all the highways, wastes, [and] open and uninclosed lands, within the said Manor and Fees and the soil and profits thereof.

He is also intituled to, and has immemorially enjoyed, all Mines and Minerals, as well in upon or under the Copyhold lands, as under the wastes, open and uninclosed lands, under which right the following Leases have been granted and now subsist:

Mathew Pryce esq. and his wife, and Thomas Pryce esq., their son, executors of Thomas Popkin esq., deceased, have by virtue of a Deed or Lease dated the first day of August 1732, and granted to the said Thomas Popkin, deceased, by the Most Noble and Illustrious Prince Henry Scudamore Somerset, Duke of Beaufort, Marquis and Earl of Worcester, Earl of Glamorgan, Viscount Grismont, Baron Beaufort of Caldecot Castle and Baron Herbert of Chepstow Raglan and Gower, deceased, liberty to work all such **veins or mines of coal** as are upon or under any of the **Customary lands of the said Thomas Popkin** within any of the Manors of the said Duke, within the Honour or Lordship Royal of Gower. To hold for the term of ninety-nine years if the said Thomas Popkin (since deceased), Robert Popkin his son ['both since deceased' in Bn only] and Thomas Popkin, son of the said Robert (now living), or either of them, shall so long live. Yielding and paying for every wey of coal that shall be raised from the said Customary lands, the sum of one shilling within one month after the same shall be disposed of. Which agreement or Lease has been assigned by the said Matthew Pryce and his wife and Thomas Pryce to Robert Morris esq. who now works the same under the said Lease or agreement.

George Owen of Hendre in the County of Pembroke esq. (deceased) held by lease dated the 23rd of December 1735, and granted to him by The Most Noble Henry Duke of Beaufort (deceased): All those **mineral waters**[33], or waters mixed or impregnated with minerals, springs, fountains, streams and currents of water, springing, running or issuing, or which at any time hereafter during the term thereby granted may be found or discovered in, upon, or under, or out of, all or any part of those several Commons or parcels of uninclosed land called **Graig Trewyddva, Mynnydd Carn Llwyd, and Treboth**, situate and being in the Parish of Langevelach in the County of Glamorgan. And all such stratums or beds of mineral earth, stone or fossils through, or out of which, the said waters might spring, run or flow, or which then were, or might seem to be, impregnated. Together with free liberty and authority to and for the said George Owen, his Executors Administrators and Assigns, to dig, bore, sink, and search for such mineral waters, or waters mixed with minerals. And to make trenches, to lay and place pipes, pumps and other machines or conveyances and reservoirs, *[Folio 91/92]* in, upon or through the said several Commons, or either of them, for the obtaining, collecting, uniting and keeping the waters aforesaid. And to erect, build, and set up on the said Commons or any part thereof, such edifices, buildings, works and conveniences for the holding, improving, strengthening, manufacturing, or meliorating the said waters, from time to time as the said George Owen, his Executors, Administrators and Assigns, and his and their agents shall think proper.

And also with full liberty and power (as far forth as the said Duke can or may in law or Equity grant and demise the same) to and for the said George Owen, his Executors, Administrators and Assigns, and his and their servants, workmen and labourers, to dig and make use of any vitriolic or other earth, stone, fossil or fossils, stratum or stratums of earth (coal, culm, lead, copper, tin and iron excepted), as well in, upon, and out of the said several Commons, or either of them, as the several Customary or Copyhold lands or tenements commonly called or known by the names of **Trewyddva Ycha, Trewyddva Yssha, Tyr Dan yr Heol and Bryth Tyr**, in the several tenures or occupations of Thomas Popkin of Forrest and Thomas Pryce of Penllergare esqs. and Mary Jones, widow, their respective undertenants or Assigns.

And also with full liberty and power (as far forth as the said Duke can or may in law and Equity grant and demise the same) to and for the said George Owen, his Executors, Administrators and Assigns, and his and their workmen and labourers to remove and carry away and make use of all such loose earth, stones or rubbish (the same not being coal or culm) as may be had, found or come at, in any colliery or coalwork now open, or during the term thereby granted to be opened, in or upon the several Commons aforesaid, by such ways and means and in such manner as the said George Owen, his Executors, Administrators or Assigns shall think fit and proper. And for that purpose to have access to the same in or through the several levels belonging to the said collieries or coalworks, and to lay and deposit upon the said Commons, or either of them, all such stones, fossils, or stratums of earth and rubbish which shall be dug or made use of as aforesaid. And also all such timber, materials, implements and things as the said George Owen, his Executors or Administrators, at any time or times during the said term have occasion for, and think fit to make use of.

And moreover, with liberty for the said George Owen, his Executors, Administrators and Assigns, to make and lay down from time to time during the term hereby granted, a convenient

---

33. This is the 'Old Alum Works' shown on Lewis Thomas' map of Trewyddfa, 1761. A tracing is in WGRO, ref. D/D WCR/Pl 24a. See also Bernard Morris: 'The Beaufort Map of the Fee of Trewyddfa', in *South West Wales Industrial Archaeology Society Newsletter*, 77, Feb. 2000.

way or road over or across the said Commons, or any part of the same, from any buildings, erections or works which the said George Owen should make, build, or set up upon the said Commons, or either of them, or upon any of the Customary or Copyhold lands or tenements hereinbefore mentioned, to any highway adjoining to the said Commons. With free ingress, egress and regress for the said George Owen and his servants, with horses, carts, coaches or other carriages, to pass and repass upon and through such way to be made as aforesaid. Provided nevertheless that neither the said George Owen, his Executors, Administrators or Assigns, or their servants or workmen, in making trenches, laying pipes or digging of any earth, stones or stratums of earth by virtue of the said lease, should do or commit any act, matter or thing whatsoever to the prejudice or damage of any colliery, coal or culm work then opened or carried on in the said several Commons by the said Duke, his Heirs, or Assigns, or his or their lessees or tenants.

To hold all and singular the premises aforesaid unto the said George Owen, his Executors, Administrators and Assigns, from the Feast Day of Saint Michael then last past, for and during the term of thirty years. Yielding and paying unto the said Duke, his Heirs or Assigns, for the first year of the said term *[Folio 92/93]* the rent of one shilling on the Feast Day of Saint Michael the Archangel next ensuing the date thereof, and from thenceforth yearly during the residue of the said term of thirty years, the rent or sum of five pounds on the Feast of Saint Michael yearly.

£5   —   —

This Lease was assigned by the said George Owen to Thos Price of Penllergare esq., who pretends[34] that he assigned the same to John Owen (son of the said George Owen) and that he gave notice of such assignment to Mr Gardiner[35]. Who *[i.e. John Owen]* is since deceased insolvent, and there is now an arrear of 17 years, which at £5 per annum comes to £85.

*   *   *

Thomas Price of Penllergare esq. holds by Lease dated 12th November 1742 and granted to him by The Most Noble Henry Duke of Beaufort, deceased: All the **coal works,** and coal and culm mines, and veins of coal and culm then found or thereafter to be found within the **Customary lands** of the said Thomas Price, by him held of the said Lord Duke, situate and lying wheresoever within the Fee of Trewyddva in the County of Glamorgan. With full power and authority to and for the said Thomas Price, his Executors and Administrators and his and their workmen, to break, dig, sink, open and lay any pit or pits, gutter or gutters, trench or trenches in and upon the soil thereof, for the searching, finding, raising, working, and landing of the said coals, culm, coal mines and veins. With liberty to take carry away, sell and dispose of the same

34. i.e. 'claims'.
35. Mr Gardiner was the Duke's Receiver (i.e. accountant). The detail in which the terms of the lease are set out here suggests concern and embarrassment arising from the arrears and Price's 'smoke-screen'.

during the term hereinafter mentioned (saving that it shall be lawful for the said Lord Duke, his Heirs and Assigns, to place and appoint one or more Wind-keeper or Wind-keepers[36]).

And also all that pond on **Mynnydd Carn Goch** in the Parish of Loughor, containing half an acre (be it more or less) with full power, liberty and authority for the said Thomas Price, his Executors and Administrators, and his and their workmen to make drains, gutters, or trenches upon the said Common to convey water to the said pond.

To hold to the said Thomas Price, his Executors, Administrators and Assigns, from the second day of February then last past, for the term of ninety-nine years, if the said Thomas Price, ['since deceased' in Bn only] Gryffydd Price his son, ['now living' in Bn only] and Thomas Mathews of Nidfwch gent. or either of them should so long live. (which said Thomas Mathews is since dead) [bracketed words are in Sa. Bn has 'since deceased']. Yielding and paying to the said Duke, his Heirs and Assigns, for each wey of coal that shall be wrought, raised and disposed of, the rate or sum of nine pence halfpenny per Wey, and so in proportion for a greater or lesser quantity than a wey. And also yielding and paying unto the Duke, his Heirs or Assigns, the yearly rent or sum of sixpence for the said pond during the said term.

And the said Thomas Price, by the same Lease, does for himself, his Executors, Administrators and Assigns, covenant to pay and satisfy such wind-keeper to be appointed by the said Duke as aforesaid his reasonable wages. And to render and give unto the said Duke, his Heirs and Assigns, a perfect account in writing of all coal or culm raised or disposed of as aforesaid, signed and attested by such windkeeper half yearly, made and delivered on the Feast Day of the Annunciation of the Blessed Virgin Mary and Saint Michael the Archangel during the said term. And [then to] pay to the said Duke, his Heirs or Assigns, all such sum or sums of money which shall then be respectively due, and shall also at all times pay and discharge all manner of taxes, tallages, taxations and charges of what nature soever, by Act of Parliament, or otherwise howsoever imposed or to be imposed on the same culm pond or coalworks.

[Folio 93/94]

Customs and Courts within the Manor of Pennard and its Fees

All the Copyhold lands within the said Manor and Fees descend according to the Rules of Common Law, but are conveyed only by Surrender, passed in the Court of the Manor and Fees, which the tenants may do either in person or by Letter of Attorney, the due execution of which must be proved in Court at the time of passing, by one of the witnesses. And if it be an Estate of a *Femme Covert*[37], she must be sole and privately examined by the Steward as to her consent, or by the witnesses to the Letter of Attorney, who must prove the same. And if the Tenants convey, or even demise or let their Copyhold lands for a longer term than a year without a Surrender or Lease obtained in open Court, it is a Forfeiture.

The Tenants may, by the Custom, intail their Copyhold lands, which intails may be barred by Surrenders where a Fine will bar at Common Law. But where there are any Remainders which

---

36. Wind-keepers acted on the landlord's behalf, and, stationed at the pit-head or the entrance to a level, kept a check on the quantity of the coal etc. extracted. The sum due to the landlord could be then be assessed.
37. A married woman.

would require a Recovery to bar them at Common Law, those can only be barred by a Recovery in the Court of the Manor by a Plaint, in the nature of a Writ of Entry *Sur Disseisin en le Post*[38].

The widows of the Customary or Copyhold tenants are intituled to their Free Bench or widow's estate in all such Copyhold lands as their husbands die seised of. But the husbands are not intituled to hold the wife's lands by the Curtesy.

If any person claims any Copyhold lands within the said Manor and Fee, he may try his right to the same in the Court of the Manor by a Plaint in the nature of a Writ of Right, upon which Pleadings are filed, and when the cause is at issue it is to be tried by a jury of twelve Copyhold tenants, sworn for that purpose.

All the tenants within the said Manor and Fees pay Heriots of the best beast if they die within the said Manor or Fees, or accidentally out of it, and holding their Estate in their own hands. But if any tenant die seized within the Fee of Kittle of Free and Copyhold lands, he then pays a Heriot of the best beast for one tenure, and five shillings for the other. And if they die out of the said Manor and Fees, and not in the occupation of their lands, or happen to have no beast, then only five shillings are paid for each tenure.

If any tenant alienates all his lands within the said Manor or Fees, he pays the Lord five shillings for the said alienation, if only part, he pays nothing.

There are two Leet and Customary Courts held for the said Manor and Fees [held] within a month of Michaelmas and Easter, at such time and place as the Steward shall by Warrant under his Hand and Seal appoint. Of which Summons [notice] ought to be given by the respective Reeves at least eight days before, at the churches of Pennard and Ilston for the Manor of Pennard and Fees of Kittle and Lunnon, and to the tenants of Trewyddva, and also [by] proclaiming it on a Market Day in the Town of Swansea. Which Courts all the tenants and resiants are obliged to attend, on pain of Amerciaments. Which Amerciaments are to be immediately Affeered by two of the tenants sworn for that purpose, and afterwards levied by a Warrant under the hand of the Steward. At Michaelmas Courts the **Reeves** and **Constables** within the said Manor and Fees are appointed and sworn, and at May Courts the **Haywards**, – the Jury presenting double the number that are appointed and sworn of each.

The tenants and resiants within the said Manor and Fees owe Suit of Mill to the Lord's mills. That is, the tenants and resiants of the Manor of Pennard and Fees of Kittle and Lunnon owe their Suit to Park Mill; and the tenants and resiants of Trewyddva to the mill which is situate within the said Fee, called Melin Vach or the little Mill.   *[Folio 94/95]*

Within the Fee of Trewyddva there is, at the bottom or south end of a meadow of Mr Thomas Jones, called Gwain Lleffrith, adjoining the south side of Mynnydd Carn Llwyd, a piece of meadow ground containing about a quarter of an acre. And also a piece of woody ground, having a few small oaks growing there, adjoining to the east and south-east corner of the said quarter. The said piece being bounded on the north by a lan[d]share separating it from the said meadow, on the east and south by a hedge and ditch dividing it from meadows of Thomas Popkin esq., and on the west by a hedge and ditch dividing it from a meadow of the said Thomas Jones. The hay and lattermath[39] of the said quarter is claimed by the Reeve for the time being, as a satisfaction for his trouble in collecting the Copyhold rent within the said Fee.

---

38. For the various legal terms, see the Glossary on p.37 & 38.
39. Grass growing after the taking of a hay crop.

[Folio 95/96]

The Manor of Oystermouth

The Manor of Oystermouth is a Member of the Seigniory of Gower, and consists of several Freehold and Customary or Copyhold tenements and is situate in the Parish of Oystermouth. The boundaries whereof are: Beginning at the mouth of the river or brook which runs by Black Pill where it empties itself into the sea, and so turning westward along the sea shore to Carswell Bay. And then turning up the bottom, along a field of Robert ['Thomas' in Bn] Popkin esq. called Green-slade near Bishopswood, and thence to a place called Jack Shoes land near Bishopswood, and thence along the western hedge of a field of William Griffiths called Broad Park, to the highway at Esperlone. And then crossing the said highway to the western hedge of the lands of Robert ['Thomas' in Bn] Popkin esq., and along the said hedge to Mourning Coomb, where the water sinks under ground. And up the said watercourse or brook to the Common called Clyne Moor, and still keeping up the said watercourse or brook till the corner of the field called Furze Parks. And turning west along the ditch which is between the Furze Parks in Manselfield and Copland, being the lands of the Lord. And along the said ditch to the Common, and still keeping the ditch of the inclosures to the old bank and ditch which divides Clyne Moor from Murton Moor. And along the said old bank and ditch to the corner of the field on the west side of the Common. And thence along the boundary of the Parishes of Bishopstone and Oystermouth, to the brook that leads up from the lands of Mr Robert Mansel called Cradocks Moor to the lands of the Lord called Broadley. And still keeping [along] the brook to Wernllaeth Lane, and up that lane to the corner of a field of the Lord's called Bryncoch. And along the western ditch of the said field to the Common, and along the ditch of a field of David Hamon's called *[blank]* to the corner. And thence crossing the Common to the north, to a well or spring of water called Funnon Dwr Da, and down the well stream or rivulet to a small river or brook called Rheed y Devid. And down along the said river or brook at the bottom of Clyne Wood to Black Pill, and thence to the mouth of the said river or brook where the boundary was begun.

There are within this Manor two large Commons or wastes, to wit, Oystermouth, also [called] Clyne Moor, and the Cliffe.

The Moor is entirely surrounded by inclosures, except part at the north end where it joins to the Manor of Weobly. The tenants of the Manor hold this Common or waste of the Lord at the yearly rent of six pounds thirteen shillings and four pence, and they do permit the tenants of Manselfield, and Murton which is a part of the Manor of Bishopstone, to turn their cattle to the same, paying two pounds nine shillings and eleven pence halfpenny yearly towards the said rent payable to the Lord.

The Cliffs which border on the sea are held by some of the neighbouring tenants of the said Manor at the yearly rent of £1 16s, to wit: Newton Cliff, twenty shillings; and Mumble Cliff, sixteen shillings; which they pay to Mrs. Mary Watkins[40], who rents the same from the Lord together with other things.

---

40. Mrs. Mary Watkins of Great Highway, Pennard.

There are on the Cliffes considerable lime stone quarries, which are let out by Mrs. Watkins to several persons who work the same and pay her the sum of two pence out of every *[blank]* ['Twenty' in Bn] shillings.

There is within this Manor a Customary Duty (called Keelage of Ships) of four ['two' in Bn] pence for every ship which lies on the sand commonly called the Mumbles Flats, and [it] is paid to Mrs. Watkins.

[Folio 96/97]

Several of the inhabitants of this Manor have particular spots on the sands under the Cliff, usually called perches, where they lay down their oysters as they catch them, until such time that they ship them off for markets, chiefly for Bristol. For which spots they respectively pay the Lord six pence yearly. Others fix poles or stakes in the sands, to which they fix nets for catching fish, for which liberty they respectively pay the Lord six pence yearly. There are others who fish for and take lobsters and crabs on the rocks or on the sea shore, for which they pay the Lord six pence a piece yearly.

The persons who paid last year are:

For Perches:

John Griffith	Mary Davies, widow	
Thomas Dunn	David Lowarch	Matthew Hall
William Maddocks	Elizabeth Russel	Daniel Cleypit
George Thomas	Richard Sheppard	John Vaughan

For fixing Nets:

Francis David	Elizabeth Williams	John Morgan
Elizabeth Powell	James Parry	
William Williams Owen David		

For catching Crabs and Lobsters:

Phillip Morgan

There are several persons who have wears erected on the sands, which belong to the Free and Copyhold tenements, and pass as appurtenant to them.

There is also in the **Mumble Cliff** a vein of **iron ore**, which has been tried by some iron masters, but not yet worked so as to yield any profit.

There are in **Clyne Wood** some veins or **mines of coal** which are held by Lease by Messrs Champion and Griffiths, who are to pay 3s 6d per wey, each wey to contain 72 bags and each bag 24 Winchester gallons. But those mines yield at present but very little profit.

The said lease has been since surrendered.

[Folio 97/98]

A Rent Roll of the Free Rent within the Manor of Oystermouth due to the Lord at Michaelmas 1761

Landlords	Tenements	Occupiers	Rent per annum		
			£	s	d
John Jennings esq.	Thistleboon	Mr Hugh Powell	–	3	4
Thomas Griffiths gent.	Readings	Joseph Evan	–	2	–
Geo. Venables Vernon esq.	Readings	The same	–	1	–
Thomas Bydder	Nottage	Thomas Bydder	–	–	10
William Griffiths	Newton	William Griffith	–	–	2½
Richard Edwards	Thisleboon	Richard Edwards	–	–	–½
John Jones	Nottage	Bennet Stephen	–	1	–
Phillip Morgan	Newton	Phillip Morgan	–	–	1
Thomas Gorton	Newton	Mary King	–	–	2½
The same	The same	Mathew Jone	–	–	3
John Thomas	The same	Phillip Morgan junr.	–	–	3½
John Russel	The same	John Russel	–	–	–½
The sameThe same	The same		–	–	4¼
Isaac Griffiths	House and lands at Newton	Ann Mathew	–	–	6¼
Mary Maddocks, widow	Thistleboon	John Kift	–	–	2
The same	Land bought of Chas White	The same	–	–	2
Hannah Sambrook, widow	Newton	Hannah Sambrook	–	–	–¾
Geo. Venables Vernon esq.	House and lands called Orchard Slade, 3 qrs at Horestone, Oak, Hollow Oak, Stubby Head &c	John Howell	–	–	3
Rachael Gamon	Lands at Newton & Horestone	Jenkin Jenkins	–	–	4

Landlords	Tenements	Occupiers	Rent per annum		
			£	s	d
William Maddocks	A barn & garden at Newton, late a house	George Thomas	–	–	–¾
Mr William Dawkin	Eight acres in Horestone Field	Rowland Morris	–	–	4
Geo. Venables Vernon esq.	House & lands at the at the north of Newton called Broad Acre, Singlewood &c	John Howell	–	–	2
James Parry	House & lands at Newton called Moor Park	James Parry	–	–	2
George Bydder gent.	Gower Cross	George Bydder	–	–	6
William Rosser	Hogland at Black Pill	William Rosser	–	–	6
Thomas Mansel Talbot esq. (was Geo. Venables Vernon esq.)	Monkyland	– Gamon, widow	–	1	–
The Rt Honble the Earl of Warwick	Part of Scurla Castle	John Clement	–	–	8
Richard Gorton, George Taylor, John Taylor, of Brufton and Philip Jenkin	Lands in Langennith	*[blank]*	–	1	2
Mary France, widow	Kennickstone	William Tucker	–	1	–
Earl of Ashburnham	Mill in Langennith	Geo. Taylor	–	1	8
Elizabeth Maddocks	Misegrove	Thomas Cornelius	–	–	3
The Earl of Warwick	Malefant's Meadow	Dd Jenkin of Norton	–	–	7½
Isaac Davies	House and garden at Newton	Anne Davies	–	–	–½
George Venables Vernon esq.	Ditto (the house is fallen down)	John Russel for garden	–	–	–½
Elizabeth Hamon	A small field by Bradley	Elizabeth Hamon	–	2	–
David Hoskin	House at Newton	David Hoskin	–	–	–½
			1	1	3

[Folio 98/99]

A Rent Roll of Customary and Moor Rent within the Manor of Oystermouth due to the Lord at Michaelmas 1761

Copyholders	Tenements	Occupiers	Customary Rent per annum			Moor Rent		
			£	s	d	£	s	d
Elizabeth Phillips, widow	Boars Pit	Thomas Bowen	–	14	8	–	3	–
The same	Mallops	Thomas Bowen	–	5	7	–	–	–
Owen Brigstock esq.	Thisleboon	Mr Hugh Powell	1	0	4	–	1	8
The same	Lands bought of Thomas Clement, Herbert Rows, Mary Thorn &c.	The same	–	3	4	–	–	–
William Dawkin esq.	Lands held by Owen Brigstock esq. and mixed with his lands	The same	–	7	–	–	–	–
Owen Brigstock esq.	Herne Acre	Joseph Evans	–	1	–	–	–	–
Mr Thomas Griffiths	Lands at Newton	Joseph Evans	–	10	5	–	1	6
The same	Land late of Thomas Russel	Joseph Evans	–	–	10	–	–	–
Mr William Dawkin	House & lands at Newton & 2 acres at Dunns	Rowland Morris	–	17	–	–	1	6
The same	House & lands at the upper end of Newton	The same	–	14	8	–	1	6
William Griffiths Newton	House & lands at	William Griffiths	1	1	11	–	1	6
Thomas Bydder	Ditto	Thomas Bydder	–	15	10	–	1	8
Isaac Griffiths	House & lands at Norton	Anne Mathew, widow	–	10	4	–	1	4
Elizabeth Maddocks, spinster	Late John Gethin's lands	Bennet Stephen junr	–	10	–	–	1	–
Richard Edward	House & lands at Newton	Richard Edward	–	5	–	–	1	6

Copyholders	Tenements	Occupiers	Customary			Moor Rent		
				Rent per annum				
			£	s	d	£	s	d
The same	Three ['Two' in Bn] houses & gardens at Newton	The same	–	–	2	–	–	–
The same	House and lands at Thistleboon bought of Thomas Parry	The same	–	3	10	–	1	–
John Jones	House and land at Nottage	Bennet Stephen	–	6	7	–	1	6
John Kift	House at Newton and lands	John Kift	–	7	6½	–	1	6
Isaac Seacomb	Five acres near Newton	Isaac Seacomb	–	3	9½	–	–	6
Thomas Gorton	A house & 3½ acres near Newton	Mary Richards	–	3	4	–	1	6
Thomas Gorton	An acre & 3 qrs at Thistleboon	Robert Jone	–	1	5	–	–	–
George Bydder	Colts Hill	George Bydder	–	12	11	–	1	–
Elizabeth Gorton, widow	Betts	Robert Phillip	–	2	8	–	1	–
Thomas Price	House & garden at Norton	Thomas Price	–	4	9	–	1	6
Mr William Dawkins	House at Norton and lands	Thomas Bowen and Thomas Price	–	9	9	–	2	–
The same	For half a wear	The same	–	–	4	–	–	–
Morgan John	For a house	Morgan John	–	–	3	–	–	–
Rachel Gamon and Jenkin Jenkin	Lands near Newton	David Hoskin	–	7	–	–	1	6
Sarah Gamon	House & 2 acres called Overland & Longland	Sarah Gamon & John Kift	–	1	10	–	–	6
David Williams and Catherine Smith	House & 2½ Acres called lady housty	Richd Phillips, David Wms & Catherine Smith	–	2	9	–	–	6

Copyholders	Tenements	Occupiers	Customary			Moor Rent		
				Rent per annum				
			£	s	d	£	s	d
Isaac Seacomb	House & croft at Newton	Isaac Seacomb	–	–	3	–	–	–
Joan Kift	One acre called Killgreen	John Kift ['Joan' in Bn]	–	1	2	–	–	–
John Russell	House at Newton & lands	John Russel *[sic]*	–	9	2	–	1	–
The same	For Norton	John Russel	–	6	9½	–	–	10
The same	For John Kneath's lands	John Russel	–	–	5	–	–	–
Geo. Venables Vernon esq.	House at Newton and lands	Thomas Nicholas, a tenant to William James	–	8	2	–	1	–
Phillip Morgan [Folio 99/100]	Half an acre called Harry pit Hay	Phillip Morgan	–	–	6	–	–	6
Susannah Mortimer	Half an acre called Harry pit Hay	Susannah Mortimer	–	–	6	–	–	6
William Dawkin esq.	House garden & croft at Norton	William David	–	–	8	–	–	6
James Parry	An acre at Boarspit	James Parry	–	–	10	–	1	–
The same	A house & garden at Blackpill	Solomon Lewis	–	–	1	–	–	–
Mr William Dawkins	Lands at Colts hill	James Parry	–	4	7½	–	–	6
William Howells	House & lands at Thistleboon	Michael John	–	5	–	–	–	6
Sarah Robbin	House & acre at Underhill	William Thomas	–	1	–	–	–	–
Hopkin Griffiths	House & lands at Thistleboon	Hopkin Griffiths	–	7	8	–	1	–
The same	Lands bought of Clement at ditto	The same	–	–	3	–	–	–
The same	Lands bought of Parry at ditto	The same	–	3	10	–	–	–

Copyholders	Tenements	Occupiers	Customary Rent per annum			Moor Rent		
			£	s	d	£	s	d
Henry Pardoe	House garden & lands at Newton	Henry Pardoe	–	–	8	–	–	–
Sarah Clement	House & garden at Thistleboon	David Murton & William Jone	–	–	4	–	–	–
Mary Maddocks	House & lands at Thistleboon	Mary Maddocks & John Kift junr.	–	5	2	–	1	–
The same	Lands bought of Charles White at ditto	The same	–	1	9	–	–	2
Matthew Hall	House fallen down	Matthew Hall	–	–	3	–	–	6
The same	An acre at Dunns	Thomas Smith	–	1	6	–	–	6
William Robbin	House & 2 fields & wood at Horse Pool	William Robbin	–	3	–	–	–	6
Sarah Rees	House & 3 acres at Underhill	Sarah Rees	–	3	6	–	–	–
John Thomas and George Thomas	House & lands at Underhill and on the Cliff	Geo. Thomas, Jno. Kift, John Bynon & John Jenkin	–	7	6	–	–	6
William Dawkin esq.	House and lands at Underhill	Thomas Rees	–	6	3	–	–	6
Richard. Jones & Wm Rosser	House & 3 acres at Dunns	Richard Jones	–	2	–	–	–	6
Elizabeth Maddox, spinster	House at Dunns & lands	Thomas Cornelius	–	2	6	–	1	–
The same	Ditto	John Matthew	–	–	9	–	–	–
The same	House & lands bought of Wm Williams	David Jenkin junr.	–	6	9	–	–	–
The same	For lands at Norton	The same	–	15	8	–	1	6
William Maddocks	For lands at Norton	William Thomas	–	12	11½	–	2	–
David Williams, mariner	An old barn & garden at Norton	David Williams	–	–	3	–	–	–

West Cross farm (see page 178), Colts Hill (see pages 173 and 174) and Mumbles in 1783, by Lieut. William Booth.

No. 660 Mumbles Road, Southend. Probably built under one of the leases listed from pages 189 to 194 below, this house is shown on the Beaufort Estate map of 1803. It is there identified as the 'Ship and Castle' public house.

Copyholders	Tenements	Occupiers	Customary Rent per annum			Moor Rent		
			£	s	d	£	s	d
Wm Williams, smith	A house and garden at Norton	William Williams	–	–	3	–	–	6
Mary Ayres	House and lands at Norton	Mary Michael	–	2	6	–	–	6
Geo.Venables Vernon esq.	Gower's Cross	Thomas Rees	–	16	–	–	3	–
William Dawkin esq.	White Stone	Mathew Jone	–	1	4	–	1	–
Mr Paul Bevan	Boar's Pitt	David Jenkin	–	–	–	–	2	6
The Lord	Three Acres at Underhill	The same	–	–	–	–	–	6
Thomas Popkin esq.	Mayalls	George Bydder	–	1	2	–	–	6
Geo. Venables Vernon esq.	Whitestone	William Lewis	–	–	8	–	1	–
John Griffiths	Mayalls	John Givelin	–	16	5	–	5	–
Francis David	Mayalls, the Lord's lands	Francis David	–	–	–	–	1	–
William Dawkin esq.	House and lands at Black Pill	Henry Morgan	–	8	6	–	1	6
The Lord	House and lands at Black Pill	Henry Tucker	–	1	8	–	–	6
[Folio 100/101]								
The Lord	The Mill & lands	Henry Tucker, mason	–	–	–	–	–	6
Geo.Venables Vernon esq.	The Meadow near Black Pill	William Rosser	–	–	3	–	1	–
Thomas Popkin esq.	Lands at Newton	John Webbern & Joseph Bynon	–	6	2	–	–	–
Elizabeth Givelin	Lands at Esperlone & New Parks	Elizabeth Givelin	–	1	4	–	–	–
Susannah Portrey	An old house and garden at Esperlane	William Lewis	–	–	4	–	–	–

Copyholders	Tenements	Occupiers	Customary			Moor Rent		
			Rent per annum					
			£	s	d	£	s	d
Geo. Venables Vernon esq.	Grange	William Bynon	–	–	–	–	2	–
The same	West Cross	John Bennett	–	–	–	–	2	–
Elizabeth Hamon	Lands near Bradley	Elizabeth Hamon	–	–	–	–	2	–
Hannah Sambroke	A quarter at Newton called Stubby Land	Hannah Sambroke	–	–	3	–	–	–
John Russel	Lands at Boars Pit late Luce Jones	John Russel	–	1	4	–	–	–
			£20	5	10½	£3	10	2

A Rent Roll of the Persons who pays Moor Rent within the Manor of Oystermouth and are not Customary or Copyholders, due to the Lord at Michaelmas 1760[41]

	£	s	d
Mr George Bidder for West Cross	–	1	–
Elinor Edward, widow	–	1	–
Owen David	–	–	6
Richard Phillip	–	1	6
Thomas Morgan, Black Pill	–	1	–
William Gwynn, Broadley	–	1	–
John Nicholas	–	–	6
David Lloyd	–	–	6
Solomon Lewis	–	–	6
Richard Griffith	–	1	–
John Rosser	–	1	–
William Hopkin	–	1	–
Owen David, or tenant	–	–	6
Anne Rees	–	–	6
Thomas Elias	–	–	6
David Rees, cooper	–	–	6
William Williams, mariner	–	–	6
Anne Mathew, widow	–	1	–
Mary Davies, widow, Thistleboon	–	–	6
Thomas Lloyd, Newton	–	–	6
George Thomas	–	–	6

41. In the Sa original, as now rebound, this rent roll has been included in the Miscellanea volume. It appears in the present position in Bn, but without the words 'due to the Lord at Michaelmas 1760'.

	£	s	d
Elizabeth Russel	–	–	6
Elizabeth Powel *[in Bn only]*	–	–	6
John Griffiths, cooper *[in Sa only]*	–	–	6
Henry Morgan, cooper	–	–	6
John Jenkin	–	–	6
David William, mariner, Norton	–	–	6
John William, Newton	–	–	6
Mary Seacomb, widow	–	–	6
John Bennett	–	3	6
William Lewis, Newton	–	–	6
Elizabeth Jones, widow, Norton	–	–	6
Henry Henry	–	1	–
John Howell, Newton	–	–	6
William Jenkin, weaver	–	–	6
Mr Hopkin Walters, or tenant	–	1	–
Leyson Bowen	–	1	–
	£1	8	–

*   *   *

A Rent Roll of the Persons that contribute to pay or make up the Moor Rent within the Manor of Oystermouth who live out of the Manor

Manselfield Hamlet:

	£	s	d
John Griffith	–	7	1
Elizabeth Givelin, widow	–	4	1
Thomas Parry	–	3	–
David Webbern 3/- ⎱ David Edward 8d ⎰	–	3	8

Murton:

	£	s	d
William Givelin	–	5	–
Thomas Watkins ['Watkins's widow' in Bn]	–	3	7
James Webbern	–	2	–
William Givelin	–	2	2
David Webbern	–	1	–
John Rowland	–	–	10
Rowland Rowland	–	–	6
David Webbern	–	2	6
Amy Webbern, widow	–	1	6
John Bydder	–	1	3
James Webbern	–	–	5
William Givelin	–	–	7
John Webbern	–	4	3

	£	s	d
Thomas Edward	–	1	4
David Bowen	–	2	6
David Hamon	–	1	6
Jacob Bynon	–	–	3
John Parry	–	–	4
John Griffith	–	–	7½
	£2	9	11½

[Folio 101/102]

An Account of the Inhabitants of Thistleboon that grazed Thistleboon or Mumbles Hill in the Year 1761

	No of Horses	No of Sheep	Rent per annum		
			£	s	d
Richard Jones	1	–	–	–	8
David William	1	–	–	–	8
William Williams	1	–	–	–	8
John Vaughan	1	–	–	–	8
David Morton	1	–	–	–	8
William Michael	1	–	–	–	8
John Griffith	1	12	–	1	8
David William	1	–	–	–	8
Jenkin Dunn	1	6	–	1	2
Leyson Bowen	1	–	–	–	8
Thomas Griffith	1	–	–	–	8
George Bowen	2	–	–	1	4
William Williams	1	–	–	–	8
Richard Edward	–	24	–	2	–
Isaac David	–	9	–	–	9
Richard Sheppard	–	10	–	–	10
Richard Burt	–	12	–	1	–
Daniel Cleypit	–	6	–	–	6
			–	15	11

Furze Cutters:

	£	s	d
Thomas Griffiths pays yearly for cutting furze on the Hill	–	–	6
Daniel Cleypit [for] the like	–	–	6
William Michael [for] the like	–	–	6
	–	17	5

An Account of the Inhabitants who grazed
Newton Cliffes in the Year 1761

	Horses	*Sheep*	£	s	d
Joseph Evan	none		–	–	–
John Kift	–	6	–	–	7½
Daniel Bevan	–	15	–	1	5
John Howell	–	5	–	–	5¾
Jenkin Jenkins	–	10	–		11¼
David Hoskin	–	2	–	–	2½
Thomas Nicholas	–	10	–	–	11¼
William Lewis	–	11	–	1	0½
James Parry	–	5	–	–	6
William Jenkin	–	6	–	–	6¾
William Griffith	–	5	–	–	6
Matthew Jone	–	8	–	–	9
Mary Lloyd	–	3	–	–	3½
Thomas Bydder	–	28	–	2	7½
John Morgan	–	23	–	2	2
Bennet Stephen	–	3	–	–	3½
William David	–	5	–	–	5¾
Bennet Stephen the elder	–	30	–	2	9¾
Thomas Bydder the younger	–	18	–	1	8¼
William Howell	–	10	–	–	11¼
William Jenkin the younger	–	3	–	–	3¼
			1	9	6½

These rents are paid yearly to Mrs Mary Watkins who rents the said Cliffes with other things of the Lord, vide folio 103.

[Folio 102/103]

The Lord is intitutled to the Several Demesne lands herein
after mentioned within the said Manor of Oystermouth

Mrs. Mary Watkins lately held by Lease, and now holds from year to year, all those Duties of **Cliffage, Oar, Keelage, Anchorage, and Herbage**, within the waste lands and cliffts belonging to the Manors of Oystermouth and Pennard, with all the rights and privileges to them belonging. Together also with that cottage situate in the Town of Swansea, in a certain place there called the Postern, and formerly in the possession of Isaac After and now in the possession of one Joan Webb, with the waste thereto adjoining from the said cottage to low water mark in the River Tawy, containing by estimation half an acre (be it more or less). For which the said Mrs. Watkins pays to the Lord the rent or sum of £20 5s yearly.   £20   5   –

William Maddocks holds several parcels of lands in the Parish of Oystermouth from year to year, paying to the Lord for the same the yearly rent of £8, which closes are as follows, to wit[42]:

	Acres	Roods
Dunns Close, containing two acres and a half, having the lane leading to Newton on the east, the lands of William Dawkin of Eagle's Bush esq. on the north and west, and the lands of Elizabeth Maddocks, spinster, on the south.	2	2
New Cross, containing one acre, having the lane leading to Newton on the north, a close of the Lord's called the Pool on the east, John Thomas's field on the west, and the lands of John Robin on the south.	1	–
A close called the little acre, containing one acre [having] the lane leading to Newton on the east and Underhill lane on the north.	1	–
A close called Underhill, containing three acres, having the lands of Mary Davies on the east side thereof. Mr William Dawkin of Eagle's Bush has an acre in this field on the south side thereof, as appears by mear stones there set.	3	–
A piece of rough ground overrun with briars, thorns and furze, called Longland, containing ten acres, meared on the east by John Russel's field called Rotherslade, and at the bottom of the steep ground by Rachael Gamon's land called Rotherslade. On the south by Mr Vernon's eastern Longland, and then comes down a piece of ground of John Russel's called Smithy's Pit, which divides the Lord's Longland in the middle. There is a long narrow piece of ground of Mr Vernon's, about ten foot broad, called the western Longland, and goes to nothing within about one hundred yards to the end where the Lord has a little clear spot. On the west by the lands of Mr William Dawkin called Peaseland, and on the north by the lands of Thomas Bydder called Heal, and a field of William Griffiths called Lowmes, a field of John Jones called Lowmes, and by fields of Mr Thomas Griffiths, Geo. V. Vernon and Owen Brigstock Esqs. called Riddings.	10	–
A rough piece of ground at Peaseland, containing two acres, having a field of John Jones lying open to it on the south called Peaseland, a narrow road called Peaseland Lane on the west, two fields of Mr Wm Dawkins on the north and east called Peaseland.	2	–

[Folio 103/104]

	Acres	Roods
Kilsplots, a rough piece of ground containing about twelve acres, having a few small oak trees growing on it, lying open	12	–

---

42. The scattered nature of these holdings and their size and descriptions, show that they are survivals from a medieval open field form of cultivation. This is confirmed by later estate maps – e.g. WGRO. D/D Beau E1 (1802).

on the west to a long piece of ground of Robert ['Thomas' in Bn]
Popkin esq. called Greenslade, on the south by Summerland
Clift, on the north by John Kift's wood, and on the east by
lands of Mr Wm Dawkin called Kilsplots, lying open to it.

Number of acres held by William Maddock:	30	2	£8	–	–

Henry Henry holds an old cottage garden and croft from
year to year, situate above the **Mayals** adjoining Oystermouth
Moor, at the yearly rent of £– 7 –

Francis David holds from year to year a small house, stable
and garden, situate on the **Mayalls**, together with the several
closes following :

	Acres	Qrs
Kae ych lawr Tuy containing 3 acres, one acre whereof is meadow ground	3	–
A close called Kae Kenol containing	1	2
A close called Kae Pella containing	1	2

Those closes are meared by the lands of Mary Griffiths, widow,
now in the possession of William Henry on the south, Oystermouth
Moor on the west and north, and the lane leading from Mayals to
the Moor on the east.

He also holds a small meadow under the said lane, called Gwain
alias Cae Bach, containing one acre; meared by the said lane on
the west, the Lord's waste at Mayals on the south, and the lands
of the said Mary Griffiths on the north and east.   1   –

Number of acres held by Francis David and rent per annum:	7	0	£2	10	–

Thomas Morgan, John Rosser and Wm Hopkin hold from year to
year a tenement of lands called **Clyne**, situate within the said Manor
of Oystermouth, consisting of the particulars following, to wit:

	Acres	Qrs
A house and garden in the possession of the said John Rosser.		
A house, garden, stall and stable in the possession of the said Wm Hopkin.		
A house and garden in the possession of the said Thomas Morgan.		
A cottage and garden let by them to one Margaret Prees.		
A cottage and garden let by them to one Richard Griffith.		
One other cottage and garden (now vacant).		
One meadow called *[blank]* containing	3	–
One other meadow called Clyne Meadow containing	12	–
The new Meadow under the Wood near the Engine in possession of William David & John Bennet	6	–
A large piece of rough ground called *[blank]* about	*[blank]*	

Three fields called David Hopkin's lands, containing four acres and a half	4	2
The Great Field containing fifteen acres	15	–
A small field lying to the east of the Great Field	3	–
Two crofts by the house in possession of Thomas Morgan ['Richd. Griffith' in Bn]	1	2
[Folio 104/105]		
Three crofts by the house in possession of Richard Griffiths, containing	1	2
Three fields in the possession of Henry Morgan called *[blank]* containing	*[blank]*	
A piece of rough ground *[blank]* in the possession of Henry Morgan, containing *[blank]*	*[blank]*	
A croft on the south side of Clyne Lane, containing	*[blank]*	

The number of acres held by Thos Morgan, John Rosser &
Wm Hopkin   *[blank]*   £26   –   –

The outward bounds of this tenement are: Clyne Moor on the west, Clyne Common and Lane on the south, and Black Pill River on the north and east. Within these boundaries Mr Thomas Griffiths, late of Newton, has a meadow containing two acres, and James Parry of Newton has a house and garden just behind the mill.

The Lord having allowed Matthew Hall of Oystermouth timber
for the building his house under the Cliff, he was by agreement
to pay interest for the said timber during the continuation of his
lease, and therefore he pays yearly the sum of   £–   10   –

Mrs Watkins of Highway pays the like yearly rent of   £–   11   9

William Williams ['Watkins' in Bn] of Oystermouth pays the like yearly rent of   £–   3   –

Henry Morgan holds by Lease dated the 22nd of July 1731,
 granted to Henry Tucker, all that water corn grist mill called
or known by the name of **Black Pill Mill,** and also a dwelling
house at Brockhole.

	Acres	*Qrs*
A small close called South Croft containing	–	1
Brock Hole croft containing1	–	
Cae Watt containing one acre and a quarter	1	1
The Meadow containing one acre1	–	
A coarse piece called Brockhole with some small trees on it	5	0
A rough piece of gorse containing	–	2

Number of acres held by Henry Morgan and rent per annum: 9   0   £12   12   –

To hold to Henry Tucker for and during the natural lives of the said Henry Tucker, Margaret his then wife, and Jane his daughter. At and under the yearly rent of £12 10s, payable at Lady Day and Michaelmas by even and equal portions, together with one couple of fat pullets, or two shillings in lieu thereof, yearly, and the sum of five shillings upon the decease of every tenant dying in possession. And the like sum of five shillings upon every Assignment or Alienation. And doing Suit of Mill and Suit of Court to the Court of the Manor of Oystermouth, on pain of five shillings for every default.

James Parry holds by Lease dated the 20th of December 1734 all that acre of land, being one moiety or half part of a certain meadow called or known by the name of **Long Meadow**, situate in the Parish of Oystermouth, on the north part of the said meadow. And having the highway and other lands of the Lord on the east part, and the lands of Mr William Dawkin and the road called Underhill Lane on the south part, and the lands of John Griffith on the west part thereof. To hold to the said James Parry for and during the natural lives of John, Elizabeth and Sarah Parry, children of the said James Parry, and the life of the survivor of them. At and under the yearly rent of *[Folio 105/106]* one shilling, payable half yearly by even portions. Paying two shillings and six pence upon the decease of every tenant dying in possession. And doing Suit of Mill and Suit of Court to the Court of the Manor of Oystermouth, on pain of three shillings and four pence for every default.

The improved rent of this amounts to   £1   –   –

Elizabeth Powell, spinster, Assignee of Phillip Powell, deceased, holds by virtue of a Lease granted to the said Phillip Powell [dated] 20th of December 1734, all that messuage or dwelling house called or known by the name of the **Horse Pool House**. And all those several closes and parcels of lands called and known by the several names following, to wit:

	Acres	Qrs
Pool Close containing by estimation two acres	2	–
The inner Meadow containing by estimation two acres	2	–
The inner Meadow *[sic]* containing by estimation one acre	1	–
The outer Meadow containing by estimation one acre	1	–
The landshare containing by estimation one acre	1	–
Acres	7	–

To hold to the said Phillip Powell for and during the natural lives of the said Phillip Powell (since deceased), Sarah Powell and Elinor Powell, his two daughters (now living), and the life of the survivor of them. At and under the yearly rent of two shillings, payable at Lady Day and Michaelmas by even portions, together with two fat pullets, or one shilling in lieu thereof. And the sum of five shillings in the name of an Heriot on the decease of every tenant dying in possession. And the like sum of five shillings upon every Assignment or Alienation, and doing Suit of Mill and Suit of Court to the Court of the Manor of Oystermouth, on pain of three shillings and four pence for every default.

Improved value   £8   –   –

Amy Webbern, widow, holds by Lease dated 20th December 1734 (and granted to Anne Owen, widow), all those two closes and parcels of lands called and known by the name of the **Four Acres**, containing by estimation four acres. And also all that close called Waterland, containing one acre, which closes are situate and being in the Parish and Manor of Oystermouth. And are meared by the lane leading from Oystermouth to Newton on the east, Grove's Lane on the south, Dumaines on the west, and the Lord's close called the Little Acre, in the possession of Richard Birt, on the north side thereof. To hold to the said Anne Owen for and during the lives of the said Anne Owen, John Owen her son, and Anne Owen her daughter, and the survivor of them. At and under the yearly rent of two shillings and one shilling in lieu of Duties yearly, the sum of five shillings in lieu of a Heriot, and the like sum of five shillings upon every Alienation. And doing Suit of Mill and Suit of Court on pain of three shillings and four pence for every default.

The improved yearly value of these closes or lands amounts to	£5	–	–

[Folio 106/107]

Mary Davies, widow, holds by Lease dated 25th of March 1749, all that old ruinous castle called **Oystermouth Castle**. And all those closes and parcels of lands to the same belonging called and known by the name of the Castle Close and Culver Close, containing by estimation three acres.

	Acres	*Qrs*
	3	–
Ledon's Close and the Hill Acre containing by estimation four acres	4	–
One meadow under Newton Hill called the Long Meadow containing	3	–
One other meadow thereto adjoining called the Pound Meadow containing	1	–
	11	–

To hold to the said Mary Davies for and during the lives of Anne Davies, Mary Davies and Elizabeth Davies, daughters of the said Mary Davies, and the life of the survivor of them. At and under the yearly rent or sum of five shillings, payable half yearly by equal portions, together with two fat pullets or one shilling in lieu thereof. And the sum of five shillings in lieu of a Heriot on the decease of every tenant dying in possession, and the like sum of five shillings for every Assignment or Alienation. Doing Suit of Mill and Suit of Court to the Court of the Manor of Oystermouth, on pain of three shillings and four pence for every default.

The improved yearly value of those closes amounts to	£8	–	–

The same **Mary Davies** holds by lease dated 15th July 1735, all those several parcels of lands situate and being in the Parish of Oystermouth, called and known by the several names following, to wit:

	Acres	*Qrs*
A field lying under Gilver's Clift Wood containing by estimation two acres	2	–
One meadow thereto adjoining, containing by estimation one acre	1	–
And also two other fields lying near Misgrove, containing by estimation	2	2
	5	2

To hold to the said Mary Davies for and during her life, the lives of Isaac Davies and Ann Davies, her son and daughter, and the survivor of them. At and under the yearly rent of one shilling, and at and under the same Duties and conditions as the next preceding lease.

The improved yearly value hereof amounts to   £4   —   —

The Representatives of Mrs Phillips hold by Lease (granted to the said Mrs Elizabeth Phillips and dated 30th September 1731), all that **house and garden situate at Norton**, now in the possession of Evan Michael, and also the closes following:

	Acres	*Qrs*
A close called the Castle Field containing one acre, having the Limekiln Close of Mr William Maddocks on the north, and the lands of Elizabeth Maddocks, spinster, on the south	1	—
A long drang containing half an acre, meared with Mr William Maddocks lands on the east, the lands of Elizabeth Maddocks, spinster, on the west, the beach on the south and the little lane on the north	—	2
One parcel of hilly ground called the Headland, containing three acres, meared by the lands of John Russel on the south, the lands of Samuel Gamon on the north, and the lands of Geo. Venables Vernon esq. called Singlewood, now in the possession of John Howell, on the west and east thereof	3	—
	4	2

[*Folio 107/108*]

To hold to the said Elizabeth Phillips, her Executors, Administrators, and Assigns, for and during the term of Ninety-nine years, to commence from the Feast of Saint Michael then last past, if Richard Phillips (since dead), Anne and Elizabeth Phillips (both now living), son and daughters of the said Elizabeth Phillips, or either of them, should so long live. At and under the yearly rent or sum of one pound and sixteen shillings, payable half yearly by equal portions, clear of all deductions whatsoever (the Land Tax only excepted). Together with two fat capons, or two shillings and six pence in lieu thereof, and the sum of 3s 4d upon the death of every principal tenant dying in possession. And doing Suit of Mill and Suit of Court to the Court of the Manor of Oystermouth, on pain of two shillings and six pence for every default.

The improved yearly value of the cott and closes amounts to   £4   —   —

Mr Paul Bevan holds by Lease dated the 11th February 1731, all that new dwelling house with the waste ground twenty yards east, twenty yards west, and forty yards south of the said house, situate at **Pwll duy** in the Manor of Pennard.

	Acres	Qrs
And also three closes or parcels of lands in the Parish of Oystermouth, one whereof is called New Cross, containing one acre. Having the lane from Dunns to Newton on the east, Mr William Dawkin's lands on the south, the little lane on the west and John Thomas's field on the north	1	–
Another field called Underhill, containing two acres. Having the lane on the north, Phillip Powell's little acre on the east, and Isaac Griffiths' acre on the west	2	–
Another close called Underhill, containing one acre. Having the lands of Isaac Seacomb on the east, of Mr Brigstock on the west, and Gilver's Cliff on the south	1	–
	4	–

To hold to him for the lives of the said Paul Bevan, James Griffiths and William Griffiths, the sons of James Griffiths of Swansea, who are both since dead. At the yearly rent of six pound, payable at Lady Day and Michaelmas, two capons or two shillings in lieu thereof, at the choice of the Lord, and 13s 4d in lieu of a Heriot. Suit of Mill and Suit of Court.

The improved yearly value may amount to	£10	–	–

[Folio 108/109]

Mary, the widow of John Jones, holds by virtue of a Lease dated 10th day of July 1741, granted to the said John Jones, deceased, all those several closes or parcels of lands, containing by estimation five acres and a half, be it more or less, called and known by the name of **Brincoch**. Situate and being in the Parish of Oystermouth, and meared by the lands of David Hamon called Higher and Lower Brincoch on the west thereof, and Clyne Moor on all other sides. To hold to the said John Jones, his Executors, Administrators and Assigns, from Lady Day then last past for and during the term of ninety-nine years, if David, Ruth and Jane, the son and daughters of the said John Jones, or either of them, shall so long live (which three lives are now in being). At and under the yearly rent of five shillings payable at Lady Day and Michaelmas by equal portions. Together with a couple of fat pullets on Saint Thomas's Day yearly, or one shilling in lieu thereof. And the sum of five shillings upon the decease of every tenant dying in possession, and the like sum of five shillings upon every Assignment or Alienation.

The improved yearly value of this tenement amounts to	£1	10	–

William Morgan, Assignee of Robert Edwards, deceased, holds by virtue of a Lease granted to the said Robert Edwards, [dated] 25th September 1704, all that messuage and tenement, with the appurtenances, called or known by the name of **Broadley**, situate in the Parish of Oystermouth and containing by estimation forty acres or thereabouts. And all that parcel of furzy and rough ground called **New Parks**[43], **alias Copley**, containing by estimation ten acres, situate and being between the lands of G. V. Vernon esq. on the south thereof, and the Lords Common called Clyne Moor on all other sides thereof. Broadley consists of a dwelling house, barn, stable, stall, and two gardens, and the several closes following, to wit:

Kae Garw containing three acres	3	–
The Orchard Close containing two acres	2	–
The Bakehouse Close containing two acres	2	–
Cae Drussy containing two acres	2	–
Broadley Lake containing three acres	3	–
Little Broadley lake containing three acres	3	–
Broadley Mead containing four acres	4	–
The Southern Close containing four acres	4	–
The Northen Close containing two acres	2	–
Cae Mawr containing four acres	4	–
Croft Cae Mawr containing a quarter of an acre	–	1
The Higher Meadow containing seven acres	7	–
The Lower Meadow containing seven acres	7	–
New Parks before mentioned contain *[Not in Sa]*	10	–
Acres	53	1

To hold to the said Robert Edward from the day of the date thereof, for and during the term of fourscore and nineteen years, if John Bynon, son of John Bynon of Gellybion; Richard Givelin, son of Joshua Givelin; and Mary, the daughter of the said Richard Edward, or either of them, shall so long live. At and under the yearly rent of seven pounds payable at Lady Day and *[Folio 109/110]* Michaelmas by equal portions, [and] two hens, or six pence, on every St Thomas's Day. And also paying the sum of five shillings in the name of a Heriot upon the decease of every tenant dying in possession. And doing Suit of Court to the Court of the Manor of Oystermouth, and doing Suit of Mill to the Lord's mill within the Manor of Oystermouth. And also doing service with horses and oxen when thereto required during the said term.

The improved yearly value of this tenement amounts to	£14	–	–

John Williams holds by Lease dated the 12th of November 1742, all those two messuages or dwelling houses and gardens situate **under the Cliff at Oystermouth**, and now in the possession of John Rees and George Thomas. To hold to the said John Williams, his Executors, Administrators, and Assigns, from the Feast Day of Saint Michael then past, for the term of ninety-nine years if John Williams [and] Sarah Williams, son and daughter of the said John Williams, and John Williams, son of Samuel Williams and grandson of the said John Williams, or either of them, shall so long live. At and under the yearly rent of seven shillings and sixpence, payable at Lady Day and Michaelmas by equal portions clear of [all] deductions whatsoever. And also

43. New Parks became the site of 'Nazareth House' orphanage, now 'Campion Gardens' nursing home.

paying the sum of five shillings upon the decease of every tenant dying in possession, and doing Suit of Mill to the Mills of the Lord.

The improved yearly value of these houses amounts to   £5   –   –

Margaret Lewis holds ['held' in Bn] by Lease dated the 8th day of February 1732, all that piece or parcel of waste ground **under the Cliff at Oystermouth**, containing twenty-four yards eastward from the lands lately granted to William Russel, and forty yards southward up the hill from the highway, together with the house lately thereon erected. To hold to John Lewis, husband of the said Margaret, and his heirs, from the second day of that instant February, for and during the natural lives of William, John, and Mary Lewis, sons and daughters of the said John Lewis, and the survivor of them. At and under the yearly rent of five shillings, together with two capons or one shilling in lieu thereof on Saint Thomas's Day yearly. And the sum of six shillings and eight pence upon the decease of every tenant dying in possession. And the like sum upon every Assignment or Alienation. And doing Suit of Mill and Suit of Court, on pain of two shillings for every default.

The improved yearly value of this house amounts to   £3   –   –
[Added note]
This lease is lately expired, and the premises lately let out for that yearly rent.

[Folio 110/111]

Thomas Huckstables, Assignee of John Russell, holds by Lease dated the 9th of August 1739 granted to the said John Russell, all that messuage and garden lately erected and made on a piece or parcel of waste ground in the Parish of Oystermouth, containing twenty-four yards in breadth eastward from an old limekiln there, and forty yards southward up the hill from the highway, situated and being in the said Parish of Oystermouth. To hold to the said John Russel and his heirs from the second day of February then last past, for and during the natural lives of the said John Russel and Martha Russel, his sister, and the longest liver of them. At and under the yearly rent of five shillings, together with two fat capons, or one shilling in lieu thereof. And the sum of 6s 8d upon the decease of every tenant dying in possession, and the like sum upon every Assignment or Alienation. And doing Suit of Mill and Suit of Court on pain of forfeiture of two shillings.

The improved yearly value of this house amounts to   £3   –   –

Mary Davies, widow, holds by Lease dated 6th February 1743, all that messuage or dwelling house on part of the stony waste ground **under the Cliff of Oystermouth**[44], together with the

---

44. This and many of the following leases relate to the foreshore cottages which made up much of the settlement of Southend. It appears from these leases, many of them 'building leases', that Southend was either created, or largely rebuilt, in the first half of the eighteenth century. Note the requirement contained in the early leases for service with horses and oxen, omitted in the later ones.

stable, outhouses and garden thereunto belonging. And also a parcel of waste ground thereto adjoining, containing by estimation one quarter of an acre, on which a new house has been lately erected. Which premises are situate in the Parish of Oystermouth, and are now in the possession of the said Mary Davies, Richard Williams and Elizabeth Button, widow. To hold to the said Mary Davies from Michaelmas then last past, during the natural lives of Isaac Davies, Mary and Anne Davies, son and daughter[s] of the said Mary Davies, and the life of the survivor of them. Yielding and paying yearly the rent or sum of five shillings, clear of all deductions whatsoever, together with two fat capons upon the Feast Day of Saint Thomas the Apostle. And also doing service with horses and oxen when and as often as she shall be thereto required. And also five shillings in the name of a Heriot upon the decease of every tenant dying in possession. And the like sum of five shillings upon every Assignment or Alienation. And doing Suit of Mill and Suit of Court, on pain of five shillings for every default.

The improved value of this amounts to   £8   —   —

Matthew Hall holds by Lease dated 15th of July 1735, all that piece of waste ground containing twenty yards square extending from the house formerly in the possession of Samuel Grove and now of Mrs. Anne Watkins, to a well situate on the waste there, together with the house thereon erected by the said Matthew Hall. To hold to the said Matthew Hall during the natural lives of Martha, the wife of the said Matthew Hall, and Matthew and Elizabeth, the son and daughter of the said Matthew Hall. At and under the yearly rent of five shillings, together with two pullets, or one shilling in lieu thereof. And the sum of five shillings upon the decease of every tenant dying in possession. And the sum of five shillings upon every Assignment or Alienation. And doing Suit of Mill and Suit of Court, on pain of three shillings and four pence for every default.

The improved value amounts to   £4   —   —

[Folio 111/112]

David Lowarch holds from year to year a house and garden situate **under the**   £5   —   —
Cliff at Oystermouth, at the yearly rent of five pounds. Which house was lately
held by lease by William Maddocks, which lease expired in July 1760.

Elinor, the widow of John Prichard, lately married to John Rees, Officer of Excise, holds by Lease (granted to the said John Prichard, deceased) dated 22nd October 1750, all that piece of **waste ground under the Clift**, containing in breadth twenty-five yards and twenty yards in length, situate at Oystermouth, and adjoining on the south side of the well called Sea Well, together with the house thereon erected. To hold to the said John Prichard, his Executors, Administrators and Assigns, for and during the natural lives of the said John Prichard (since deceased), Elinor his wife, and Margaret Prichard, daughter of Anne Prichard of the Town of Swansea, and the survivor of them (which said Elinor and Margaret are now living). At and under the yearly rent of five shillings, clear of all deductions whatsoever. Together with two fat pullets, or one shilling in lieu thereof on St Thomas's Day yearly. And the sum of five shillings in the name of a Heriot on the decease of every tenant dying in possession, and the like sum of five shillings upon every Assignment or Alienation. And also yielding and doing constant Suit of Mill to the Lord's mill called Black Pill Mill, and Suit of Court to the Court of the Manor of Oystermouth, on pain of three shillings and four pence for every default.

The improved value amounts to   £8   –   –

William Williams, mariner, holds by Lease dated 20th July 1736, all that piece of waste ground being in the whole twenty-five yards square, situate at **Thistleboon** in the Parish of Oystermouth, adjoining to a piece of waste ground of William Maddocks, mariner, of the one side, and the small piece of waste ground of the Lord's on the other side, together with the house and garden thereon erected and made. To hold to the said William Williams and his heirs for and during the natural lives of the said William Williams, Elinor his wife, and John Williams, their son, and the survivor of them. At and under the yearly rent of five shillings, together with two pullets or one shilling in lieu thereof, on St Thomas's Day yearly. And the sum of five shillings for and in the name of a Heriot on the decease of every tenant dying in possession, and the sum of two shillings and six pence upon every Assignment or Alienation. And doing Suit of Mill and Suit of Court to the Court of the Manor of Oystermouth, on pain of forfeiture of 3s 4d for every default.

The improved yearly value amounts to   £2   10   –

[Folio 112/113]

Mrs. Anne Watkins, Assignee of Samuel Groe, holds by Lease dated the 20th day of December 1734 (granted to the said Samuel Groe), all that piece of ground containing in the whole twenty-five yards square, adjoining on the east side to **the old salthouse**, together with the house and garden thereon erected and made. To hold to the said Samuel Groe and his heirs for and during the natural lives of the said Samuel Groe, William Groe his son, and Mary Groe his daughter, and the survivor of them. At and under the yearly rent of five shillings, clear of all deductions whatsoever, together with two pullets or one shilling in lieu thereof yearly. And the sum of two shillings and six pence in the name of a Heriot, on the decease of every tenant dying in possession, and the sum of two shillings and six pence upon every Assignment or Alienation. And doing Suit of Mill and Suit of Court, on pain of 3s 4d.

The improved yearly rent amounts to   £3   –   –

William Williams, blacksmith, holds by Lease dated 25th of March 1749, all that messuage or **dwelling house and smith's forge** lately erected and built by the said William Williams on the beach at Oystermouth. And also all that piece of waste ground to the said messuage and smith's forge adjoining, containing in the whole (the ground whereon the said messuage and smith's forge stands being included) eighty feet in length, and twenty feet in breadth, with the appurtenances. Having the highway on the west, and the beach on all other sides thereof, situate in the Parish of Oystermouth. To hold to the said William Williams, his Executors, Administrators and Assigns, for and during the natural lives of the said William Williams, Martha, his wife, and Elizabeth, their daughter, and the life of the survivor of them (which three lives are now living). At and under the yearly rent of five shillings, clear of all deductions whatsoever, together with two fat pullets or one shilling in lieu thereof yearly. And the sum of five shillings in the name of a Heriot on the death of every tenant dying in possession, and the like sum of five shillings on every Assignment or Alienation of the said lease. And doing Suit of Mill to the Lord's mill called Black Pill Mill, and Suit of Court to the Court of the Manor of Oystermouth, on pain of three shillings and four pence for every default.

The improved yearly rent amounts to	£2	–	–

Thomas Griffiths, mariner, holds by Lease dated 29th September 1749, all that messuage or dwelling house and garden lately erected and made **on Oystermouth Clift, opposite the oyster perches**, having the waste piece of ground lately granted to Elizabeth Morgan, spinster, on the north side thereof, the beach on the east, and the beach and Clift on the south and west sides thereof, containing twenty-four yards square, situate and being in the Parish of Oystermouth in the County of Glamorgan. To hold to the said Thomas Griffiths, his Executors, Administrators and Assigns, for and during the natural lives of Mary, the wife of the said Thomas Griffiths, Thomas Griffiths and Mary Griffiths, son and daughter of the said Thomas and Mary Griffiths, and the life of the survivor of them. At and under the yearly rent of five shillings, and one shilling duties. And five shillings in the name of a Heriot on the decease of every tenant dying in possession, and the like sum of five shillings upon every Assignment or Alienation. And doing Suit of Mill and Suit of Court, on pain of three shillings and four pence.

The improved yearly value amounts to	£2	10	–

[Folio 113/114]

Jenkin Dunn holds by Lease dated 22nd of October 1750, all that piece or parcel of waste ground containing twenty-four yards square, situate and being at Oystermouth Clift, and bounding on the north-east side of the Hill at Oystermouth, together with the house thereon by him lately erected. To hold during the natural lives of Elizabeth, the wife of the said Jenkin Dunn, George Dunn and John Dunn, sons of the said Jenkin and Elizabeth, and the life of the survivor of them. At and under the yearly rent of five shillings, and one shilling duties. And the sum of five shillings in the name of a Heriot on the decease of every tenant dying in possession, and the like sum of five shillings upon every Assignment or Alienation. And doing Suit of Mill and Suit of Court, on pain of three shillings and four pence.

The improved yearly value amounts to   £3   —   —

David Lowarch holds by Lease dated 22nd October 1750 (granted to Leyson Bowen of Oyster-mouth, shipwright, and by him afterwards mortgaged, together with the lease on Willoxton, to Sir Robert Long, Baronet, Narborne Berkley and John Talbot esqs., Executors of his Grace, Charles, late Duke of Beaufort, deceased, for the sum of four hundred and four pounds. And by them assigned to the said David Lowarch by the direction and appointment of the said Leyson Bowen, who at the same time conveyed the equity of redemption of the said lease to the said David Lowarch for the sum of forty pounds). All that piece or parcel of **waste ground lying on Oyster-mouth Cliff**, containing twenty-four yards square, on the north-east side from the oyster perches, together with the house and gardens thereon lately erected and made by the said Leyson Bowen. To hold to the said Leyson Bowen, his Executors, Administrators and Assigns, from the Feast of Saint Michael then last past for and during the term of ninety-nine years if the said Leyson Bowen, Mary Bowen and Magdalen Bowen, daughters of the said Leyson Bowen, or either of them, should so long live (which three lives are now in being). At and under the yearly rent of five shillings, and one shilling duties. And the sum of five shillings in the name of a Heriot on the decease of every tenant dying in possession, and the like sum of five shillings upon every Assign-ment or Alienation. And doing Suit of Mill and Suit of Court, on pain of three shillings and four pence for every default.

The improved yearly value amounts to   £5   —   —

[Folio 114/115]

Daniel Cleypit holds by Lease dated 18th November 1754, all that piece or parcel of waste ground containing twenty-four yards square, situate **upon part of the Clift at Oystermouth**, near and adjoining to the dwelling house there in the possession of Thomas Griffiths, together with the house and garden thereon lately erected and made. To hold to the said Daniel Cleypit, his Executors, Administrators and Assigns, during the term of the natural lives of the said Daniel Cleypit, Mary, his wife, and Mary Cleypit their daughter, and the life of the survivor of them. At and under the yearly rent of five shillings, and one shilling duties. And the sum of five shillings in the name of a Heriot on the decease of every tenant dying in possession, and the like sum of five shillings upon every Assignment or Alienation. And doing Suit of Mill and Suit of Court, on pain of 3s 4d. for every default.

The improved yearly rent amounts to   £2   —   —

John Lowarch has **liberty to build ships at Norton's End** in the Parish of Oystermouth, paying to the Lord yearly the rent or sum of one shilling.   £– 1 –

Elinor, the wife of John Rees (and late widow of John Prichard, deceased), **has liberty to build ships**, and to lay down timber on the beach, at the **Mumbles**, paying to the Lord yearly the rent or sum of one shilling.   £– 1 –

Leyson Bowen has liberty to build ships, and lay down timber on the beach at the **Mumbles**, paying to the Lord yearly the rent or sum of one shilling.   £– 1 –

[Folio 115/116]

Customs and Courts
within the Manor of Oystermouth

The Lord claims and is intituled within this Manor to all Royalties whatsoever, in as large and extensive manner as he enjoys them within the Seigniory.

He is also entitled to all highways, wastes, open and uninclosed lands within the said Manor, and the soil and profits of the same.

The Copyhold or Customary lands within this Manor descend and are conveyed and all customs in regard to them are exactly the same as within the Manor of Pennard.

Heriots and Alienations are the same as in Pennard. Vide Folio 94 *[p.166 & 167]*.

There are two **Leet and Customary**[45] **Courts** held for the said Manor yearly, to be appointed and summoned in the same manner as the Courts for Pennard. And the tenants and resiants are to attend on pain of Amerciaments in like manner as in Pennard.

At Michaelmas Leet are appointed and sworn the **Reeve**, **Constables**, and **Aletaster**. And at May Leet, [are appointed] the **Lear Keeper** and **Heywards**.

The Lord has within this Manor a water corn grist mill called Black Pill Mill, to which all the tenants and resiants within the Manor owe Suit.

The tenants have usually gathered and carried away sea weed called kelp, and also sand from the sea side for manuring their lands, without paying any acknowledgement to the Lord for so doing.

There is within this Manor an ancient castle which was formerly one of the Seats of the Lords of Gower, but it is now ruinous and in great decay.

---

45. Customary Courts are the Courts Baron.

[Folio 116/117]

Bishopston Manor

This Manor was formerly held by the Bishops of Landaff, of the Seigniory in Free Alms, and was alienated by one of the Bishops to *[blank]* Mathews of Landaff esq., who went afterwards and settled in Ireland. And [it] was enjoyed by them until about the year 1703 when it was sold by George Mathews, of Thomas Town in the County of Tipperary in the Kingdom of Ireland, to Gabriel Powell, gentleman, who immediately parted with it to the then Duke of Beaufort.

This Manor is bounded by the sea on the south from Pwll duy, by the Manor of Pennard and Fee of Kittle on the west, by a brook or watercourse running from Cradock's Moor on the north, and the Hamlet of Manselfield and Manor of Oystermouth down to Caswell Bay on the east

It consists of several Freehold tenements which are held in Common Soccage by Fealty, Rent, Suit of Court and Heriot; and several Customary or Copyhold tenants who hold their lands by Copy of Court Roll at the Will of the Lord, according to the Custom of the Manor.

There are within this Manor several pieces of waste, open, and uninclosed land, commonly called by the several names of Hankins Cliff, Bareland, Bishopston Hills, the Green by and near the Church, Parsonage Hills, Murtons Green, and Cobbin's Cliff. The soil whereof belongs to the Lord, but the tenants of the Manor have time immemorially had common of pasture on the same as appurtenant to their several Freehold and Copyhold tenements, without paying any particular rent or other acknowledgment for the same.

The tenants of Murton Hamlet intercommon with the tenants of Oystermouth on Clyne Moor, for which they pay one pound twelve shillings and one penny towards making up the rent which the Oystermouth tenants pay the Lord. And the tenants within Bishopston Hamlet also intercommon with the tenants of Pennard and Kittle on Pennard's Moor, for which they pay 13s 4d to the Lord, which is collected by a person appointed by themselves, by a proportionable rate.

A few of the inhabitants of the Manor pay six pence yearly for fishing in the sea, to wit: John Webbern and William Phillip for fixing nets on the sands; and David Hugh for catching crabs and lobsters in the rocks.

A Rent Roll of the Free Rents
within the Manor of Bishopston

Freeholders Names	Tenements	Occupiers	Rent per annm		
			£	s	d
The Earl of Warwick	Harrols ['Harolds' in Bn]	Robert Bydder	–	–	8
Thos Mansel Talbot esq., infant	Half an acre in Robert Jone Combmeads		–	–	–½

Freeholders Names	Tenements	Occupiers	Rent per annm		
			£	s	d
G. V. Vernon esq.	A water corn grist mill called Old Mill	Thomas Jones	–	8	–
Late Mayzod Dawkin, widow	A water grist mill, 2 cottages & 9 acres of land	Edwd Lloyd & Robt Jone	–	–	10
The same	Half an acre of meadow in Coomb Meads	[blank]	–	–	2
The same	Two acres of ground in the Coomb meads called the Mill Meadow	Edwd Lloyd & Robt. Jone	–	–	2
Rachel Mansel, widow	Backinstone	William Groe	–	3	3
The same	Longash	David Bowen	–	2	–
William Hamon	Bishopston	John Griffiths	–	3	–
Thomas Richards, tanner	Bishopston	John Rowland	–	6	5½
Rachael Mansel, widow	Allslade[46]	Jacob Bynon	–	2	–½
Rachael Mansel, widow	Allslade	Jacob Bynon	–	1	6
Thomas Bydder	A messuage near the Cross at Bishopston	Thomas Bydder & 16 acres of land	–	2	–
[Folio 117/118]					
William Richards gent.	Part of the Coomb Meadows	John Gwyn	–	–	2
Phillip Kneath	Part of the Coomb Meadows	Phillip Kneath	–	–	2
William Gamon, infant	Backinstone	John Thomas	–	–	5
The same	Backinstone	John Thomas	–	–	4
John Parry	Barland and Pile Fields	Thomas Parry	–	1	1½
Thomas Parry	A house and 16 acres at Bishopstone	Thomas Parry	–	–	3½
Jane Griffith, widow	Bishopstone	John Griffith	–	1	5½

46. Allslade, later known as 'Hareslade' [Brandy Cove].

Freeholders Names	Tenements	Occupiers	Rent per annm		
			£	s	d
Jane Rowland, spinster	Part of a house and a close called Barland	John Rowland	–	–	2
Samuel Griffith	Culverhouse	Mary Griffith	–	–	–½
David Hugh	A house & garden	David Hugh	–	–	1
William Givelin	Redly	John Phillip	–	–	5
John Webbern	Cutters Acre	John Webbern	–	–	1
Elizabeth Givelin & Sarah Edward, widow	New Parks	Elizabeth Givelin & Sarah Edward	–	–	9
Richard Gamon	A House at Murton	Richard Gamon	–	–	–½
			£1	15	8

A Rent Roll of the Customary Rent within the Manor of Bishopston[47]

Copyholders Names	Tenements	Occupiers	Rent per annm		
			£	s	d
The Earl of Warwick	A messuage and tenement of lands at Bishopston, by estimation 16 acres	John Gwyn	–	5	6
The same	Another tenement at Murton, about 14 acres	William Givelin	–	5	8
The same	Another tenement of lands, about 9 acres	Thomas Parry	–	3	3
The same	Another tenement of lands	Thomas Richards	–	–	10
The same	Another tenement at Murton, about 9 acres	David Webbern and Anne Sheppard	–	5	8
Rachel Mansel, widow	One croft adjoining to the house at Longash containing one acre	*[blank]*	–	1	–
William Hamon	A house, stall & barn and those closes or parcels of	John Griffiths	–	7	6

47. As in Oystermouth Manor, many of these holdings are derived from scattered strips in former open fields.

Copyholders Names	Tenements	Occupiers	Rent per annm		
			£	s	d
	lands viz: western Hay, Gough's Hay, One Acre in Rips, Great Pitland, little Pitland, Redlyway, with Park, Allslade Hill, and a little parcel thereto belonging in Cuddyburgh, two large parcels in Great Pile, Martens Cross, Gerrard's Hill, two acres of wood in Bishops Wood, & a house & garden near the Cross				
The Lord	One tenement containing one house called the Stone House and one toft & garden, two crofts containing one acre at Bishopston	Rowland Rowland	–	1	6
David Webbern	A house & lands at Murton	David Webbern	–	2	6
Rowland Rowland	Northway	John Rowland	–	1	6
George Bowen	The eastern two Acres, the western two Acres, Silken Mead, Hillhouse, Burroughs, one piece of wood called Peterwell Wood, great Withy Bed, Sker Grove, Sker, Longland and Caswell Hope, containing 20 acres situate at Murton in the possession of Jno. Webbern of Herbert's Houses	John Webbern	–	8	8
Anne Watkins, widow	A house & lands at Murton	William Morgan	–	7	4½
David Webbern	Lands at Murton	David Webbern	–	5	–

[Folio 118/119]

This should be mentioned to Jas Wibbern: one close called oldway, 1 acre; one close called Mansel Croft, 1 acre; & 2 acres of short meadow hay in Wm Givelin's Norway[48]. *[Added note in Sa only.]*

Copyholders Names	Tenements	Occupiers	Rent per annm		
James Webbern	Lands at Murton	James Webbern	–	–	10
William Givelin	The eastern parcel in great	William Givelin	–	1	2

48. Northway.

Copyholders Names	Tenements	Occupiers	Rent per annm		
			£	s	d
	Northway, and the western parcel in the same close, and two little meadows called Park's Meads, the whole containing by estimation five acres				
Jennet Hopkin, widow	One messuage with the appurtenances at Murton, and those closes of lands, called the two eastern Crofts, the Hay door Park, Redleyway Longland, Withy Bed, Sker Grove, an acre of wood at Bishopswood with the Spot thereunto belonging, the whole containing twelve acres	James Wibbern	–	4	4
Jane Griffiths, widow	Lands at Murton	John Griffith	–	5	6
Jane Rowland, spinster	Northway & Blindwell	John Rowland	–	2	1
William Givelin	A messuage with the appurtenances at Murton & all those closes of lands vizt: Killhouse, the two Milson Acres, Burroughs, two Peter's Wells, Moormote Hill, the little Acre, the Longland and the Wood, the whole by estimation 9 acres	John Phillip	–	5	4

[Folio 119/120]

William Givelin & George Thomas	A messuage with the appurtenances at Murton and the closes of lands following: the two Peter Wells, Burroughs, Broadway, Sker Grove, Limekilles, The eastern Croft & the Croft by the House, by estimation nine acres	John Dawkin	–	3	4
Thomas Parry	A messuage with the appurtenances at Bishopston & the closes following: the Croft by the House, the Park	Thomas Parry	–	3	10

Copyholders Names	Tenements	Occupiers	Rent per annm		
			£	s	d
	by the House, Withybed, the two closes at Northways, Withy Park, one acre in a close called three acres and one acre of wood at Bishop's wood, one acre in Harold alias Southfield & half an acre in Rips adjoining the Orchard ['belonging to a tenement of Lord Warwick called Butcher's land, in the possession of Morgan Thomas' in Bn only]				
William Givelin	Northways	William Givelin	–	–	8
John Webbern	A messuage with the appurtenances called Herberts' Housen [*sic*] and these closes and parcels of lands vizt.: Markin's lands, the two Killhouses, the two half acres, Bushland, the four closes by the House, a quarter of an acre in Carswell hope, Carswell Croft, a parcel of rough and woody ground at Bishop's wood and one cliff	John Webbern	–	7	–
Thomas Jone	One messuage with the appurtenances & a croft thereto adjoining, a close called Gerrards Hill, and a parcel of lands lying in a close called three acres Close and a small parcel lying in the higher end of Edward Bowen's Croft near the Church and two little houses and a garden, the whole by estimation 4 acres	Thomas Jone	–	1	4
John Parry	One close of lands called Payland and the western Acre in a close called Headland and one croft under Bishopston Hill, in all about three acres and a half	Thomas Parry	–	3	6

[Folio 120/121]

Copyholders Names	Tenements	Occupiers	Rent per annm		
			£	s	d
Thomas Edward	A messuage with the appurtenances at Murton and the Closes following viz: Hooks, Sheepherds Lone, Longland, two closes at Northway, one acre in Bishop's wood, one little parcel of land wherein is an old drying kiln adjoining Garbs Hay, the whole by estimation 9 acres. He also holds one half acre called Sker Grove	Thomas Edward	–	3	3
Jennet Bowen	One messuage with the appurtenances at Bison and the closes of land following viz: Pwll dy land two acres, an acre in South Field, an acre in Cuddybourgh, New park, the three acres, an acre in Broad Acres, two acres , in Payland, two acres & a half in Gomers Pit, three quarters of an acre in Waterfords, an acre in Vensland, half an acre in Rips, one croft by the Churchyard, one other croft lying between the Sker and Parsonage Hills, one quarter of an acre in broad Meadow, and an acre and a half of wood in Bishop's wood, and one acre in the middle of great Pile. The whole by estimation 18 acres	John Rowland	–	8	–
David Webbern	A messuage with the appurtenances at Bishopston. One parcel of land thereto adjoining called the Hayes, one close called the eastern Barland Parke, and an acre lying in a close called Marten's Crosse	David Webbern	–	1	2
Mary Rees	A house & small garden at Bishopston	John Webb	–	–	1
			£5	7	4½

[Folio 121/122]

The Lord is Entitutled to the several Demesne Rents herein after mentioned within the said Manor of Bishopston

Jonathan Rees lately held by Lease [dated] the 25th December 1734, all those two pieces of ground called the **Drangs**, and all that water corn grist mill, with the appurtenances, called **Pennard Mill**, situate and being in the Parish of Pennard. To hold to the said Jonathan Rees from the Feast of Saint Michael then past, during the lives of the said Jonathan Rees, Jane, his wife, and Thomas Owen, son of John Owen of the Parish of Oystermouth, and the survivor of them. At and under the yearly rent of five pounds, and a shilling duties. But the said Jonathan having run greatly in arrear, he on the *[blank]* day of *[blank]* surrendered the said Lease, as appears by a memorandum of that date indorsed on the said Lease.

The said mill hath been since let to David Bevan from year to year, at the yearly rent of £5 1s. ['of which he has since taken in lease.' *in Bn*].

This mill is situated in the Manor of Pennard, but by mistake was inserted in the last rent roll in Bishopston.

Thomas Jones holds by Lease dated 18th July 1737, all that **tucking or fulling mill** situate in the Parish of Bishopston, with all the streams of water, water courses, ponds, floodgates, and appurtenances thereto belonging. To hold to the said Thomas Jones, for and during the natural lives of the said Thomas Jones, Thomas and David, his two sons, and the life of the survivor of them (which three lives are now in being). At and under the yearly rent of ten shillings and one shilling duties, and the sum of five shillings in lieu of a Heriot on the decease of every tenant dying in possession.

$$£ - \quad 11 \quad -$$

John Morgan holds from year to year part of the stable adjoining to the west pine end of his house at Bishopston, at the yearly rent of

$$£ - \quad - \quad 6$$

* \quad * \quad *

[Folio 122/123]

Customs and Courts within the Manor of Bishopston

The Lord claims and is intitutled to all Royalties whatever, in as full and extensive a manner as in the Seigniory. He is also intitutled to all highways, wastes, open and uninclosed lands, and the soil and profits of the same.

The Copyhold or Customary lands within this Manor are **Burrough English Tenure**[49], and descend not only to the youngest son or daughter, but also in the collateral line to the youngest brother, sister, uncle, aunt and all others. But they are conveyed only by surrender passed in the

---

49. See the Glossary on p.37 & 38 for the legal terms.

Courts of the Manor, which the tenants may do either in person, or by letter of Attorney, the due execution of which must be proved in Court at the time of passing by one of the witnesses. And if it be an Estate of a *Femme Covert*, she must be sole and privately examined by the Steward as to her consent, or by the witnesses to the letter of Attorney, who must prove the same. And if the tenants convey, or even demise, their lands within this Manor without a surrender or licence obtained in open Court, it is a forfeiture – if for a longer term than three years.

The Tenants may by their Custom entail their Copyhold lands, which entails may be barred as in the Manor of Pennard. Vide Folio 94 *[p.166 & 167]*.

The widows of the Customary or Copyhold tenants are intituled to the Free Bench or Widow's Estate in all such Copyhold Estate as the husband died seized of an inheritable Estate in. But the husband is not intituled to hold the wife's Estate by the Curtesy.

All the tenants of the Manor, as well Free as Customary or Copyhold, pay Heriots of the best beast if they die within the Manor, or in occupation of their lands within the same. And if any tenant die seized of Free and Customary lands then they pay a Heriot of the best beast for one tenure, and five shillings for the other. And if they die out of the Manor, and not in the occupation of their lands, or happen to have no beast, then five shillings only are paid for each tenure.

If any tenant alienates all his Freehold or all his Customary or Copyhold lands within the Manor, he pays five shillings for the alienation of each tenure. And if only part of each or either tenure, [then] he pays nothing.

There are two Leet and Customary or Baron Courts held for the said Manor within a month of Michaelmas and Easter, on such day and place as the Steward shall, by a Warrant under his hand and seal, appoint. Of which notice ought to be given by the Reeve in the church yard of Bishopston and proclaimed on a Market Day in the Town of Swansea at least eight days before the holding of the said Courts. But Customary or Baron Courts, merely for the passing of surrenders, may be held at any time or place within the Manor upon shorter notice or summons to a few of the tenants.

All the tenants, both Free and Customary or Copyhold, owe Suit and ought to attend the general Leet and Baron Courts on pain of Amerciaments, but none are to attend the casual Courts but such as are particularly summoned.

At the Michaelmas Leet and Baron Courts are appointed and sworn the **Reeve** and **Constables**, to wit: one for Bishopston Hamlet; and another for Murton; and formerly an **Aletaster,** but that was disused many years before my time. And at Easter Courts, **Heywards** for Bishopston and Murton are appointed and sworn, to wit: one for each.

The Tenants claim and have enjoyed a prescriptive right to gather and carry away sea weed and sand from the sea shore for manuring their lands within the Manor, and also power to cut, and convert to their own use, all such timber and wood as grow on their Customary or Copyhold lands.

[End of Folio 123. Folio 124 is blank. 'The Seigniory or Lordship Royal of Kilvey' begins on Folio 125 .]

[Folio 125]

The Seigniory or Lordship Royal
of
KILVEY

This Seigniory was an ancient Lordship Marcher of Wales, always held by the Lord of Gower, who had and enjoyed with it all Royal Jurisdictions in as large and ample manner as he enjoyed in Gower, and [it] was by the same Statute[50] annexed to and made part of the County of Glamorgan. It was anciently considered as part of, and passed under the general name of, Gower. It was part of the Cantref Eginoc in the County of Carmarthen, and still continues with Gower in the Bishopric of St Davids although all the rest of the County of Glamorgan is in the Bishopric of Landaff.

It lies on the east side of the River Tawy and includes the whole Parish of Lansamlet and one Hamlet of the Parish of Swansea, and is bounded as follows, vizt: From the black Rock by Neath River[51] on the east, and from thence in a line up to Crumlyn Bridge lying in the highway from Swansea to Neath. And from thence keeping on the north or east side of Crumlyn Brook or the Great Ditch, unto the great Pool in Crumlyn Marsh called Pwll Kynnan. And from thence to Rhyd Ycha ar y Crumlyn, and from thence to a little brook called Nant y Feene, and from thence on the north or east side of the said brook to the road called Fordd Rhyd y Keyrt. And from Fordd Rhyd y Keyrt, as the said road or lane leadeth west into the great road, then as the said great road leadeth northward, then it turneth north-east into a little close by a wood side. And through the middle of another close northward to a hedge which runneth north-east unto a well called Funnon Illtyd, thence to a little marsh ground. And thence along a way or genfordd upon Mynnydd Drymme to a well called Funnon Dwym, and thence along Mynnydd Drymme, keeping along the east side of Kae Veirig to Kist Faen. And thence turning to a well where Curnach Brook taketh its rise, and thence along the north-east side of Curnach Brook, leaving the same wholly within this Manor, till the said brook falleth into Clais Brook. And then along Clais Brook side, leaving the said brook entirely within this Manor, till it empties itself into the River Tawy. And thence along the said river till it empties itself into the sea below the Town of Swansea. And thence along the sea side to the River Neath, and then up along the River Neath to the black Rock, where the boundary first began. Vide Kilvey Roll for October 1756.

A Disputed Boundary[52]

This Lordship adjoining the manor of Cadoxton, some differences happened a few years ago in regard to the boundaries, between Mr Gabriel Powell and the then Steward of the said Manor.

---

50. The first Act of Union, 1536.
51. The Black Rock(s) lay in the Neath estuary, approximately due south of the present-day Jersey Marine. The Llansamlet tithe map, dated 1846, shows the eastern boundary of the parish following the eastern edge of Crymlyn Bog as it nears the sea. The eastern boundary of the parish, and of the marcher lordship of Gower, reached the sea just over a mile to the east of the present parish, and City and County of Swansea, boundary.
52. For an account and discussion of this interesting encounter see Prys Morgan 'The Glais Boundary Dispute, 1756'. *Glamorgan Historian* IX (Barry 1973), pp.203-210.

George Rice, Hans Stanley and Henry Compton esqs., the Lords of Cadoxton, having ordered a general Survey to be made of their Manor, the persons employed, for some interesting reasons, had an intention to take into their boundaries the brooks of Kurnach and Claise and part of the River Tawy. Which Mr Powell hearing of, and being told that they intended to perambulate their boundaries with a Jury of Survey, he determined to give them a meeting on Mynnydd Drymme, in order to take care that they did not incroach on the rights of the Lord of Gower and Kilvey. And as several disputes arose on that occasion it may be of use hereafter to set forth the particulars of what then passed.

Mr Gabriel Powell went on the 17th May 1756 to the top of Mynnydd Drymme, attended by his Clerk, Mr James Jones; Richard Morgan, an Agent of Herbert Mackworth esq.; and David Woodwall, a tenant within the Manor of Kilvey. Soon after they saw Mr Thomas Edwards of Cardiff, who acted as Steward for the Lords of the Manor of Cadoxton; Mr John Gwyn, Deputy Steward; Mr Thomas Williams, Agent and tenant of Mr Rice and Mr Compton's share of the Manor; attended by a Jury made up of their own tenants (there not being one Freehold tenant of the Manor); a few of their own *[Folio 125/126]* colliers; and about eight or ten collier boys. They came up from a place called Gelly, along a road upon the hill lying upon the east side of a wall of Mr Daniel Jones's Coed Kae, to a well called Funnon Dwym. From thence they went along the same road to a place called Kist Faen, (or Stony Chest), which is a square hollow stone in the shape of a chest, and appears to be found at the bottom of a large heap of stones thrown up like a Burrough.

From thence they turned off to the southward, to a well called Curnach. Just below this well Mr Powell stood across the brook, declaring no one should pass that way without throwing him down, by reason it was not their boundary, for their bounds went on the north-west side thereof. And not far from thence [he] removed a stake, which was placed in the brook, to the same side, and saying these were their bounds and that if they would look in their ancient books and surveys they would find it to be described so, which Mr Edwards did – where it mentioned the north-west side. A little above the gate that leads off the hill they put up some stones in the brook, which Mr Powell removed and laid them on the north-west side, declaring that was their boundary. And a little below the road that crosses the same brook to a gate leading to Penyrhiwisfa, Mr Powell again stood across the brook, declaring as before. And on a boy's attempting to go between his legs he took him by his left arm and moved him to the bank on the north-west side of the said brook. And also said he protested against their going through the brook as their boundary and desired they would take notice of what he said and insert it in their Presentment. And that he thought the opposition he had given was sufficient to show the bounds they walked were litigated as wrong, but that it was impossible for him to stop so many people. He also removed several stones from out of the brook, on Mr Edwards desiring the boys to take notice of the stones as their boundary.

Mr Powell stood across the brook just below where Curnach empties itself into Clais, and stopped the boys and turned them to the north-west side. And below that, where they crossed Claise to go to Penyrhiwisfa, he and Mr Jones by his directions stood across the brook on horseback, where the boys passed them on the north-west side. From thence they went down Claise to the River Tawy, Mr Powell still calling to them and declaring their boundaries were along the side of the brook, but that no part of the brook belonged to them.

When they came to Tawy both Mr Edwards and Mr Williams declared they claimed no right to the river and their boundaries were only along the banks. But the Lords of Cadoxton claimed a right to fish in particular pools, by virtue of an old Grant from the Lord of Gower, which Mr Powell agreed to and said he was willing they should fish [as] far as their Grant extended.

They then said they claimed to *[Folio 126/127]* fish half Claise Pool, and wetted their net in it. They then walked to Ynispenllwch Wear and said the Wear was tied to their lands, which Mr Mackworth had no right to do. Mr Cross, Agent to Mr Mackworth, answered that Mr Mackworth had a wear on the river at that place time out of mind, which was tied to the land on their side, and therefore insisted he had a right to do so. Mr Edwards then said that the pool above Ynispen-llwch Wear was called Llyn Immon, and ordered their net be put in. But William Hopkin Leyson, the tenant of Ynisymmon[53], told him it was not; for that pool lay higher up the river. They then walked about half a mile along the banks of the river till they came to Llyn Immon, and there the said William Hopkin Leyson showed in the bottom of the river a few stakes which looked like the foundation of an old wear.

From thence they proceeded up the river and claimed some acres of land on the Gower side, and it also appeared there was about three acres, belonging to a tenement of His Grace's called Graig y Trebannoes, on the Cadoxton side. But the banks of the River Tawy on the Cadoxton side were agreed to be the boundary, and so they were walked till they came to Mr Mackworth's Manor of Neath Ultra, and then [they] turned up to the brook called Llecha, when Mr Powell left them and returned home, not being acquainted with the boundaries any further.

On the 19th of May 1756, Mr Edwards called on me, and told me he was come to satisfy me that I was mistaken in regard to the claiming of the whole brooks of Curnach and Claise to be within the boundaries of Kilvey. And then produced to me the old grant of John de Mowbray to the Abbot and Monks of Neath Abby *[sic]*. After I had read it over, I told him I thought that grant rather confirmed my opinion, for where [the] boundary is set forth in the grant it is expressed to be "*Usque ad Fonnon Doym et inde directe <u>in</u> Rivulum qui vocatur Gleys et inde <u>per</u> eundem Rivulum usque ad illum locum ubi idem Rivulus cadit in Tawe*", for that "*in*" signified "to" or "unto" the river which is called Gleys, and that "*per*" signified "by". But he insisted that "*in*" signified "into" and "*per*" "through", and so would claim to the middle of the brook. To this I answered that taking it in that sense rendered the boundary uncertain, for [if] it was "into" the river, it did not distinguish whether it was an inch or a foot, but could never carry them into the middle of the brook. Besides, if they were taken in the sense I argued for, it would appear reconcilable with the Surveys of Gower, but according to his construction they would not only contradict the Gower Surveys, but be repugnant to their own. For in the Cadoxton Surveys, and in the notes made to explain their maps, they are mentioned as I insist on, the boundary being set forth to be to the brook called Curnach and thence by the said brook of Curnach until the fall thereof into the River Claise, and from the fall of Curnach it runneth by the river of Claise south-west, then turning northward by the said river of Claise until the fall thereof into the River Tawy. Mr Edwards at last said he believed there would be no dispute between the Lords of Kilvey and Cadoxton and so parted – but dropped a hint – that there would be no dispute if no grant was made to anyone of the water[54].

---

53. Ynys y mond.
54. But note that on 20.6.1757 a lease of these waters was granted to Chauncey Townsend for the use of his copperworks. See below, p.213 & 214.

Customs and Courts within the Lordship Royal of Kilvey

The tenants within this Manor hold their lands in Soccage Tenure, by certain Chief or Quit Rents, payable at Lady Day yearly, Fealty, Suit of Court and Heriot.

There are two general **Leet** and **Baron Courts** held for this Manor within a month after Michaelmas Day and Easter Day yearly, upon Summons by Custom time out of mind, to be held at the Guildhall of the Town of Swansea on Monday. Which Summons or Notice of the time is to be proclaimed on a Market Day in the Town of Swansea, and at the Church of Lansamlet, at least eight days before the Courts are to be held. At which Courts all the tenants and resiants of the Manor are to attend to do their Suits, on pain of Amerciaments. And there are also Baron Courts held for this Manor at the Guild Hall of Swansea every three weeks, upon adjournment from three weeks to three weeks, for the trial of all actions under forty shillings, which Courts are to be held before the Steward.   *[Folio 127/128]*

Heriot within this Manor is only five shillings, and an Alienation of five shillings upon every tenant departing with his whole estate within this Manor.

There are several veins or **mines of coal** wrought within this Manor, for which the Lord receives a Customary payment of four pence a wey, for every wey of coal shipped to be exported over the Bar of Swansea. Each wey to contain forty-eight bags, and every bag twenty-four Winchester gallons.

The inhabitants of this Manor claim a **right to pass over the Ferry Boat** at Swansea, paying yearly a small Customary sum, to wit: they of the Lower Division, four pence; and [of] the Higher Division, two pence.

There are no wastes or Commons within this Manor of any extent, except the beach between Swansea Ferry Boat, and the old chapel belonging to the Lord, which is now destroyed by the sea. And also Crymlyn Burroughs and Crymlyn Gorse or Marsh, all or the greatest part of which is claimed by the Honourable George Venables Vernon esq. in right of the Britton Ferry Estate. But how he can make out such right I can't guess.

The River Tawy runs by this Manor. The brook Mynrod[55] runs through it, and part of the brook and lake of Crymlyn is within it; the soil and water as well as the sole and separate fishery of which belong to the Lord.

There are four **fishing wears** on the salt sands within this Manor, called Hicket Wear, Globert Wear, Syl Wear, and y Gored Ddee, which Mr Vernon now claims as his freehold, paying for the three first six pence each yearly, and for that last, one shilling, which wear, called y Gored Ddee, was formerly thought to be held from year to year.

There are two other fishing wears on the salt sands, held by Daniel Fabian from year to year, at the yearly rent of ten shillings. And no tenant or other person can set up any wears, engines or other devices for the taking fish within the said Manor without the Lord's licence and consent.

The tenants and resiants of this Manor pay twenty pounds for **Mises**, as mentioned in Gower Anglicana. *Vide Folios 26 & 27 [p.76].*

I have seen it mentioned, in the copy of an ancient paper, that the Lord was intituled to four

---

55. Now known as Nant y fendrod.

pence for **Keelage** of every vessel lying within the Manor, two pence for **Anchorage**, and two pence for each **Top** belonging to every vessel. And one halfpenny by way of toll for every horse load or horse pack carried through the Borough of Bettws (that is by St Thomas's Chapel), and four pence for every score of hogs driven through the said Borough, but I never knew or heard it was paid.

The Lord is intituled to the several Demesne rents hereinafter mentioned within the said Seigniory or Lordship Royal of Kilvey.   *[Folio 128/129]*

A Rent Roll of the Demesne Rents within the said Manor of Kilvey

Daniel Fabian holds some pieces of lands adjoining **the old salthouse** (now in ruins), called the **Salthouse Green**, now lying open and uninclosed, having the sea on the south and west parts thereof, and the Lord's waste and highway leading from Swansea to Briton Ferry on the north and east parts. With liberty to gather the wood thrown up by the sea between the mouth of the lane called Heol y Twad and St Thomas's Chapel, at the yearly rent of   £–   12   –

The sea gains every year on the said house and lands, so that in a few years there will be nothing left of it.

Daniel Fabian holds a **fishing wear** on the east side of Swansea River, and also another fishing wear lying on the salt sands, to the east of the wear in the possession of Thomas Edward, at the yearly rent of   £–   10   –

Daniel Fabian holds from year to year two pieces of land called Tyr Watty Daniel, and Tyr Perkin otherwise Cae Sychan. These pieces of land cannot now be found, but they lie in the tenement of lands of George Hutton gent., called Tyr Glan y Bade, and for which the tenant of that tenement has paid at Michaelmas yearly the rent of   £–   10   –

David William holds from year to year a parcel of arable, meadow and pasture lands, called **Kae Verch Eynon Dduy**, lying to the west of his dwelling house, containing by estimation three acres. But I believe some part of it has been inclosed off; so that the measure is now short. The tenant pays for it the yearly rent of   £1   –   –

Mr John Phillips holds from year to year two parcels of land at a tenement called **Llwyn Hernin**. One called Enherraeg Vach, containing about half an acre lying in the upper end of a field called Kae ych lawr Tuy Llwyn Hernin, having the lands of the Honourable George Venables Vernon esq. on all sides thereof, and being fenced on the east, south, and west parts. Mear stones have been lately laid down by Mr David Rees, now Agent to Mr Vernon, and me, on the north part. The other piece of land lying in a close called Kae Hwnt yr Tuy Llwyn Hernin, lying on the west of the house, containing half an acre of Customary measure, and lying on the eastern side of the said close, having a lane leading from Llwyn Hernin house on the north; a fence or hedge on the east, and mear stones lately laid down by Mr Rees and me on the west and south sides thereof. For both [of] which the tenant pays yearly   £–   6   8

Thomas Voss holds from year to year the parcels of land called **Kae Vadock Ycha**, containing one acre; a rough piece of ground called Cwm Vadock; [and] one parcel of arable land called the Croft, containing one acre. Which are bounded by the lands of Mr Edward Evans on the north; the highway leading to Heol y Sarney on the west; the lands of the Hon. George Venables Vernon esq. called Tyr Yssha on the south; and a field of the Lord called Cae Vadock Ysha on the east. He also holds a meadow called Wain Tuy Coch, containing two Customary acres, and having the highway on the south and east parts, and the lands of the said Mr Vernon on the west, and of the said Mr Evans on the north.

The tenant pays for the whole the yearly rent of   £2   5   –

Thomas Pryce of Dyffryn esq. holds a field called Kae Vadock Yssha, containing *[Folio 129/130]* two acres and a half, as part of a tenement of lands called **Tyr Yssha**, which he holds by lease from the Hon. Mr Vernon, and insists it is part of that tenement. It is bounded by Cae Vadock Ycha on the west; the lands of Edward Evans esq. on the north; part of a tenement now called Tyr Yssha (but formerly Tyr William Hopkin Tom Will Goch) on the south; and the highway leading from Dan y Graig to Pont y Moch on the east. *[No rent quoted in Sa or Bn]*

William Voss holds a house called **Tuy Coch**, situate on the highway near Wain Coch, together with a parcel of waste lands thereto adjoining, which piece of waste doth extend itself into a brook, or small rivulet, which falls into Cwm Vadock. *[No rent quoted in Sa or Bn]*

Mr Walter Howell holds from year to year a piece or parcel of land called Tre Quarter Hirion, lying in a field called Kae Newydd belonging to a farm of Mr Vernon's called **Gwernllestre**, the breadth of one field to the south-east of the dwelling house. And having a hedge or fence on the west and north parts thereof; the lane or way leading to Gelly Gasseg farm house on the east; and mear stones on the south lately laid down by Mr Rees and me, and being the whole length of the field from east to west, and from the hedge on the north side forty-six yards to the mear stones. For which parcel of land the said Walter Howell pays the yearly rent of: £–   5   –

The same **Mr Walter Howell** holds from year to year a piece of land called **Clones**, containing one acre of Customary measure, having a hedge on the south; a field of the Hon. Mr Vernon's called Kae Keven Coed on the east; a ditch on the north; and mear stones lately laid down by Mr Rees and Mr Powell on the west to divide it from Mr Vernon's part of the Clones. For which Mr Howell now pays the yearly rent of: £1   –   –
['(now held by Catherine Jones)' in Bn]

Rees Howell holds from year to year a cottage and garden, situate on the north-west corner of a field called **Kae maes y Bar** where the highways divide, one leading from Lansamlet Church to Swansea, the other to Neath. For which he has agreed to pay the yearly rent of: £–   5   –

Rees Howell also holds from year to year part of a field called **Kae maes y Bar**, having the highway leading from Lansamlet Church to Swansea on the north; the highway leading from Lansamlet Church to Neath on the east; the way leading to Llwyn Crwn house on the south; and mear stones lately laid down by Mr Rees and Mr Powell on the west. For which he pays yearly the sum of: £–   10   –

[Folio 130/131]

The Honourable George Venables Vernon esq. holds from year to year a parcel of land containing sixteen acres of Customary measure, called **Koed hyr Draeth**, lying on the west side of Crymlyn Marsh or Burroughs, having the lands formerly purchased by Bussy Mansel of Briton Ferry esq. from Mr Gibbs on the east side thereof. This parcel of land is not at present known, but Mr Vernon pays for it the yearly rent of: £–   1   8

The same **Mr Vernon** holds from year to year a parcel of land called **Erw'r Ishim**, containing two Customary acres, adjoining to a lane leading by a messuage called Llan y wern ycha to Gwernvarre, and being on the south side thereof; the lands of the said Mr Vernon on the north; and the Freehold lands of the Hon. Mr Vernon called Gellydowill on the east and west parts thereof. And also one parcel of meadow and pasture ground called Gwain y Bedw, containing by estimation three acres of Customary measure, and bounded with the highway leading from Dan y Graig to Pont y Moch on the west; the said tenement called Gellydowill on the north and east sides thereof; and the lands of Mr Watkin Howell called Lan y Wern Ysha on the south, at the yearly rent of: £1   10   –

Mr Hurst and Mr Calvert Richard Jones, in the right of their wives, hold an acre of land lying on the south-west of the barn at **Tyr Glandwr**, having the Marsh on the west and south parts thereof; the said barn to the north; and a field of the said tenement called Tyr Glandwr on the east, at the yearly rent of   £–   –   8

Mr John Jones holds from year to year a close or parcel of land called **Tyr David Taylor**, containing by estimation three acres of Customary measure, adjoining the highway near the Beacon on the east and south sides thereof; and the lands late Mr John Popkins of Knap Coch, but now of the Hon. Mr Vernon, on the west side thereof, at the yearly rent of   £1   –   –

Mr Thomas Morgan held by lease (which it is apprehended is expired) all that water corn grist mill called **Braen Mill**[56] and the house adjoining to the mill and two or three spots of waste on which the tenants of the mill used to winnow, a saw pit where they used to saw timber to repair the mill, and a drying kiln. And the several closes of land following: that is to say, Bryn y Garthen, lying in the middle of a meadow called Park yr Ystrad (but now Gwain yr Ystrad), containing by estimation half an acre Welsh measure. Which parcel was formerly surrounded with scattered trees and bushes, but was lately shewn me by Mr Thomas Morgan, the present tenant, to be in the corner of a meadow, having a hedge or fence on the south and east parts, and

---

56. On the brook called Nant Bran.

some small trees on the west; Tyr y Gwr Coch yn y Gwnlyn, abutting to the highway leading towards Neath, and contiguous to the lands of Mr Morgan called the Gwnglin *[sic]*, on the west; to a brook called Nant Brane on the north; to a pathway leading to a parcel of pasture ground called Koed Kae through a gate towards Nant Braen, which divideth the said parcel called Tyr y Gwr Coch yn y Gwnglin, on the east; and the said pasture parcel called Koed Kae on the south; containing by estimation three *[Folio 131/132]* quarters of an acre, which parcel hath some timber trees growing thereon.

A parcel of furzy ground called Tyle Garw, which lieth in a tenement called Tyr Llon Llaes, which parcel is bounded by a brook called Crymlyn on the east; the wood called Coed Llonllaes on the north; a scattered hedge in the middle of the said field on the west; containing about half an acre Welsh measure. The above boundary is now altered, the wood being cut down, and the furze grubbed up, and it appears now to be one entire field of arable land.

Treboth Ycha, Treboth Yssha, divided into four parcels, abutting to the lands of Llewelyn Rogers called Tuy Milwr on the west; to the hill called Mynnydd Drymme on the east; to the lands of the said Llewelyn Rogers called Brane blane ycha, and a ditch that leads to Mynnydd Drymme on the north; and to the brook running by the lands of Mr Morgan called Gellydeg on the south.

The above parcels are now divided into the following parcels, to wit: Treboth Ycha, six acres; Treboth Yssha, two acres; Treboth Genol, four acres; Treboth Vach, one acre; Wain Newydd, three acres and a half; Kae Brin Reeg, one acre and half; two crofts containing about two acres. All [are] within the above boundaries and are held by the tenant of Gellydeg. They lie high, and seem poor. But Mr Thomas Morgan now insists that Wain Newydd and Kae Brin Reeg are not part of the premises, though they appear to be within the above boundaries.

Enherrag Maes Ychel, containing by estimation half an acre of Customary measure, lies in the middle of a field of Mr Daniel Jones of Glan Braen, called Kae'r Kappel.

For which mill and lands Mr Thomas Morgan pays yearly   £10   –   –

[Folio 132/133]

Richard Lockwood of Deweshall in the County of Essex, esquire; **John Lockwood** of the City of London esquire; and **Robert Morris** of the Town of Swansea in the County of Glamorgan esquire; hold by Lease dated 24th of June 1754 all that messuage and tenement with the appurtenances called or known by the names of **Forrest Ysha**, Davaden Vawr and Fee Vach containing the several closes of land following:

	Customary Acres	
Maes Treharne	6	Now in one large field called Maes Treharne & [a] small one behind the barn.
Two small closes above the house	2½	
The House Meadow with the Gorse	8 1	Now in one field called the Great Meadow

Dav<u>o</u>den Penygored	1½	The same now with a little island in the river.
Traws Kae Ycha	4	Now in two fields called
Traws Kae Yssha	5¼	the Cross Fields.
Coed Mawr	1	
Maes y Calch Ycha	3¼	Where the mills[57] are built and houses,
Maes y Calch Genol	3½	with one field above the mills, and
Maes y Calch Yssha	4	one long field below the mills.
Davoden Evan	3½	
The two Davodens	8	The same now at the lower end of the Estate.
Upper Maes y Nya	11¼	Now the same and called so.
Middle Maes y Nya	4½	Now in one field and called Middle Maes Nya.
Little Maes y Nya	3	
Lower Maes y Nya	7	The same now.
The Gwerns & Kae Prees	10	Now divided into 5 fields, of which three are
The Great Marsh	13	called Gwerns and the other two the Upper
		Marsh & the Lower Marsh.
Acres	100¼	

To hold to the said Richard Lockwood, John Lockwood and Robert Morris, their Executors, Administrators and Assigns, from the Feast of the Annunciation of the Blessed Virgin Mary which was in the year of our Lord 1746, for and during the term of 99 years thence next ensuing and fully to be complete and ended. At and under the yearly rent of seventy-four pounds and fifteen shillings (but there is included in the said rent of £74 15s a piece of ground called the Lord's Marsh for which they pay yearly £4 5s, and five shillings for the piece of waste whereon the **copperworks** now are erected. So that the yearly rent is only £70 5s) payable half yearly, to wit: at Lady Day and Michaelmas by equal portions. And also the sum of five shillings in the name of a Heriot on the decease of every tenant dying in possession. (here write ye Boundary) *[sic].* Bounded by the lands of Thomas Popkin esq. called Forrest Ycha on the north; the River Tawey on the west; and the brook called Mynrod[58] on the east and south parts thereof. *[Folio 133/134]*

Chauncey Townsend esq. holds by Lease dated 20th day of June 1757 (and granted to him by The Most Noble Elizabeth, Dutchess Dowager of Beaufort, Mother and Guardian of The Most Noble Henry Duke of Beaufort, Lord of the said Manor of Kilvey), all those brooks streams and currents of water commonly called and known by the several names of **Claise**[59] and **Nant brane**, and all and every other brook, stream or current of water which then did, or of right ought to go or run to an ancient mill of the said Duke's called Brane Mill, situate and being within the said

---

57. The 'battery mills' on the east side of the Tawe, opposite Lockwood and Morris' Forrest copperworks.
58. Now the Nant y fendrod, which forms the lake in the Swansea Enterpise Park.
59. For the disputed boundary at Glais see p.205-207.

Manor of Kilvey. With free liberty and authority for the said Chauncey Townsend, his Executors, Administrators and Assigns, to make any dam or dams, wear or wears, or other device in upon and across the said brooks, streams and currents of water, and the channels, ground and soil through and over which the same then did, or ought to, run, for the diverting of the same out of their present and ancient channels and courses. And also free liberty and authority to and for the said Chauncey Townsend to cut, make and dig, any gutter, or gutters, trench or trenches, channel or channels, in, upon, through, and over a certain piece of waste ground of the said Duke's called Pen yr Rusva. And in, upon, through, and over, any highway or waste, open, and uninclosed lands adjoining to any highway which he or they shall have occasion to cross, pass, or go over. And also in, upon, through, and over, certain inclosed land of the said Duke, called by the several names of Gwyndy Bach and Caer Wern Vawr, situate and being in the Parish of Lansamlet and within the Manor of Kilvey aforesaid, for the conveying to the use of, and working [of] any engine or engines which the said Chauncy Townsend, his Executors or Administrators should at any time thereafter erect or set up for the draining any water, or waters, which should at any time thereafter be hurtful or prejudicial to any coal works which the said Chauncy Townsend, his Executors, or Administrators, should at any time thereafter carry on, or be concerned in, upon or under any lands of George Venables Vernon esq. and Mary Morgan, widow, or either of them, in the Parish of Lansamlet, and for the conveying of the said waters for the use of the new works[60] lately erected for smelting and refining of copper by the said Chauncy Townsend and Partners, at or near a certain place called Middle Dock in the Parish and Manor of Kilvey aforesaid, or for the use of any works he or they shall erect for the manufacturing the said copper within the said Parish and Manor. He, the said Chauncy Townsend, making satisfaction to the tenant or occupier of the said inclosed lands for all such losses or damage as he or they shall suffer by reason or means thereof. And also full and free liberty for the said Chauncy Townsend, his Executors and Administrators, to scour and cleanse the said gutters, trenches and channel, and to lay down the mud, gravel and filth raised and thrown up in scouring and cleansing the same, on the banks and sides thereof, or of any waste, open or uninclosed lands near the same, [but] so that no obstruction or any nuisance be done to any highway or road whatsoever. To hold to the said Chauncy Townsend from the 25th day of March then last past, for and during the term of ninety-nine years, at and under the yearly rent of twenty-one pounds, payable at Lady Day and Michaelmas by equal portions, clear of all deductions whatsoever.   £21   –   –

[Folio 134/135]

George Venables Vernon esq. holds by Lease dated 6th of February 1743 (and granted to the Honourable Bussy Mansel, esq, deceased) all that close or parcel of lands called or known by the name of **Caer Wern Vawr**, situate and being in the Parish of Lansamlet and in the said Manor of Kilvey, having the lands called Gwyndy Bach on the north, and the lane leading from White Rock to Bone Maen on the east and south part, and the lands of Mr Vernon on the west, and having the **waggon way** of Mr Townsend across it. To hold to the said Bussy Mansel, his Executors, Administrators and Assigns, from the Feast of Saint Michael then past, for and during

60. The Middle Bank copperworks.

the term of 21 years. At and under the yearly rent of forty shillings, payable half yearly by equal portions, clear of all taxes and deductions whatsoever.   £2   –   –

    The improved yearly rent thereof may amount to   *[blank]*

[Folio 135/136]

Elizabeth Anthony holds by virtue of a lease dated 10th of December in the year of our Lord 1705 (and granted to Jenkin Joshua her father, deceased) all that messuage or tenement of lands with appurtenances called or known by the name of **Gwyndy Bach**, situate in the Parish of Lansamlet within the said Manor of Kilvey. To hold to the said Jenkin Joshua, his Executors, Administators and Assigns, from the date thereof for and during the term of 99 years, if the said Jenkin Joshua, Elinor, his then wife (both since deceased), and the said Elizabeth should so long live. At and under the yearly rent of forty shillings, payable half yearly at Lady Day and Michaelmas by equal portions, clear of all deductions. And two capons, or one shilling in lieu thereof, on the Feast of the Circumcision of our Lord yearly, and the sum of five shillings in the name of a Heriot on the decease of every tenant dying in possession. And planting two young trees or saplings, either of oak, ash, or elm, yearly on the premises. And doing Suit of Court to the Manor of Kilvey during the said term, and Suit of Mill to the mill of the Lord within the Manor aforesaid, and doing service with horses and oxen when thereto required.

Gwyndy Bach consists of a messuage, and a field above the house called Cae Ych lawr y Ty, containing 1½ acres. Having the house and garden and the lane leading from White Rock to Bene y maen on the west; the lane joining the three small fields on the north; the garden on the east and Cae ych lawr y Ty on the south. And three small fields situate below the house, having Gwern Gwyndy on the west and north part; Gwern Llestre on the east; and the lane on the south; and containing about 2½ acres. And one other large parcel of rough wood ground before the house, having the said lane leading to Bene *[sic]* y maen from White Rock on the east; Cae Wern Vawr on the south; a small marsh, formerly of Mr John Popkin and now of the Hon. Mr Vernon on the west; and part of Gwern Llestre tenement on the north; and having the waggon way of Chauncy Townsend esq. running through the middle of it. Containing about 5 acres.

    The improved yearly value amounts to   £4   –   –

Evan Edward holds by Lease dated 25th March 1749, all that cottage, garden and croft situate, lying and being near the **Boat Side**[61] within the Parish of Swansea and Manor of Kilvey, and then and now in the possession of the said Evan Edward. To hold to the said Evan Edward from the Annunciation of the Blessed Virgin Mary then last past, for and during the natural lives of the said Evan Edward, Mary, his wife, and Catherine Edward, their daughter, and the life of the survivor of them. At and under the yearly rent of one pound and one shilling, payable half yearly by equal portions, without any deduction whatsoever. Together with two fat pullets, or one shilling in lieu thereof, on St Thomas's Day yearly. And the sum of five shillings in the name of a

---

61. The Swansea ferry.

Heriot on the decease of every tenant dying in possession, and the sum of five shillings upon every Assignment or Alienation. And doing Suit of Mill and Suit of Court, on pain of three shillings and four pence for every default. £1 2 –

Daniel Fabian and **Thomas Reynold** pay yearly to the Lord the sum of six pence, for the use of **a level by the salt house** to drain their meadows.

N.B. That wherever the improved yearly value is set down, the present rent of the respective premises is included.
[Folio 136/137]

A Rent Roll of the Chief Rent within the Manor of Kilvey

Freeholders	Tenements	Occupiers	£	s	d
Honble G. V. Vernon esq.	Erw Vawr alias Tyr Crew	David Woodwall	–	–	8
The same	Tyr y Gwll	Evan David	–	–	8½
The same	Therwes	*[blank]*	–	–	7½
The same	Gwern Llestre	Hopkin Davies	–	–	8
The same	Tyr Engharud Vach William	Thos Reynold	–	3	–
The same	Tyr y Gwaydd & Tyr Willm ab Evan ab Henry	The same	–	–	10
The same	Tyr Gwillim ab Evan called Dan y Graig vach	Roger Jones	–	–	3
The same	Tyr Neast Vrase alias Dan y Graig Genol	The same	–	2	–
The same	Llys newidd	Jonathan Williams	1	–	–
The same	Morva'r Kyrse	The same	–	10	–
The same	Morva'r Byth Allt	The same	–	6	8
The same	Tyr Edmond	John Edward	–	–	4½
The same	Gelly Gravog	The same	–	–	3
The same	Lands called *[blank]* late in possession of Edward Thomas	Edward Thomas	–	1	–

Freeholders	Tenements	Occupiers	Rent per annm		
			£	s	d
The same	Lands late in possession of Thos Richard Robert	Chauncy Townsend esq.	–	1	–
The same Church called *[blank]*	Lands near Lansamlet	Owen David	–	1	5
The same	Lands late in possession of William ab William	John Jones	–	–	7½
The same	Kilbury	The same	–	1	10
The same	Llwyn Krwn Ycha	Thomas Edwards	–	–	4
The same	Llwyn Krwn Yssha	Rees Howell	–	–	8
The same	Lands near Lan y Werne	Rees David	–	1	7½
The same	Tal y Choba	Evan Jenkin	–	–	3
The same	Tyr Evan Lliky	The same	–	–	4½
The same	Lands at Kevenhenvod	John Jones	–	–	1½
The same	Pant y Blawd	Owen David	–	–	9
The same	Lands at Kevenhenwood	John Jones	–	–	9
The same	Tyr Morgan Cadwgan	Peter King	–	–	2
The same	Tyla'r Dengis, Bon y maen & Kae mawr	John Jones	–	1	4
The same	Lands late in the hands of Wm Hopkin ['ditto' in Bn]	*[blank]*	–	–	2
The same	Tyr y Ddyan alias Tyr Wm Lewis	David Woodwall	–	–	9
The same	Tyr y Vord	Thomas Lemuel	–	–	8
The same	Pant y Geville & Pwll Mawr	Thomas Hopkin	–	–	11
The same	Pudew Glase	David Woodwall & Chauncy Townsend esq.	–	–	9
The same	Lands at Dan y Graig late in the hands of John William ab William	David William	–	–	7½
The same	Tyr y Wyllt	Hopkin David	–	–	4

Freeholders	Tenements	Occupiers	Rent per annm		
			£	s	d
The same	Wayn Wen	John Jones	–	–	4½
The same	Lands late in the hands of Hopkin David called Funnon Vadocke	David Woodwall	–	1	–
The same	*[blank]*	*[blank]*	–	1	–
The same	Lands late in the hands of Jane Elias	Howell Harry	–	–	3½
The same	Lands late in the hands of Morgan Howell	Daniel Fabian	–	1	–
[Folio 137/138]					
The same	Tyr Evan Llewelyn Goch	David Woodwall	–	–	2
The same	Gelly'r Gasseg	Walter Howells	–	2	–
The same	Llwyn Hernin	Mr John Phillips	–	–	10
The same	Tregove	William Thomas	–	1	–
The same	Tyr Evan Jenkin Treharn	Margt Rees, widow	–	–	2
The same	Lands late in possession of Rees Woodwall widow & M. Llewelyn	Catherine David	–	–	9½
The same	Lands late in possession of Cecil Hopkin	John Jones	–	–	6
The same	Land late in hands of Jno. Richard Owen	Thomas John	–	–	4
The same	Tyr Madock Wayth, Coed Hyr Draeth and Tyr Gwillim Gronow Ddee	Morgan Thomas	–	–	6½
The same	Tyr Evan Lloyd	*[blank]*	–	–	5
The same	Tyr Griffith David Ddee	Thomas Llewellyn	–	–	9
The same	Y Ty Duy alias Mawr	Morgan Thomas	–	1	–
The same	Gelly Dowill	*[blank]*	–	1	–
The same	Knwffe Coch	*[blank]*	–	1	5
The same	Kavenhenvood	John Jones	–	1	–

Freeholders	Tenements	Occupiers	Rent per annm		
			£	s	d
The same	Gwern y Maen Llwyd	[blank]	–	–	1½
The same	Gelly Dowill	Wm Lloyd	–	1	–
The same	Glan Mynrod	Howell Harry	–	1	5
The same	Tyr Evan Jenkin Treharn	[blank]	–	–	2
The same	Lands late in the hands of Robt Bodicwm called Tyr Neast	David Woodwall	–	–	4
The same	Y Gored Dduy	Roger Jones	–	1	–
The same	Hicket Wear	John Edward	–	–	6
The same	Globert Wear	The same	–	–	6
The same	Syl Wear	John Jenkin	–	–	6
			£4	3	7½
Walter Howell	Tyr Jenkin ab Evan Ychan alias Tyr Glan y Bade	Chauncy Townsend esq.	–	2	4
The same	Tyr Llewellyn Bevan Tew	The same	–	–	9
The same	Lands late in possession of Wm John alias Lanerch	Walter Howell	–	–	9
			£–	3	10
Mr Thos Morgan	Gellygynoon	[Most of this column is blank]	–	–	9
The same	Tyr Phillip Tew		–	–	5
The same	Tyr Thos Griffith ab Hopkin Lloyd		–	1	4
The same	Tyr Evan Bach		–	–	3
The same	Gwain Evan Ddee	Chauncy Townsend esq.	–	–	3
The same	Gwern Vare	David Hopkin Francis	–	–	3
The same	Tyr Thomas Lya		–	–	7
The same	Tyr Madock Bach & Evan Goch ab Richd.		–	4	5
The same	Tyr Meyrick Ychan		–	4	8

Freeholders	Tenements	Occupiers	Rent per annm		
			£	s	d
The same	Tyr Evan Jenkin Treharn		–	–	2
The same	Lands late in possession of Evan and Robert Rosser		–	1	10
[Folio 138/139]					
The same	Tyr Trimme	John Jenkin	–	1	9
The same	Tyr y Pray		–	–	6
The same	Clyn y Gorse		–	–	8
The same	Tyr y Grose *[sic]* Llwyn	Widow of Zech. Evan Jenkin	–	–	3
The same	Park y Brin Rose Velin		–	1	–
The same	Tyr Evan Gwyn		–	–	4
The same	Croft y Gething		–	–	3
The same	Tyr Thos Griffith ab Hopkin Llwyd		–	–	1
The same	Tyr Evan Madock Goch, Tyr y Mynnydd and Gwerne Bwll	John Jenkin	–	–	5½
The same	Pant y ffynnon Lase		–	–	5
The same	Gellydeg and Llechwood Dwene	Joseph Owen	–	1	8
The same	Cwm Curnach	Phillip Eynon	–	–	8
The same	Tyr y Prydd		–	–	4
The same	Tyr Jenkin ab Gwillim & Llwyn y wydir		–	1	11
The same	Tyr Llon Llase	David Hopkin Francis	–	–	5
The same	Clyn Cadwgan		–	–	6
The same	Tyr Hopkin Rosser Vaine		–	–	4
The same	Tyr Powell ab Evan Jenkin		–	–	5
			£1	6	10½

Freeholders	Tenements	Occupiers	Rent per annm		
			£	s	d
Edward Evans esq.	Llanerch elydir	Mr Walter Howell	£–	1	9
Thos Popkin esq.	Tyr Forest Ycha	His own possession	–	2	2
The same	Tyr Tanglwst alias the Ynis	William Rees	£–	1	4
			£–	3	6
Mary Nicholas, widow	Ynisdderwe	William Thomas	–	1	3
The same	Tyr Duy alias Mawr	The same	–	2	6
The same	Tyr yn y Llwyn	The same	–	–	5
The same	Tyr Madock Goch	Rees Howell	–	–	5½
The same	Tyr y Browne	The same	–	–	3
The same	Tyr y Bwla 1½ Tyr David Dduy ¾	The same	–	–	2¼
The same	Tyr Verch Llewelyn Ychan	The same	–	–	4½
The same	Tyr y ffunnon Vared	The same	–	–	8
The same	Tyr Evan Griffith	The same	–	–	7½
The same	Tyr Morgan Cadwgan	The same	–	–	2
			£–	6	10¾
Mr Daniel Jones	Blaen Braen	His own possession	–	–	9
The same	Kill y Vrane	Ditto	–	–	10
The same	Tyr Griffith Milwr	Ditto	–	1	7
The same	Tyr Meyrick Ychan at Mynnydd Drymme	Ditto	–	–	11
The same	Lletty Maen	Ditto	–	–	2
The same	Tyr John Rosser ab Howell Ychan	Ditto	–	–	11½
			£–	5	2½

[Folio 139/140]

Freeholders	Tenements	Occupiers	Rent per annm		
			£	s	d
David Samuel	Lands in Kilvey late in possession of David Samuel	Lewelyn Sims	£–	–	1½
John Jenkins late Wm Rees	Tyr Reynallt	William Rees	–	1	1½
The same	Tyr y Von ddare & Ynis arlla	The same	–	–	9
The same	Tyr Thomas Meyrick	The same	–	–	4
			£–	2	2½
Mr George Hutton	Tyr Glan y Bade	Daniel Fabian	£–	2	4
Mr Hurst & Mr Jones	Tyr Glan Dwr	Thomas Evan	£–	3	–

The end of Folio 140 is the end of the description of Kilvey Lordship, and is the end of the main body of the Gabriel Powell 1764 Survey.

Fabians House, 1849, by William Butler. The farmhouse of Tir Glan y Bad and home of Daniel Fabian and his family (see pages 209, 216 and 218). They gave their name to Fabian's Bay, now the site of Swansea Docks, and to the modern Fabian Way.

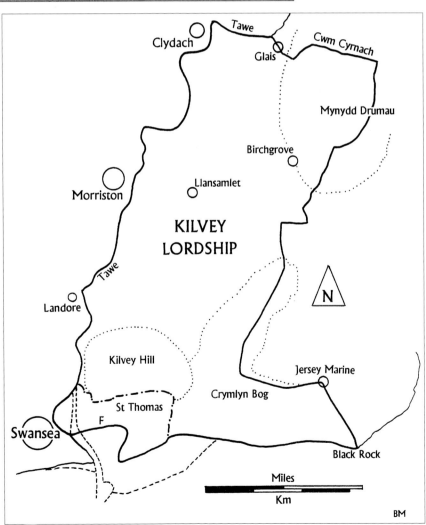

The Lordship of Kilvey. 'F' shows the location of Fabian's House.

Several appendices now follow, some contemporary with the Survey and others added as indicated.

Original Appendices to the 1764 Survey

[All now bound in the Miscellanea volume of Sa]

[Folio 141]

Appendix I

The Stewards and Deputy Stewards of the Seigniory of Gower

1.	John Owen, Steward	Anno	3 Edward 1st	*[1274-75]*
2.	Rees Hacklett		11 Edward 2nd	*[1317-18]*
3.	Lord John Deymle		15 Edward 2nd	*[1321-22]*
4.	Rees de Penrice		2 Edward 3rd	*[1328-29]*
5.	Thomas de Harfford		6 Edward 3rd	*[1332-33]*
6.	Thomas Lacon ['Lord' *deleted*]		16 Edward 3rd	*[1342-43]*
	John Dalaber, Deputy Steward		41 Edward 3rd	*[1367-68]*
	Robert ap Thomas, Deputy Steward		2 Richard 2nd	*[1378-79]*
7.	William Gwynn, Steward		19 Richard 2nd	*[1395-1396]*
8.	John St John		9 Henry 5th	*[1421-1422]*
	Richard Maunsell, Deputy Steward in the time of Henry 5th			
9.	Sir William Thomas, Knight, Steward		22 Henry 6th	*[1443-1444]*
10.	Sir Roger Vaughan, Knight		10 Edward 4th	*[1470-1471]*
11.	Thomas ap Roger Vaughan		3 Richard 3rd	*[1485]*
12.	Sir Rees ap Thomas, Knight of the Garter		3 Henry 7th	*[1487-88]*
13.	Sir Mathew Cradock, Knight		6 Henry 7th	*[1490-91]*
14.	Morgan Kidwely		7 Henry 7th	*[1491-92]*

15.	Sir Mathew Cradock, Knight	12 Henry 7th	*[1496-97]*
16.	Sir George Herbert, Knight, in the time of Queen Mary		
17.	Sir Edward Mansell, Knight, in the time of Queen Elizabeth		
	Lyson Price, Deputy Steward to Sir Edward Mansell		
18.	Jenkin Francklen	20 Elizabeth	*[1577-78]*
19.	Sir Thomas Mansell, Knight	28 Elizabeth to 22 James	*[1585-1625]*
	Phillip Mansell, Deputy Steward to Sir Thomas Mansell		
20.	Edward Lord Herbert, Steward Walter Thomas, Deputy Steward to the Lord Herbert	6 Charles	*[1630-31]*

William Thomas, Steward   12 Charles 2nd   *[1660-61]*

Walter Thomas   16 Charles 2nd   *[1664-65]*

Bussy Mansell esq.
Christopher Midleton esq.   20 Charles 2nd   *[1668-69]*

William Herbert esq.

David Evans esq.   23 Charles 2nd unto 2 William & Mary   *[1671-91]*

Sir Humphry Mackworth
Henry Crow, esq.   3 William & Mary to 5 Anne   *[1691-1707]*
Robert Price esq. } Baron of the Exchequer & Judge of the Common Pleas.   *[R. Price is not in Bn]*

Sir Humphry Mackworth
Henry Crow esq.
John Watkins esq.
William Dawkins esq.   5 Anne   *[1706-07]*
Lewis Thomas esq.
Thomas Price esq.
Gabriel Powell esq.

John Somersett esq.
John Burgh esq.   1 George 1st   *[1714-15]*
Gabriel Powell esq.

John Burgh esq.
Gabriel Powell esq. } 2 George 2nd   *[1728-29]*
John Powell esq.

John Powell esq.
Gabriel Powell esq. } 7 George 2nd   *[1733-34]*

John Powell esq.
Gabriel Powell esq. } 17 George 2nd   *[1743-44]*

John Powell esq.
Gabriel Powell esq. } 1 George 3rd   *[1760-61]*

Thomas Morgan esq., Penderry   28 George 3rd   *[1787-88]*
['Penderry' and regnal year, and also the following note,
  are in Bn only]

I have compared the above copy, the original of which is in the possession of Mr Edward Hancorne of Burry *['Burry'*
in Sa, 'Berry' in Bn. The latter is correct] in the Parish of Landewy in Gower, and find it (verbatim) just correct and
true.

Tho Morgan   Steward.   *[Signature]*

[The list has been continued in a different script as follows;]

 [The regnal years following are in Bn only]
Edmund Estcourt esq.   44 George 3rd   *[1803-04]*
John Jeffreys esq. Deputy

Zouch Turton esq.*   53 George 3rd } *[1812-13]*
Deputy John Jeffreys esq.*   *[Those marked * are in Bn only]*
John Jeffreys esq.*   54 George 3rd } *[1813-14]*

Robert Nelson Thomas esq. *['Nelson' is in Bn only]*   56 George 3rd   *[1815-16]*

Lewis Thomas esq.   3 George 4th   *[1822-23]*

[In Sa the list has been further extended, in pencil, as follows:]

Serj[eant]t Ludlow [with a question-mark]

F.P. Hooper

C. Baker

R.W. Beor

[F.H. Glynn Price should be in at this point but has been omitted]

Francis Hobbs (1921).

*   *   *

[Miscellanea volume, Folio 142.]

Appendix II

The Reeves of Kilvey

Lewis Thomas esq.	1705	Mr John Jones	1730
David Jenkin	1706	– Sidney esq.	1731
Sir Thomas Mansel	1707	David Samuel	1732
Mr Evan Evans	1708	Mr Franklyn Mathews	1733
Mr David Nicholas	1709	Robt Popkin esq.	1734
Roger Morgan	1710	Mr George Hutton	1735
John Jenkin	1711	Mrs. Eliz. Herbert	1736
Morgan Horsel	1712	Thos Popkin esq.	1737
Mr John Popkin	1713	Mrs. Nicholas	1738
William Browne	1714	Jenkin David	1739
Mr William Thomas	1715	Rd Evans esq.	1740
Mr Thos Popkin	1716	Roger Morgan	1741
Richd Herbert esq.	1717	Walter Howel	1742
Rees Thomas	1718	Honble Bussy Mansel esq.	1743
Jane Morgan	1719	Lady Leicester	1744
George Hutton	1720	David Samuel	1745
Jenkin David	1721	Mrs. Rose Griffiths	1746
Roger Morgan	1722	Mrs. Jane Mathews	1747
Mr Robt Popkin	1723	Robt Popkin esq.	1748
Mr Edward Evans	1724	Mr George Hutton	1749
Mr William Rees	1725	Roger Powell esq.	1750
Mr John Jones	1726	Mrs. Nicholas	1751
Mr David Nicholas	1727	Thos Popkin esq.	1752
Walter Howels	1728	Jenkin David	1753
Mr John Popkin	1729		

Appendix III

A Rent Roll of his Grace the Duke of Beaufort's Cottages, leased to John Lockwood Esquire and Company from Michaelmas 1775 to Michaelmas 1776

[The following rent roll, dated 1775-76, is bound in the 'Miscellanea' volume. It is a little over ten years later than the 'Survey', but can be compared with the list of cottages in the Lockwood and Morris lease of 1754 on Folios 89 and 90 [p.160-163]. The most notable addition is that of 24 dwellings at "Castle", i.e. Morris Castle on Graig Trewyddfa, built in c.1774 by John Morris, the first purpose-built flats for workers in Britain.]

Where Situate	No.	Tenants Names	Rent for the Year ending Michaelmas 1776		
			£	s	d
Brinmelin	1	John Jenkin	..	2	..
Cwm Rhyd y Vilast	2	In ruins	..	2	..
Treboth	3	Eleanor Morgan	..	2	..
	4	David William	..	2	..
	5	John John	..	2	..
	6	David Morgan	..	2	..
	7	John Thomas	..	2	..
	8	Ditto for Croft Llewellin	..	2	..
	9	John Lewis	..	2	..
	10	Edward Jenkin	..	2	..
	11	Thomas William	..	2	..
	12	David Phillip junr.	..	2	..
Knap Llwyd	13	John Grey	..	2	..
	14	John Mordecai	..	2	..
	15	William John Richard	..	2	..
	16	John Jones	..	2	..
	17	Lewis John	..	2	..
	18	Thomas Lloyd	..	2	..
Castle[62]	19	David John Rees	..	2	..
	20	Richard William	..	2	..
	21	William John	..	2	..

62. This entry is important. It provides a list of the early tenants of Morris Castle, John Morris' pioneering block of workers' flats, then lately completed. Its ruin is still a well-known landmark above Landore.

Where Situate	No.	Tenants Names	Rent for the Year ending Michaelmas 1776		
			£	s	d
	22	Samuel Charles	..	2	..
	23	Thomas John	..	2	..
	24	John Watkins	..	2	..
	25	William Lewis	..	2	..
	26	John Jenkin	..	2	..
	27	Jenkin Zacharias	..	2	..
	28	Jenkin Richard	..	2	..
	29	Morgan David	..	2	..
	30	John Thomas	..	2	..
	31	Thomas Evan	..	2	..
	32	David John	..	2	..
	33	John Morgan	..	2	..
	34	John Vulk	..	2	..
	35	John Rees	..	2	..
	36	John Daniel	..	2	..
	37	Jenkin David	..	2	..
	38	John Lewis	..	2	..
	39	Richard Thomas	..	2	..
	40	Thomas Richard	..	2	..
	41	Richard Hugh	..	2	..
	42	John Thomas	..	2	..
Trewyddva	43	John Franklen	..	2	..
	44	David Phillip	..	2	..
	45	Evan Grey	..	2	..
	46	David Lott	..	2	..
	47	William Powell	..	2	..
	48	Edward Lewis	..	2	..
	49	Catherine Grey	..	2	..
	50	James Lewis	..	2	..
	51	William Hugh	..	2	..
	52	Thomas John Hugh	..	2	..
	53	Honor *[sic]* William Hugh	..	2	..
	54	Thomas William Hugh	..	2	..
	55	John Thomas Hugh	..	2	..
	56	Thomas Jenkin	..	2	..
	57	Hopkin Terry	..	2	..
	58	William Lewis	..	2	..
	59	Anne Isaac	..	2	..
	60	Elizabeth Frank	..	2	..
	61	Henry David	..	2	..
	62	Evan Jenkin	..	2	..
	63	John Thomas	..	2	..
	64	Joseph Morgan	..	2	..
	65	Thomas Lewis	..	2	..
	66	Thomas David Lewis	..	2	..

Where Situate	No.	Tenants Names	Rent for the Year ending Michaelmas 1776		
			£	s	d
	67	David Jenkin	..	2	..
	68	William Hopkin	..	2	..
	69	John Morgan	..	2	..
	70	Sarah David	..	2	..
	71	Thomas Jenkin	..	2	..
	72	William John	..	2	..
	73	Christmas Miles	..	2	..
	74	Benjamin John David	..	2	..
	75	Thomas Grey	..	2	..
	76	Lewis Morgan	..	2	..
	77	Joan Morris	..	2	..
	78	Samuel Jones	..	2	..
Heol Hen Sage	79	Mary Woolcock	..	2	..
Place y Marl	80	Hopkin Perkins	..	2	..
	81	John Abraham	..	2	..
	82	Elizabeth Abraham	..	2	..
Marsh Side	83	John Thomas – smith	..	2	..
	84	John Thomas – mason	..	2	..
	85	Martin Bevan	..	2	..
	86	William Powell	..	2	..
	87	John Evan	..	2	..
	88	William Morgan	..	2	..
Landore	89	Lewis Lewis	..	2	..
	90	Rees William	..	2	..
	91	David Evan	..	2	..

Mynnydd Carn Llwyd: a cottage mentioned in the Schedule with the lease, now occupied by John Franklen.

Thomas Lott (Signature)

Appendix IV

Some original working notes

[These notes are included in the Miscellanea volume of Sa. and appear to be some of Gabriel Powell's working notes for the Survey. They are on both sides of a scrap of paper c.2½" wide and c.10" long [6cm x 25cm].

Kille
[Killay]

? who owns Pen y pool
   do.   Girland
? Mr Walters Christian name

Lunnon

? aubrey wido. Christian name

Trewyddva

? Mr Morris's tent[ant]s. name in the lands he bought of Bennet
? The name of Franklen infant
? wt. do they call Mr Popkins land wch. adjoin Mr Vernons marsh
? the particular fields of lower Forrest

Oystermouth

? name of Francis Davids meadow
? Paticulars of Thos [?] gains & taking
? Boundaries of James Parry's lands

*   *   *

Lord Ashburnham ? the land he pays for & who is tenant

? lands bo[ough]t of Thos Clo—

? lands of Mr Wm Dawkin late held by Mrs Lloyd

? Thos Russels' lands late [held?] by late Mr Griffiths

? Isaac Griffiths Ten[an]t

? tenement to late Jon. Gell [*cut off*–. ? Gethin] lands

Appendix V

George Grant Francis' Introduction to the Survey – 1876

[This is Grant Francis' manuscript introduction to the Sa original of the Gabriel Powell 1764 'Survey of Gower', written soon after he had acquired the volume. It is now bound in the 'Miscellanea' volume starting at Folio VII.]

This important manuscript relates to one of the most interesting of the marcher lordships in Wales, Gower, in its more recent condition.

It may be recollected that it was this very Seigniory which caused so much discord between Edward II and the Barons in the middle ages, and at length brought about the disastrous battle of Boroughbridge on the 22nd of March in the year 1322, with the death of no less than nineteen of the rebellious nobles including the then Lord of the Seigniory, de Mowbray himself, who was decapitated at York in the *[blank]* year of his age.

The manuscript was compiled by that earnest and painstaking agent of the Duke of Beaufort, Mr Gabriel Powell of Swansea, in the year 1764 – than whom no great landowner ever had a more faithful Steward.

This gentleman had the advantage of special training for the particular duties of the office, having been brought up to the law, under his father, who for many years had preceded him in the management of the Beaufort Estates in Glamorgan.

Thus, the details of every portion of land and its occupiers – the practice in the several Manor Courts, the rights of the Lord and the Commoners in the various Divisions & Mesne Manors comprising the Seigniory, came under his immediate ken and were practically and thoroughly well-known to him. Indeed, he himself says that when he compiled this 'Survey' he held the Offices of Steward, Coroner, Recorder and Bailiff of the Liberty of Gower, and that he derived his information from ancient and authentic evidences, combined with an experience, between himself and his father, of nearly three quarters of a century: moreover, that he prepared it at the especial request of the Dowager Duchess of Beaufort, who had been left Guardian to her son, Henry the fifth Duke, then a minor.

These facts assure us that no efforts would be left unemployed to produce a record of the utmost correctness, and the minute additions and emendations he from time to time made (in his peculiar handwriting) on almost every page of the work are the best possible evidence of the watchful care he bestowed on each particular. No higher praise can be accorded him either as Author or Steward.

Mr Powell has added his *Imprimatur* by appending his autograph signature to the title page, thus giving weight and validity to the contents of the pages which follow.

When this Survey was eventually placed before Her Grace of Beaufort there can be little doubt but that two fair copies would be directed to be made for use and reference. One for the Muniment Room of the Ducal residence at Badminton in Gloucestershire; the other for the Estate offices at Swansea; the chief town of Gower itself. I have seen both, but I regret to say without power of inspection or extract, a disadvantage I felt much while bringing together and publishing my volume of the 'Surveys of Gower and Kilvey', in 1861.[62]

It may therefore be easily imagined with what pleasure I heard of the existence of this – "the Original Survey", which had, it appears, never left the Powell Family, having passed by descent into the possession of a great-grandson of the Author, another Mr Gabriel Powell, also a Solicitor at Brecon. At his death it was acquired by my friend Mr Joseph Joseph F.S.A., Banker of Brecon, who kindly spared it to me with the remark that "He felt the book ought to pass into my hands, looking to the great interest which I took in everything relating to Swansea itself, and the time & money I had devoted to the History of Gower and the surrounding Districts".

The volume when it came into my possession was in a sadly dilapidated condition even to the extent of its back being torn off and many of the leaves worn through at the folds. My appreciation of its importance allowed me to lose no time in causing it to be carefully cleansed, properly rebound and so interleaved as to receive notes and additions, but in a manner which should not interfere with the original text, nor in any way destroy the integrity of the work itself. By way of frontispiece I have added the very rare portrait of the Author, Mr Powell, drawn from the life when giving evidence on the Swansea Paving Act before the House of Commons in the year 1787[63]. Though at one time there may have been [more] copies of this now scarce portrait about, it must have been at all times rare, for during more than fifty years I have never seen but four impressions of it. One, with Mr O.G. Williams; one with old Mr S. Padley; a coloured copy, which I obtained in London in 1830; and this, which belonged to Mr Lewis Thomas, formerly the Duke's Steward in Gower. A map of the lordship and surrounding districts seemed to be a natural addition to a work embracing so considerable a topographic area[64]. These are very humble contributions to a work which I consider of remarkable value and interest to the place of my birth.

George Grant Francis FSA [signature]
President of the Royal Institution of South Wales
Swansea
December 1876

62. *The Lordship of Gower in the Marches of Wales.* Ed. by George Grant Francis and Charles Baker (Cambrian Archaeological Association, 3 parts, 1861, 1864 & 1870).
63. Reproduced on p.31. This is now in the Swansea Museum collection.
64. G.G.F. used a small-scale printed map to show the lordship boundaries.

THE EDITOR

Bernard Morris MBE, FRICS, FSA, FRSA is a retired chartered surveyor who was for twelve years the City Estate Agent to the former City of Swansea Council, a major landowning authority. He has a long-standing interest in local history and archaeology and has published extensively on those subjects. He is a past President of the Royal Institution of South Wales and of the Gower Society, and has edited the Society's annual research journal *Gower* for over twenty years. In 1998 he was made an Honorary Fellow of the University of Wales Swansea in recognition of his contributions to local historical research.

As well as many articles, his publications include: *The Houses of Singleton*; *Old Gower Farmhouses and their Families*; *Swansea Castle*; *Thomas Baxter – the Swansea Years* (with John O. Wilstead) and *Thomas Rothwell – Views of Swansea in the 1790s* (with Michael Gibbs). In 1992, on behalf of the R.I.S.W., he edited for publication the second volume of W. H. Jones *History of Swansea and the Lordship of Gower* which had languished at galley-proof stage since its author's death in 1932.

His acquaintance with Gabriel Powell's 'Survey' goes back to at least 1960, but his commitment to putting it into print began just under two years ago. For forty years he has hoped to see its contents made more generally available and he is gratified that the Gower Society has at last made this possible.